NORTH COUNTRY RIVER VALLEY WALKS

Tony Stephens

Published by Sigma Leisure – an imprint of
Sigma Press, 1 South Oak Lane, Wilmslow, Cheshire SK9 6AR, England.

British Library Cataloguing in Publication Data
A CIP record for this book is available from the British Library.

ISBN: 1-85058-486-9

Typesetting and Design by: Sigma Press, Wilmslow, Cheshire.

Cover photograph: Burnsall from Burnsall Fell

Maps and photographs: A.D. Stephens

Printed by: Manchester Free Press

Disclaimer: the information in this book is given in good faith and is believed to be correct at the time of publication. No responsibility is accepted by either the author or publisher for errors or omissions, or for any loss or injury howsoever caused. Only you can judge your own fitness, competence and experience.

Preface

I have long been of the view that the best way to appreciate the Pennines is to walk its river valleys. A combination of the idyllic sections adjacent to the riverbank and others higher up the hill-side with fine views, produces walks which are not only highly scenic, but also allow visits to the many sites of historic interest.

Since the Pennines cover such a large area, it would not be practical to cover all its river valleys in a single book. I decided therefore, to concentrate first on the southern Pennines, the relatively compact Peak District. The result was 250 miles of walks down 12 river valleys, published as Peakland River Valley Walks by Sigma Press in 1995.

The present book, covers the much larger northern section of the Pennines, known as the Pennine Dales, with over 500 miles of walks down the 20 river valleys lying between the Calder and the Tyne. Together, the two books cover all the main river valleys in the Pennines.

As a youth I had the good fortune to live on the banks of a river in the Yorkshire Dales. If I had any slight concern, before I started the walks, that revisiting places fondly remembered from youth might not live up to my high expectation of them, I need not have feared. The Pennine Dales remain simply England's most beautiful and interesting region.

Although you should be able to find described most of the best known and loved river valley locations throughout the Pennine Dales, you will also find many equally attractive places which are less well known and are relatively little visited. My hope is that readers will derive as much pleasure as I have in discovering these more out-of-the-way places.

Tony Stephens

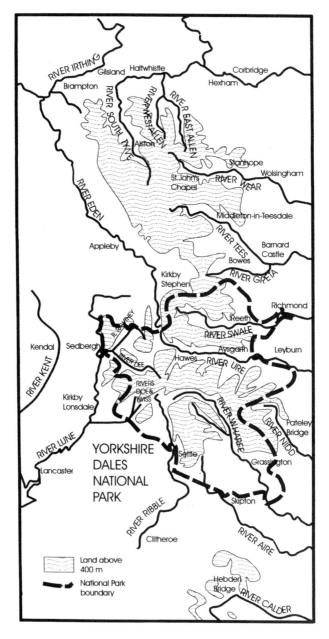

Rivers of the Pennine Dales

Contents

Due to a printer's error, the photographs on pages 38 (River Dee walk) and 79 (River Lune walk) have been transposed.

Walking the River Valleys

The northern Pennines, an area of some 5000 square miles between the Calder and the Tyne rivers, has some of England's finest scenery. It is drained by numerous river valleys, and it is the walks along these dales which are the subject of this book. (The river valleys of the southern Pennines are described in the author's companion book, "Peakland River Valley Walks", also published by Sigma Press.)

In addition to the renowned scenery, the dales have had a continuously rich history from the time of the last Ice Age to the present day, and the walks have been carefully planned to include the best of both the scenic beauty and the features of historical interest. Over 500 miles of walks of great variety and interest along 20 river valleys are described. Nearly all of the walking has been confined to paths and green tracks. In lowland England, routes used by Romans, medieval monasteries, packhorsemen and cattle drovers were often upgraded to turnpikes at the beginning of the Industrial Revolution. In the Pennines, these ancient routes were largely unsuitable for wheeled vehicles, and have, by default, been inherited by the walker. Since most people find it intriguing to know the history of the paths on which they walk, I have indicated the provenance in the text where known.

For convenience of the narrative, I have split the descriptions of the walks

The author, in the Kent valley

into sections of 8-10 miles. These could be combined to make longer walks or subdivided. For most of the walks there is sufficient official and unofficial parking to allow walks to be planned to suit any taste, whether this is a short stroll along a riverbank or a strenuous hike which includes the hilltops.

For each river valley I have aimed to provide a good balance of sections along the valley bottom and on the hilltops. There is something intensely satisfying in seeing from above the valley bottom you have just walked or are about to walk, and also in being able to peep over into adjacent valleys. After a few such walks you begin to get a unique feeling for the geography of the area which it is not possible to gain in any other way.

The walks are mainly continuous, and only a very few sections have had to be excluded because they lack interest or require an undue amount of road walking. More often there are alternative routes for you to choose between or to combine into circular walks.

One of the practical difficulties of describing 500 miles of walking is to produce maps which are sufficiently accurate but not too large. In the 17th century, the cartographer Ogilby overcame this problem when mapping roads by producing strip maps, several of which were displayed on a page. Since rivers generally flow in one direction, I have been able to adopt the same approach. Not all river valleys oblige by flowing for any great distance in the same direction and, when the need arises, wider maps are used. For each river, the maps are numbered consecutively so that you will move from one map to the next as you progress down the valley.

The symbols used should be self explanatory, with a consistent set of line thicknesses used to differentiate between river, walk, road, woodland etc. Perhaps the only symbol needing further explanation is the "special" direction symbol. You will see that the direction of progress along the walks is indicated periodically by a "standard" direction symbol (→). At the beginning and end of many of the maps, but not necessarily at the exact edge, you will notice a "special" direction symbol (⇨). These symbols mark the same place on adjacent maps, and are particularly useful when there is an overlap of maps due to a change of orientation.

The maps have been drawn so that the walks start at the bottom of the page and progress upwards. Whilst this may at first seem strange to the Western eye, which is used to reading from the top of the page to the bottom, it has the very considerable benefit that the relative position of places on the ground and on the map in front of you are the same. No more turning maps upside down!

You may wish to augment the maps in the book with Ordnance Survey maps, and I have indicated in the text the relevant Outdoor Leisure Series (1:25 000) and Landranger (1:50 000) maps. The Outdoor Leisure maps 2, 7, 10, 30 and 31 together cover about half of the area of interest. They show detail down to field boundaries, which can be extremely useful in establishing your bearings when lost! The Pathfinder Series, also at 1:25 000, is available for the whole area, but each map covers only a restricted area and so this is an uneconomical option. On one walk down the South Tyne valley, I found that I was covering approximately £2 of map an hour!

When doing the initial research for the walks, it soon became apparent that some really excellent walks could be devised along 20 river valleys. My only concern was the logistics of carrying out these mainly linear walks. To my surprise, the difficulty turned out to be much less of a problem than I had feared as most of the Pennine valleys are tolerably well served by public transport.

Most of the walks described were carried out by driving to a bus or a train, taking the public transport and then walking back to the car. I am less enthusiastic about walking away from the car to catch public transport for the return journey – it may not always be reliable. Since the availability of public transport changes from time to time, and is also seasonal, I have indicated its availability in general terms only. For detailed information on transport and accommodation matters, you should contact the local Tourist Information Centres which I have always found to be most helpful. In the descriptions of the walks I have included the telephone numbers of the local Tourist Information Centres. Two very useful transport booklets which cover nearly all the area of interest, and which are available on request from Tourist Information Centres, are:

"Dales Connections" (covers the southern dales up to and including Swaledale),

"Bus and Train Services Across the Roof of England" (covers the Tees to the Tyne).

For a number of walks, I managed to persuade friends to bring another car so that we could have the luxury of walking between two cars. It always surprises me that so few people seem to do this since it is an excellent way of carrying out linear walks. If you do walk in this way, you have to be very disciplined to change into walking boots at the right time and leave your ordinary shoes in the right car. Walking away from your ordinary shoes is very unfortunate if you are planning to go into a posh pub at the end of the walk. You may laugh, but don't say I didn't warn you!

Taxis may seem an expensive option, but can be economical when there is more than one person. I have used taxis mainly in the upper reaches of a few of rivers where there is no public transport. Again, the local Tourist Information Centre is the best source of advice.

As so much of the landscape of the river valleys can be properly understood only from a knowledge of the underlying geology, I have included information on the fascinating topic of Pennine geology immediately after this section.

For those interested in history, the Pennines is a truly wonderful area.

So little has been disturbed, and there are features to be seen associated with nearly every period since the end of the Ice Age. At the end of each chapter there is a section indicating places of interest. The entries in these sections are cross-referenced to the maps using reference numbers within roundels. The appendix at the end of the book gives a more structured summary of the history of the region.

Geology and the formation of the Pennine Dales

From the diagram, it may be seen that most of the surface rocks in the Pennine dales were deposited between 280 million and 370 million years ago. This is known as the Carboniferous period for it was then that most of the world's coal reserves were formed.

Northern England was then a shallow tropical sea, located just north of the equator. Some 100 miles to the north, there was a land mass of continental size from which flowed enormous deltaic rivers similar to today's Nile and Mississippi. The combination of tropical sea and coastal strip next to a large land mass resulted, over tens of millions of years, in the deposition of vast quantities of calcareous shells, silts and sands.

The shells were later to compact to limestone, the silts to shales and the sand to gritstone. Many areas contain all three deposits due to the ever changing sea level and the changing directions of the discharges from the deltaic rivers.

The greatest deposits of limestone are the Great Scar limestones of the Craven district, such as the exposure seen at Kilnsey Crag in Wharfedale. Also in Craven, a coral barrier reef was established, stretching between the Ribble and the Wharfe, which later weathered to the line of reef knolls which may be seen today. Further north, the influence of the deltaic rivers limited the limestone to thinner deposits, sandwiched between shales and gritstones. The shallow marshy areas must have supported dense primeval forests as the shales and gritstones are interspersed with thin coal measures.

Over most of the Pennine Dales, we see repeated sequences of limestone, gritstone and shale. As this rhythmic sequence is at its most pronounced in Wensleydale, the sequences are called the Yoredale series; Yoredale being the medieval name for Wensleydale.

Although the majority of the rocks in the Pennines are of the Carboniferous period, around Sedbergh and in several valley bottoms in Craven there are older rocks more characteristic of the Lake District (Silurian and Ordovician). Red sandstones, younger rocks laid down when the area was an arid desert, are seen in the Eden valley. Even younger rocks must have been deposited across the Pennines, and it is probable that chalk, which is still seen on the east coast, covered the whole of the Pennines during the period known as the Cretaceous.

The importance of these rocks, which have long since disappeared, is

Sedi-
mentary
rocks
200 Myrs

Triassic

Permian

280 Myrs
Carbon-
iferous

Reef
knolls

370 Myrs
Devonian
(missing)

415 Myrs
Silurian
Ordovi-
cian

515 Mrs

Igneous
rocks

Fault line

Mineral
field

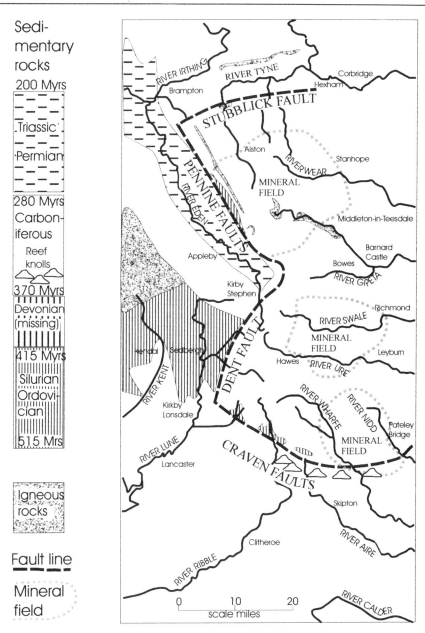

Rock types, faults and mineral fields

that they played an important role in the initial formation of the Pennine Dales. Rivers which eventually cut the valleys we see today, first flowed through these chalk deposits. Once the direction of the valleys had been established in the chalk (predominantly west to east), the rivers continued to flow along the same valleys when they reached the harder rocks below.

The west to east flow of the central rivers of the Pennine dales is the result of great earth movements which started towards the end of the Carboniferous period. This was a period of major mountain building in central Europe. Although the Pennines were a long way from the centre of this activity, they were, nevertheless, subjected to considerable stress.

Under stress, rocks may either fold or fracture. Further south, in the Peak District, the stressing led to the formation of a dome and the eventual establishment of a radial pattern of rivers. In the north Pennines, enormous fault lines developed along a line which has the approximate shape of a capital Greek letter (Σ), as shown in the diagram.

Although the individual sections of the fault were not all active at the same time, the eventual result was the lifting of the whole area contained within the fault lines. The process has been likened to the lifting of a lid which is hinged along its eastern edge. On the western edge, the vertical displacements were of the order of 5000 feet (over 1500m).

The result of this massive uplifting was to bring together, on opposite sides of the fault, rocks of widely differing ages, and it is along the edges of the fault that we see the oldest and youngest rocks:

* the oldest (Silurian and Ordovician) along the Dent and Craven Faults,
* the youngest (Permian and Triassic) along the Pennine Fault.

In addition to the Σ-shaped fault lines around the periphery of the Pennine Dales, there were three areas within the Σ which became highly fractured:

* Alston moor,
* Swaledale – Wensleydale,
* Grassington and Greenhow moor.

Lead and other minerals later migrated from the earth's magma and were deposited along these faults, producing mineral fields which were of great economic importance to the Pennines from Roman times to the end of the 19th century. A number of the villages and towns we find so attractive today were built largely on the profit from lead mining (Kettlewell and Grassington in Wharfedale, Reeth and Richmond in Swaledale and Alston in South Tynedale).

The period of stressing which accompanied the mountain building resulted in another phenomenon which is important to our story – the creation of the Whin Sill. Vast sheets of magma, typically 100 to 250 feet (30m to 75m) thick, were squeezed between the horizontal strata in the northern Pennines. The resulting rock, which is extremely hard and is known as the Whin Sill, mainly lies unexposed, below the surface. Where exposed, it leads to highly visible features. The ones seen on the walks are:

- High Force and Cauldron Snout in Teesdale,
- High Cup Nick,
- Lambley gorge (South Tyne),
- the ridge along the north of the Tyne valley on which Hadrian built the wall which was to be the northern boundary of the Roman Empire.

One of the delights of the Pennine Dales is the large number of waterfalls, many of which are spectacular. The waterfalls occur where a river crosses exposures of rocks of different hardness:

- the limestones, gritstones and shales of the Yoredale series (Wensleydale),
- the interface between Carboniferous and Silurian or Ordovician rocks (e.g. Doe-Twiss walk, Stainton Force (Ribble valley)),
- intrusions of igneous rocks (upper Teesdale).

The hard rock forms the upper lip of the waterfall, resisting erosion better than the softer rocks beneath. Waterfalls in Yoredale rocks, such as Hardraw Force, cut back along the water course to form long deep valleys.

With the exception of a few peaks such as Cross Fell, Ingleborough and Pen-y-Ghent, the ice sheet covered the whole of the Pennines during the Ice Age. Further south in the Peak District, the melt waters from the ice were the agents which initiated the formation of many of the river valleys, but in the northern Pennines the valleys had already been established. Here, the main action of the ice was to deepen valleys such as Littondale and convert them from V to U shape. Perhaps the most spectacular U-shaped valley is at High Cup Nick (Tees valley walk) where a glacier has cut across the Pennine Fault to expose a rim of Whin Sill.

In the valleys, boulder clay was formed into round deposits known as drumlins. Seen in many of the Dales, drumlins are most evident at Ribblehead and in the Ribble, in the Eden valley between Brough and Appleby and in the Aire valley between Hellifield and Skipton. These last deposits actually blocked the former channel of the Ribble (which had been down Airedale), and diverted the river westward to its present course. Drumlins are not to be confused with the similarly shaped reef knolls of Craven, whose origins have already been described.

At the end of the Ice Age, the Pennines were littered with rock debris deposited by the glaciers. In the millstone areas, stagnant acid conditions have led to the formation and accumulation of peat, whereas in the limestone areas there has been surface erosion averaging 0.5 to 1 metre.

The limestone scarps in Ribblesdale and Wharfedale, where we can still see the outlines of the hut settlements of Iron Age man, are now so bare that they would be uninhabitable today. Perhaps the most striking evidence

Glacial erratic in Ribblesdale

of erosion is the glacial "erratics" such as those seen at the start of the Ribble walk. The "erratics" have preferentially protected the rocks directly beneath, which in turn keep the "erratics" suspended above the local ground level.

In the first half of the nineteenth century, the British were pre-eminent in the field of geological research, and it was then that the fascinating story of the origin of the Pennine rocks was unravelled. John Philips, Curator of Fossils at York, wrote the classic book on the geology of Yorkshire in 1836. He named the recurring gritstone, shale, limestone sequences as the Yoredales, after Wensleydale, which he regarded as the typical locality.

Adam Sedgwick (1785-1873), son of the Vicar of Dent, and for many years Professor of Geology at Cambridge University, collaborated with Roderick Murchison in the first systematic study of pre-Carboniferous rocks. Sedgwick gave the names to the Cambrian and Devonian periods.

It can be no coincidence that, as a youth, Sedgwick would have seen pre-Carboniferous rocks, which he was later to make his life's work, in the riverbeds and hillsides around his home in Dent. Sedgwick is commemorated by a large granite memorial in the centre of Dent, and also by the Sedgwick Geological Trail in Garsdale which was opened to celebrate his bicentenary in 1985. The trail follows a short section of riverbank as the river crosses the Dent Fault. Only metres apart, you can see coral fossils in Carboniferous limestone and primitive graptolites which are millions of years older in Silurian rock. (To get the most out of a visit, it is a good idea to pick up a leaflet on the trail from the Tourist Information Office in Sedbergh).

Walk 1: River Aire

Section 1: Malham Tarn to Gargrave: 9 miles
Section 2: Gargrave to Skipton (via Sharp Haw: 8½ miles)
Information Centres: Skipton 01756 792809; Malham 01729 830363

Malhamdale, the name for the upper Aire valley, is one of the best known and loved limestone areas of the Yorkshire dales. The walk, which is described in two sections, is through the attractive countryside between Malham Tarn and Skipton, where the river passes out of the limestone into a sinuous gritstone valley, on its way to industrial Yorkshire.

Malham, Skipton and the intervening villages are of Anglo-Saxon and Danish origin. Skipton, with its attractive, wide high street, has one of the finest castles in northern England and the Craven Museum, in Skipton High Street, has an excellent collection of artefacts relating to the history of the Dales.

Section 1: Malham Tarn to Gargrave

Starting at Malham Tarn, the walk descends to Malham over the spectacularly exposed Craven Fault at Malham Cove. It then follows the crystal clear river past a number of villages of Anglo-Saxon and Danish origin before reaching Gargrave.

At Gargrave, "drumlins", well-rounded hillocks formed under glaciers, fill the valley bottom, while gritstone hilltops dominate the skyline. Malham has long been a major tourist attraction and is best visited outside peak periods.

Distance: 9 miles

Starting point: Malham Tarn car park, SD895658

Public transport: There is a bus service from Skipton via Gargrave.

Maps: 1.1 and 1.2 plus Outdoor Leisure 10 or Landranger 98 and 103.

The walk starts at the rather rough and muddy car park just to the east of the stream which flows out of the Malham Tarn. Cross the stream and follow it away from the tarn. In a short distance you will come to the Water Sinks, where the stream flows underground.

Follow the dry valley for about a mile to Malham Cove. Until 1824 the

View from the top of Malham Cove

stream occasionally flowed down
this valley to produce what must
have been a magnificent waterfall
at the Cove. The limestone pavement above the Cove gives excellent views of Malham Beck 250
feet (75m) below, with Malham
village nestling in the valley bottom behind. On the far horizon,
you should be able to see the
pointed gritstone hilltop of Sharp
Haw, which will be visited on the
second part of the walk.

From the top of the Cove, field
systems can be seen which span
a period of two millennia:

- small Celtic fields in the valley
  bottom (almost levelled and
  best seen in side lighting in the
  morning or evening),

- long strip lynchets produced
  by ox teams from Anglo-Saxon
  to late medieval times,

- enclosures of the 18th century,
  built when the dales changed
  from arable to pastoral farming.

Cawden, the rounded hill just to
the east of Malham, is a reef knoll,
one of a line stretching between
the Ribble and the Wharfe. Others
will be seen from the top of Sharp
Haw on the second section of the
walk. Cross the pavement to the
west side of the Cove and take the
path down to the village.

It might seem logical to sup-
pose that the beck which you see
appearing at the base of the Cove
is the same stream which disappeared underground at the Water
Sinks. In fact, the collecting
ground for Malham Beck is the

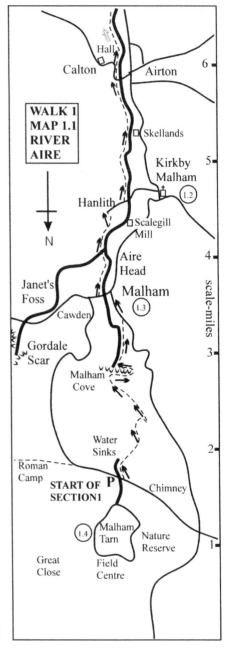

area to the South West of Malham tarn and the water from the Water Sinks reappears at Aire Head, to the south of Malham.

From Malham, there are footpaths down both sides of the river. My preference is to take the path down the east side of the river, which follows the Pennine Way. Shortly after passing a sign to Janet's Foss, you will see the springs of Aire Head on the other bank, the re-emergence of the water from Malham Tarn which went underground at the Water Sinks.

The path climbs a small hillock from which there are excellent views looking back to Malham Cove and Gordale Scar. Below, on your right, you will pass Scalegill Mill. There has been a mill here at least back to the time of the Domesday Book. Although the mill has now been converted into holiday flats, it is pleasing to see that water power is still used to generate electricity (using a turbine).

The path reaches the village of Hanlith at some farm buildings which are well up the hillside from the river. Take the lane downhill, past Hanlith Hall to the river, and enter the field at the bridge.

(Not directly on the line of the walk, but only about a quarter of a mile to the west and well worth a detour to see if you have the time, is the attractive village of Kirkby Malham with its 15th century church.)

Below Hanlith Bridge, after traversing a long field and then passing a small wood on your left, you will see some farm buildings across the river, on the Airton to Malham road. This is Skellands, the home of Dr. James King who circumnavigated the world with Captain Cook.

As you come into Airton, there is an 18th century cotton spinning mill on the opposite bank, now converted into flats. From Airton the walk proceeds down the river, but you could take a short cut here to the second section (cutting out Gargrave) by bearing left up the hill at Airton to Friar's Head. If you decide to take this short cut, do look out in Calton for Calton Hall (on the Hetton Road). A plaque commemorates James Lambert, a distinguished General in Cromwell's army, who lived in the Hall.

Follow the riverbank down from Airton to the next river bridge. At Newfield Bridge, cross the bridge and follow the opposite bank for a short distance before recrossing at a footbridge. From the footbridge, climb uphill, walking diagonally across a large field at Eel Ark Hill. Ark is a medieval word for trap and the medieval monks would have caught their eels in the stream here.

About three-quarters of a mile after crossing the footbridge below Eel Ark Hill, you will come to a sign at the crossing of two footpaths. Leave the Pennine Way, bearing right towards an old limestone quarry at Haw Crag. From the crest of the hill there are fine panoramic views of the Aire valley below, with the gritstone hilltops of Pendle Hill and Sharp Haw dominating the skyline. The road and railway thread their ways through the drumlin-filled valley to Settle. Before the last Ice Age, the River Ribble also came down this valley from Settle, but glacial debris between Hellifield and Gargrave forced the river westwards.

Descend from the quarry to Mark House Lane which will take you to Gargrave. Hollow-ways in the lane suggest ancient usage – before the opening of the Keighley to Kendal turnpike in 1750, this quiet track was one of the main routes up Airedale.

As you descend into Gargrave, you will see the 15th century tower of St Andrew's Church ahead. The road will take you over the Leeds – Liverpool canal to the main square.

Section 2: Gargrave to Skipton (via Sharp Haw)

The walk from Gargrave to Skipton climbs 800 feet (240m) to pass over Sharp Haw, a gritstone hilltop, from which there are good panoramic views not only over the Aire valley below, but also over to the Ribble and Wharfe valleys beyond.

Just outside Gargrave, the walk passes a small Elizabethan Hall, Friar's Head, which is an architectural gem.

Distance: 8½ miles

Starting point: The Square, Gargrave SD932542

Public transport: There is a regular bus service between Gargrave and Skipton.

Maps: 1.2 plus Outdoor Leisure 10 or Landranger 103.

From the Square, take the road towards Skipton and then turn left towards Malham (Eshton Road). The Eshton Road has a good footpath on the left side.

About two thirds of a mile from the village centre, you will see a footpath to the left. Take this, crossing the field diagonally. In the next field bear left a further 30 degrees to make for the gate into the wood ahead. After the wood, the path takes you back to the Malham Road, which you cross. The next field path leads to a lane over the Eshton Beck to Brockabank. Pass to the left of Brockabank, and in a short distance you will come out onto Winterburn Lane.

A short distance up the lane is Friar's Head, an exquisite small Elizabethan Hall which is said to have 365 windows (see Appendix for the history of the hall).

At Friar's Head, take the path to the right, which climbs uphill, following the line of the wall. At the second field boundary, bear right to cross the next field diagonally to an orange marker with the numbers "58.2". This is

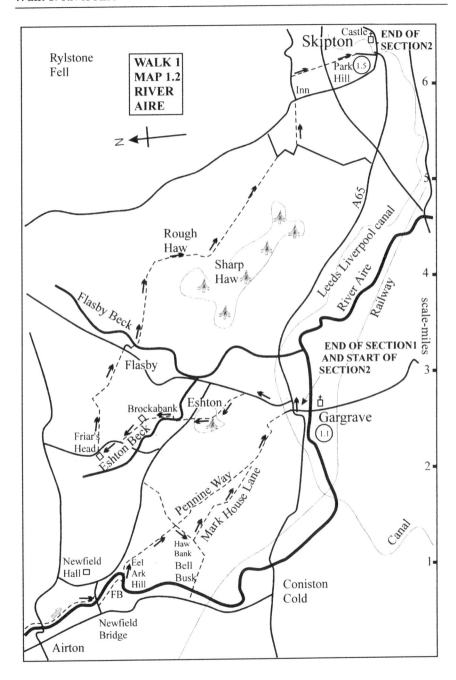

WALK 1
MAP 1.2
RIVER
AIRE

Rylstone
Fell

Skipton

Castle

END OF
SECTION2

Park 1.5
Hill

Inn

6

5

Rough
Haw

Sharp
Haw

A65

Leeds Liverpool canal

River Aire

Railway

4

Flasby Beck

Flasby

END OF SECTION1
AND START OF
SECTION2

scale-miles

3

Brockabank

Eshton

Gargrave
1.1

Friar's
Head

Eshton Beck

2

Pennine Way

Mark House Lane

Canal

Haw
Bank

Newfield
Hall

Eel
Ark
Hill

Bell
Busk

Coniston
Cold

1

FB

Newfield
Bridge

Airton

the marker for an ethylene pipeline from Teesside to Cheshire, the number indicating the distance from the production plant.

From here there are good views of Sharp Haw and Flasby Fell ahead. Follow the left-hand wall of the field ahead then bear right at the next corner. Stay in the same field, but cross it towards the gate in the opposite stone wall. When the gate is reached, cross the stile which is next to it and follow the line of the wall down to the village of Flasby.

In Flasby, cross the road and take the lane down to and over Flasby Beck. When you come to a signpost, take the road ahead marked Grassington Road 2½ miles. At the end of the track you will enter open moorland which can be boggy in places. There is a small stream to your right, and as you walk uphill, you will be forced to your left to a wall.

The line of the wall points towards Rough Haw, which you may care to climb. Rough Haw is, however, flatter topped and lower than Sharp Haw, and there is little you can see from Rough Haw which is not better viewed from Sharp Haw.

To gain access to Sharp Haw, find the break in the wall which is on a line almost directly between Rough Haw and Sharp Haw. Climb directly from here to the trig point. Although this is not marked on the maps as a right of way, it is a permissive path. There is a gritstone ridge in front of Sharp Haw, but because it is slightly lower, it does not impede your view of the valley. On a clear day Sharp Haw gives excellent panoramic views:

- to the north west are the limestone outcrops above Malham Cove,

- to the south west, in the foreground is the Aire valley, with Pendle Hill in the Ribble valley in the distance,

- to the south east is Skipton, with the narrow gritstone valley behind it through which the Aire travels towards industrial Yorkshire,

- to the north east, at Cracoe, the reef knolls on the west side of the Wharfe valley can be seen.

The centre of Skipton is about 3 miles away and you start the gentle descent over open moorland with skylarks overhead. In about a mile you join a track coming down from the wood on the western face of Sharp Haw. This track takes you down to a small road, which you turn right to join. At the third bend, as the road swings right, you should take the path ahead, down the fields. Cross the Grassington Road and take the lane ahead for about a quarter of a mile before turning right onto a path which will take you to Skipton. The path crosses the A65 before climbing a small hill, Park Hill, which has a commanding view of the castle. During the Civil War, the Parliamentary forces took advantage of this position by placing a cannon battery here with which they besieged the Royalists in the castle.

Places of interest in the Aire valley

1.1 Gargrave

Although settled in Roman times (one of the few Roman villas in northern England was close to the village), Gargrave's period of greatest prosperity came at the end of the 18th century because of its position in an important transport corridor across the Pennines. First to arrive, in 1750, was the Keighley – Kendal turnpike (The White Swan was a coaching Inn), followed by the Leeds – Liverpool canal in 1777.

Gargrave was the canal's western terminus for 39 years as the canal company were unable to afford to complete the section between Gargrave and Liverpool. The main cargoes were coal (being brought into Craven), and lead and zinc (being shipped out).

Gargrave is overlooked by the gritstone outcrops of Sharp Haw and the valley bottom is dominated by "drumlins", rounded hillocks of glacial debris formed during the last Ice Age.

Although restored in Victorian times, the church foundation goes back to pre-Norman times. The tower is of the 15th century, a time when the church was the benefice of Sawley Abbey.

Johnson and Johnson, the medical supplies company, has a large factory at Gargrave. The quality of the air was one attraction of the location.

1.2 Kirkby Malham

Kirkby Malham is a most attractive village with many 17th century buildings. The church, known as the Cathedral of the Dales, is of the 15th century. It was once the benefice of West Dereham Abbey and consequently has many features normally associated with Norfolk. The name Kirkby suggests that the church foundation is of a much earlier age, being already established when the Danes settled the village. There is a three-seater stone stocks dated 1677 in the churchyard.

One of Oliver Cromwell's generals, James Lambert, lived in the neighbouring village of Calton. Although successful as a general, Lambert was one of those imprisoned at the Restitution of the Monarchy and ended his life in Plymouth gaol. Cromwell visited the village in 1657 and his signature appears in the church register.

Another famous son of Kirby Malham is Dr James King who lived at Skellands (on the road between Kirby Malham and Airton). Dr King made the first circumnavigation of the world with Captain Cook.

1.3 Malham

An attractive village with several 17th and 18th century houses, Malham is a farming settlement of great antiquity. The fields in the valley around Malham show farming over a period of two thousand years:

- Celtic (small fields delineated by rubble remains),
- Anglo-Saxon (strip lynchets produced by ox teams),
- 18th century enclosures.

Just to the north of Malham, the Craven Fault is spectacularly exposed at Malham cove (250ft) and Gordale Scar (150ft). Cawden Hill, just to the east of Malham Beck, is one of the series of reef knolls which lies along the southern edge of the Craven Fault.

1.4 Malham Tarn

The tarn is one of only two natural lakes in the Yorkshire Dales (the other being Semer Water). It owes its existence to a layer of impervious Silurian slate. The south-facing slopes around the tarn have produced the greatest concentration of microlithic flints in the Dales, and suggest that the tarn was a favoured fishing spot in Mesolithic times.

Mastiles Lane, the road which runs to the south of the tarn was, from the 13th century, used by the monks of Fountains Abbey to take sheep from their western granges to Kilnsey for shearing. The road may be much older for it passes through a Roman fort just over a mile to the east of the tarn.

Great Close, Malham Tarn was one of the most important centres of the droving trade. Animals were fattened there and sold at great fairs. In the mid-18th century, a Mr Birtwhistle of Skipton rented the 732 acres of the Great Close. As many as 20,000 cattle would pass through in a year. At any one time 10,000 cattle could be on the road to Malham – typically in herds of about 200.

In the late 18th and early 19th centuries, zinc was mined on Malham Moor and smelted at the tarn before being transported to Gargrave by packhorse for shipment down the Leeds – Liverpool canal. The chimney of the smelter may still be seen to the south east of the tarn.

Tarn House was built as a shooting lodge by Lord Ribblesdale and later became the home of Walter Morrison, eccentric Liberal MP and philanthropist. During his ownership the house was visited by a stream of well-known people including John Ruskin, John Stuart Mill, Charles Darwin and Charles Kingsley, who wrote "The Water Babies" there.

Today the house is a field centre for Tarn Moss, a wetland Nature Reserve of international importance.

1.5 Skipton, "The Gateway to the Dales"

A 7th century Anglo-Saxon settlement, Skipton ("Sheep town"), is strategically placed to command the access to the Aire Gap, one of the easiest passages through the Pennines. The Aire Gap was of military importance for many centuries and the Normans built a castle at Skipton in the 12th century. Originally owned by the de Romilles, the castle later passed to the Cliffords. The castle was under siege for three years (1642-5) during the

Civil War, but was restored to its current glory by Lady Anne Clifford between 1655 and 1658.

Although many of the buildings in the High Street are of 18th century origin, the earlier medieval layout has been largely preserved. The infilling in the narrow alleyways behind the High Street is on the gardens of the houses which originally fronted the High Street.

The coming of the turnpike, canal and railway down the Aire valley led to a rapid growth in Skipton's size and prosperity in the 18th and 19th centuries. Today Skipton is a busy market and tourist centre. The castle is open daily and the Craven Museum has an interesting display of the history of the Dales.

Walk 2: River Allen

Section 1: Whitfield to Haydon Bridge 9½ miles
Section 2: Allendale Town to Haydon Bridge 10½ miles
Information Centre: Hexham 01434 605225

The Allen rises as two tributary rivers, the West and East Allen. After the confluence, near Cupola Bridge, the river, which is now simply the Allen, flows northwards through a deep, spectacular gorge, on its way to the Tyne.

The delightful National Trust property at Allen Banks is well known, and is made accessible by a large car park. The upper end of the gorge at Staward Peel and the tributary rivers above Cupola Bridge attract fewer visitors.

The two walks described start respectively on the West and East Allen rivers, and end at Haydon Bridge on the Tyne. You could choose shorter sections from the walks described, perhaps walking the upper tributaries only, or the lower valley starting form Cupola Bridge or High Staward. Buses from Haydon Bridge and Hexham allow you to reach the starting point using public transport.

Section 1: Whitfield to Haydon Bridge

This walk comprises three main sections: a first section on the plateau above the West Allen, with good views over the valley below; a middle section through delightful woodlands, following the Allen gorge between Cupola Bridge and Allen Bank and passing the fortified tower at Staward Peel; a final section which climbs through the famous deciduous woodlands at the National Trust's Allen Banks before descending to the Tyne Valley.

Distance: 9½ miles

Starting point: Whitfield, NY782570

Public transport: A mid-morning bus from Haydon Bridge will take you to Whitfield. To shorten the walk, get off at High Staward or Cupola Bridge.

Maps: 2.1 plus Landranger 87.

In Whitfield, take the road from the public house towards Allendale Town. Cross the river and take the footpath into the woods on the left. When you come out into the open, bear left across the field towards the farmhouse at

The Allen gorge near Staward Peel

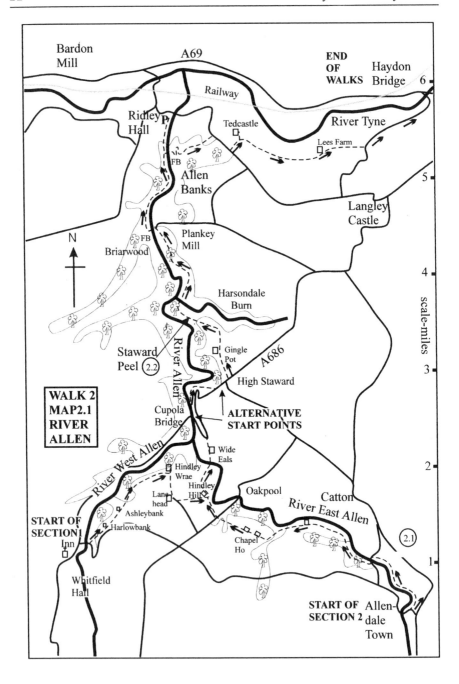

Bardon
Mill
A69
END
OF   Haydon
WALKS   Bridge   6

Railway

Ridley   Tedcastle   River Tyne
Hall
Lees Farm
FB
Allen   5
Banks
Langley
Castle
N
FB   Plankey
Briarwood   Mill   4

Harsondale
Burn

Staward   River Allen   Gingle
Peel (2.2)   Pot   A686
High Staward   3

WALK 2
MAP2.1   Cupola
RIVER   Bridge   **ALTERNATIVE**
ALLEN   **START POINTS**
River West Allen
Wide
Eals   2
Hindley
Wrae
Lane   Hindley
head   Hill   Oakpool   Catton
River East Allen
START OF   Ashleybank
SECTION   Harlowbank   (2.1)
Inn   Chapel
Ho   1

Whitfield
Hall
START OF Allen-
SECTION 2 dale
Town

scale-miles

Harlowbank. Cross the track in front of the farmhouse and keep to the right of the building. Now make for the next building, at Ashleybank, descending across the fields to reach it. Again, pass to the right of the building.

Follow the hillside, enjoying some good views down the valley towards the confluence with the East Allen. When the path reaches the track going down to Hindley Wrae, turn right and follow the track uphill until you come to Lanehead. Here you take the path on the left to Hindley Hill.

At Hindley Hill, go around the farm, bearing left. From the farm, take the track which is roughly parallel to the East Allen river. After passing a muddy patch at the top of a small gully, go to the edge of the plateau. Below you is the alluvial plain of the East Allen.

Drop down the hillside, making across a bridge to the farmhouse at Wide Eals. Skirt to the left of the farm, and follow the farm road up to the A686. Here you bear left and go down to the Cupola Bridge. (Next to the bridge there is space to park a few cars.) This handsome bridge with three arches was built following an Act of Parliament in 1778, and was named after the adjacent lead-smelting mill.

Just before the river, take the path on the right into the woods. Shortly, the river curves to the right and the path climbs steeply through the woods. When you come out of the woods, the path divides, one leg forking left and staying in the woods and the other going into the field. Take the path into the field and go to the road.

Follow the road uphill for a short distance until you come to a road on the right to Allendale Town (take care since there is no footpath). Opposite the end of a large wall, take the gate into the fields on the left. Follow the track which passes to the right of the ruined building at Gingle Pot.

Follow the path to the end of the field where it goes into the woods along a promontory between the Allen and Harsondale valleys. There are some excellent views from this promontory, looking out over the two valleys. Shortly you will come to Staward Peel.

From Staward Peel, take the path ahead which descends steeply to join a path in the Allen valley below. When the path meets the riverbank, carry on downstream for about three-quarters of a mile to come to Plankey Mill. At Plankey Mill, there is a footbridge over the river which you should take.

Pass through the edge of Briarwood Bank, a woodland thought to have been undisturbed since the Ice Age and now owned by the Northumberland Wildlife Trust. The path then takes you into property owned by the National Trust. (The 194 acres of woodland were given to the National Trust by a member of the Queen Mother's family.)

Just less than a mile from Plankey Mill you will reach a suspension bridge over the river at Allen Banks.

Cross the suspension bridge, and turn to Section 3 of the Tyne walk for directions for the next part of the walk down to Haydon Bridge.

Section 2: Allendale Town to Haydon Bridge

Much of the first part of this walk is along the East Allen riverbank as it crosses an attractive former lake bed. At Hindley Hill you will join the walk down the West Allen, and the description of the walk down the Allen gorge and across to Haydon Bridge is found in Section 1.

Distance: 10½ miles

Starting point: Allendale Town, NY835558

Public transport: There are several buses a day from Hexham to Allendale Town. From the end point of the walk at Haydon Bridge there are frequent buses back to your starting point at Hexham (there is also a train).

Maps: 2.1 plus Landranger 87.

The walk starts about 100 metres from the bridge over the East Allen at Allendale Town. A signpost indicates Allen Mill ¾ and Oakpool 2¾.

As you follow the river below the town, you will pass a culvert going into the hillside, just before you cross a small stream. This was built to drain the Allendale lead mines. At the first road bridge downstream, cross to the other side of the river and take the path into the woodlands.

When you come out of the woodlands, you will go onto a flat alluvial plain which is a former lake bed. This runs all the way down the valley to the confluence with the West Allen near Cupola Bridge, and is a most attractive part of the walk.

Just under a mile after leaving the woods, you will come to a small stream coming down a wooded gully. Take the footpath over the stream and follow the path which climbs up the hillside. When you reach the plateau above, look for the chimney high up on the skyline to the left. The chimney was connected to the lead smelter in Allendale Town by a flue which ran up the hillside.

The path follows the top of the wooded gully until you reach a stile opposite to Chapel House. Cross the stile here and make for the left of the farmhouse. At the stile turn right. Do not go into the farmyard, but follow the rather inconspicuous waymarker on the left, pointing towards the next farm.

At the next farmhouse, there are two footpaths. The first, just to the left of the farmhouse, you should ignore (this would take you back to the bottom of the valley). Take the stile about 50 metres to the left of the farmhouse and follow the line of the wall across two fields to come to the narrow road coming up from Oakpool. Drop 50 metres down from this road and then take the farm road to Hindley Hill. Go through the farmyard and take the track which maintains a general direction parallel to the river valley to your right. You have now joined the walk which started at

Whitfield, and for the description of the rest of the walk, you should turn to Section 1.

Places of interest in Allendale

2.1 Allendale Town

At one time, Allendale produced a sixth of Britain's lead, and it was the lead which justified the building of a town in such an isolated location.

The chimneys of the former lead operations may still be seen on the hilltops. (The building of a two mile flue up the hillside gave the Allendale Town smelter a chimney with an effective height of 700 feet (212m)!)

Apart from tourism, which is today revitalising the local economy, the town's two main claims to fame are:

* a medieval fire festival, known as Baal Fire, on New Year's Eve,

* a position said to be at the centre of the country (disputed in 1995 by Plenmeller in the Tyne valley).

2.2 Staward Peel

Staward Peel was built in 1273 and given to the Friars of Hexham in 1386. With walls seven feet (2.1m) thick, sheer drops to the Allen and Hardondale valleys and a drawbridge on the approach from High Staward, the peel was an ideal place to which the monks could retreat during the frequent Scottish raids.

The peel was a popular tourist attraction during the Victorian period, with passengers alighting at Staward Peel and taking refreshments at Gingle Pot. With the closing of the railway line, the peel is today less accessible and less frequently visited. Only two sides of the peel are now standing, and the views are rather restricted by the trees. From nearby on the approach ridge, however, there are excellent views of the two valleys below.

Walk 3: River Calder

Section 1: Todmorden to Hebden Bridge via Blackshaw Head and Heptonstall, 8 miles
Section 2: Hebden Bridge to Todmorden via Stoodley Pike, 6½ miles
Information Centres: Halifax 01422 368725;
Hebden Bridge 01422 843831; Todmorden 01706 818181

Although the valley bottom is industrialised, and the River Calder is not particularly attractive, Calderdale offers some splendid walking along the hilltops. Throughout the dale, you will see evidence of the development of the cloth-weaving industry:

* farmhouses with a large number of small, mullioned upstairs windows which gave light to the handloom weavers,
* the grander houses of the yeomen clothiers,
* water and steam-powered mills,
* extensive paved packhorse ways over the hilltops which were used to bring wool to the weavers.

Before the dissolution of the monasteries, much of this wool would have come from monastic houses such as Whalley Abbey.

Although prehistoric settlement in the Pennines was mainly on high ground, by Saxon times the valley bottoms had been cleared and settled. The Calder valley was an exception, and even in late medieval times settlement was confined to the hilltops where cloth weaving supplemented meagre farm incomes. Only towards the end of the 18th century did the demand for textiles cause manufacture to move from the hilltop homes in Heptonstall to the valley bottom factories at Hebden Bridge. Heptonstall was left intact and is largely as it was in the 18th century.

The two walks described, which could be amalgamated into a single circular walk, are confined to the valley above Hebden Bridge. For a more complete understanding of the history of the textile industry, you might like to complement the walks with a visit to Halifax to see the Piece Hall and adjacent Industrial Museum (a good use of a wet day).

The walks make extensive use of the Calderdale and Pennine Ways. Although these are reasonably well signposted, waymarking is not sufficient for you to dispense entirely with a map or guide. The Calder valley is particularly accessible to public transport, with regular trains from Manchester, Leeds and Preston. Using the train to get from one end of a walk to the other also solves a parking problem. There is only limited car parking in the Calder valley, but rail users can park at the station.

Section1: Todmorden to Hebden Bridge via Blackshaw Head and Heptonstall

This walk begins with a steep climb out of the valley from Todmorden, before following medieval packhorse routes to Heptonstall, a unique pre-Industrial Revolution textile village. There is then a steep descent to Hebden Bridge (which took over from Heptonstall when weaving moved out of the home into the mill). The route crosses the Hebden Water by a 16th century packhorse bridge at the site of the first settlement at Hebden Bridge.

Distance: 8 miles

Starting point: Todmorden Town Hall SD936242

Public transport: There are regular trains between Hebden Bridge and Todmorden, making it easy to plan this linear walk

Maps: 3.1 plus Outdoor Leisure 21.

From the road junction at the Todmorden Town Hall, take the A646, the Burnley Road. After passing under the railway viaduct, pass, in turn, the Cricket field, Centre Vale park, a mill and the High School.

At the end of the school playing field, follow Stoney Royd Lane (on the right), which for a short distance follows the Calder riverbank. Pass under the railway viaduct and follow the path in front of Stannally Farm. The path zigzags uphill and as you climb higher, there is a deep gully to your left. Towards the top of the gully, the path bears right through a gate onto moorland.

After passing a farm on the right, a zigzag leads you to a paved packhorse way above. Follow this to the right. Cross Whirlaw Common and after going through a gate, descend below Whirlaw Stones over a paved way. Below, you should be able to see your starting point – Todmorden Town Hall and the railway viaduct. As you come round the end of the hill, Stoodley Pike appears high above you on the other side of the valley. The Pike will remain in view for most of the rest of the walk.

After passing a farm on the right, cross a stile and take the path on the right which follows a wall downhill. In about 5 minutes you will reach a small stream running under the path. Here there is a choice of paths. Ignore the track which continues down the clough and take the path ahead, which climbs upwards. In about 50 metres, take the stile on the left. The path passes some huts and then a golf club.

Turn left at a road, but when you reach a house on your left, turn right, off the road and go through a gate. Pass a farm on your right and cross two fields to a hollow-way. After the hollow-way, cross a small patch of moorland back into the fields.

Pass two more farms on the right to come to another sunken way. You

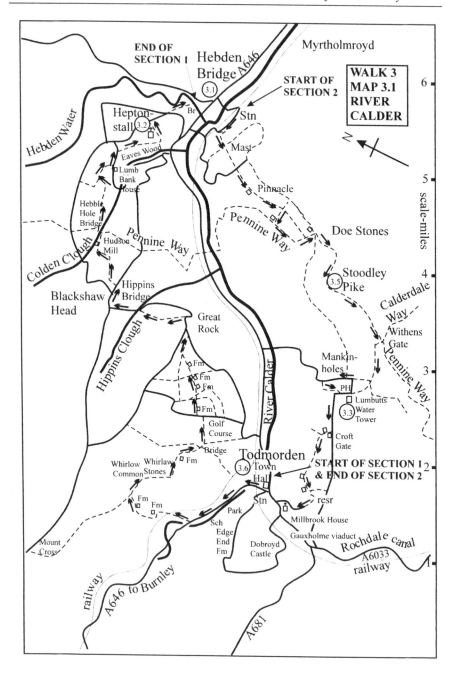

should cross this and a gully then skirt to the left of a holly bush to reach the next farm. After passing to the left of the farm, follow a hollow-way upwards. Keep climbing until you reach a level path above, which you follow to the right. This path will take you forward to a road. Bear left onto the road, but then right at the T-junction to come to Great Rock. From here, there are wonderful views across and up and down the valley.

From Great Rock, take the path to the left. In about half a mile this path descends steeply to rejoin the road from Great Rock at Hippins Bridge. Cross the bridge, and follow the road up to Blackshaw Head. (In antiquity, Blackshaw Head was the crossing point for several important hilltop tracks.)

Turn to the right at the T-junction in Blackshaw Head and, ignoring the turning to Hebden Bridge via Heptonstall, go down Badger Lane, past the cemetery (in medieval times, a badger was a corn-dealer). Take the path on the left into the fields. Cross the hill ridge and descend diagonally across the fields towards Colden Clough. When you reach a hollow-way, follow it downhill to the left to a house. Bear left here onto a metalled road, and then right to follow the clough.

Pass Hudson Mill, originally a corn mill, on your left and you will shortly reach the Pennine Way making its way northwards. Turn left onto the Pennine Way and descend steeply to the bottom of the clough where there is a delightful clapper bridge (Hebble Hole Bridge). The builders of this bridge must have used considerable ingenuity to manoeuvre the massive stone slabs in such a difficult place!

From the bridge, the path climbs upwards along ancient pavings to the corner of a wood, and then crosses several fields, some of them flagged.

Ignore a path joining you on the right, but when you reach a T-junction, bear right and detour around a derelict building. From here there are fine views of the steep-sided clough below as it turns away towards the valley bottom.

Follow the line of the wall down to a crossing of several paths. Here take the path (between walls) which leads ahead towards the edge of the woods. Bear left onto the metalled road which comes up from Lumb Bank House, and follow the road until it swings to the left. Here take the path to the right. (This path will shortly cross the top of some gritstone outcrops with considerable drops to the right, so if the visibility is poor, it is better to keep to the metalled road into Heptonstall.)

If you have taken the field path, go along the top of Eaves Wood. The terrain is uneven, with the path crossing a boulder field. When you reach Eaves Rocks, there are excellent views over the valley below. From the rocks, there is an inclined path on the right down to the valley bottom. However, if you wish to visit the delightful medieval weaving village of Heptonstall, take the path on the left through an estate of modern stone houses to the two churches. (If you have the time, it is well worth exploring the many interesting buildings in Heptonstall – see places of interest.)

When you reach the main road, Towngate, the building to your left, is a 16th century cloth hall, the earliest in Yorkshire. Turn right here and follow the road downhill. Some care is needed as the road is narrow and there is no footpath. However, the steepness of the road is an advantage since it keeps the traffic speed low. In about a quarter of a mile you can leave the road to take the steps on the left. From here there is a bird's eye view of Hebden Bridge. This is even more attractive at night when the valley lights twinkle below.

When you reach a road, bear right for a short distance before taking the steep cobbled path on the left which goes down to the Old Bridge below. This is the old road to Heptonstall from the valley and is more than four centuries old. During the Civil War, this hillside was the scene of fierce fighting between Royalists from Halifax and Parliamentary forces camping in Heptonstall above. The Royalists were repulsed, and as they retreated, the Roundheads rolled boulders down the hillside onto them. To add to the Royalist woes, the river was swollen and some of their number were drowned as they attempted to recross the packhorse bridge.

Medieval bridge at Hebden Bridge

Section 2: Hebden Bridge to Todmorden via Stoodley Pike

In comparison with the other side of the valley, the north-facing slopes of the Calder valley receive little sunlight, and were ignored by the early settlers. The few settlements established, such as Sowerby Bridge and Mankinholes, were by the Norse – the more favourable sites on the other side of the valley having been previously taken by the Anglo-Saxons.

The Normans reinforced the wilderness nature of the south side of the valley by making it a hunting park (Errington Park) which was not dispaled until the 15th century. (If you study the Leisure series Ordnance Survey map, you will see several place names which reflect the hunting history of the hillside – Buckley Stone, Doe Stone.)

This fine walk, which incorporates parts of the Pennine Way and the Calderdale Way, climbs steeply out of the valley and crosses a plateau before climbing to Stoodley Pike. At 1300 feet (394m), this gives excellent panoramic views over much of the Calder valley. The delightful ancient village of Mankinholes is visited and an interesting water-wheel tower is seen at Lumbutts before descending to Todmorden.

As with the walk on the other side of the valley, several sections are former packhorse routes and are paved. The most impressive section of paving is from Withens Gate down to Mankinholes.

Distance: 6½ miles

Starting point: Hebden Bridge railway station SD995268

Public transport: There is a regular train service between Todmorden and Hebden Bridge, making it easy to plan this linear walk.

Maps: 3.1 plus Outdoor Leisure 21.

From the Hebden Bridge railway station, walk away from the direction of the town centre. Go under the railway line, climb uphill and turn right along Palace House Road. Towards the end of Palace House Road, as it descends towards the railway line, take the lane on the left before some traffic lights. About 100 metres up this lane, take the path between walls on the right as it climbs diagonally upwards across a field.

At the end of the field, a wall-line is reached. Here you are in line with the Hebden Water as it flows under the old packhorse bridge and, after only a small climb from the valley bottom, you get an excellent view over the town below.

Bear left uphill through the wood. At the top of the wood, cross the roadway (there is a mast on your left) and follow the sign to Pinnacle Lane. In the third field above the wood, you reach a plateau and Stoodley Pike comes into view. Looking back, you will see that you are now at the same level as Heptonstall on the other side of the valley.

After two more fields, cross the road coming up from the valley onto Pinnacle Lane, and pass the farmhouse of Pinnacle with its small mullioned windows. At the end of a long straight stretch, the way goes through a sharp double bend. After a gate, the lane peters out and you cross the fields ahead towards the Pike. When a lane is reached, turn right and walk down to a farm where you turn left onto the Pennine Way.

At the end of a long thin field, reedy moorland is reached. The OS map shows the path going forward here, but by custom and practice the track bears left to cut to the corner of the next field. Here follow the line of the wall and start the gentle ascent from the plateau. At the end of the wall, cross a track from a smallholding on your left and follow the path up to the Pike.

Stoodley Pike is undoubtedly the best vantage point from which to view the panorama of the Calder valley. In front of you, it is possible to see most of the route from the Pike to Todmorden. Over the other side of the valley, the route from Todmorden to Heptonstall which was described in the first section can be traced as it passes identifiable farmhouses across the patchwork of fields. To the south is bleak moorland as far as the eye can see.

Leave the Pike along the path to the south. The path follows the hilltop edge, which is strewn with gritstone boulders. Follow the edge as it swings towards the east, ignoring smaller paths off to the left and right. In just under a mile from the Pike, you will come to a large standing stone and a signpost. This is Withens Gate, where the Pennine Way and the Calderdale Way cross.

Bear right onto the Calderdale Way and follow a magnificent paved packhorse way for half a mile as it descends steeply across the hillside.

This is a relatively modern paved way, having been built in the cotton famine of the 1840s to generate employment for millworkers. Ironically, the construction of the paving more or less coincided with the end of centuries of packhorse trade. The main beneficiaries of the generosity of the Victorian millowners have been hill walkers!

Do not descend all the way to the Lumbutts millponds. When you reach a gate, take the track on the right to Mankinholes. As you go through this ancient village, note the drinking troughs on the right (for the packhorses and cattle) and the delightful 17th and 18th century houses. Go slightly beyond the village and take the path on the left, again flagged, towards Lumbutts.

In Lumbutts, bear left past the Top Brink Inn and descend to the road, where you turn right, passing the Lumbutts water-wheel tower. Follow the road uphill. Just less than half a mile from the bottom of the clough, on the right, you will reach Croft Gate cottage with a lintel dated 1598.

Turn to the right here and walk down the lane. At the farm, go through a gate onto a walled track. At the end of the field, go through squeeze posts on the left. The path follows the line of the wall across three fields and then crosses a further two fields to reach a farm.

Go to the left of the farm and take the path across the field to the next farm. Your path through the farm takes you between stables. Bear left along the farm road. At a T-junction bear right, and then right again below the bank of a reservoir.

The roadway will now take you downhill into Todmorden, passing on the way the Unitary church built by the Fieldens, the local mill owners. No expense was spared, and a most unusual feature was a waterwheel beneath the church to drive the organ!

At the bottom of the hill you will reach Fielden Square. Bear right here, cross the Rochdale Canal and follow the Rochdale road to the Town Hall.

Places of interest in the Calder valley

3.1 Hebden Bridge

When the Calder valley was first settled, the valley bottom was waterlogged and the settlements were established on the hilltops. A wooden bridge was built across the Hebden Water to serve travellers crossing the valley, and it was around this bridge that the settlement of Hebden Bridge grew. In the 16th century, the wooden bridge was replaced by a stone packhorse bridge, and it is this structure, with later modifications, that we see today.

During the Industrial Revolution, textile manufacture moved out of the home into water-driven mills, and the valley bottom displaced the hilltop weaving settlements. In many parts of the country water-driven textile manufacture was relatively short-lived as steam power began to displace water. However, with its excellent transport infrastructure – turnpike 1772, Rochdale Canal 1798, Manchester and Leeds Railway 1840 – Hebden Bridge was ideally placed not only to survive this technological change, but to profit from it. Hebden Bridge became an important textile centre.

An interesting example of the change from water to steam power may be seen looking upstream from the 16th century packhorse bridge. Its chimney might suggest that the mill on the east bank of the river was built to be steam powered. However, the path which allows you to walk under the eastern arch of the bridge is built on top of the goit of an earlier watermill. The watermill was converted to steam in 1820.

The narrowness of the valley at Hebden Bridge meant that much of the housing for the textile workers had to be built on the steeply sloping hillside. This led to the rows of buildings which are so characteristic of the town; buildings which have two houses on top of each other. The two houses are accessible from different sides. After years of neglect, much has been done to renovate the buildings and the canal, and Hebden Bridge is now a popular tourist centre.

3.2 Heptonstall

Heptonstall (Hep – tonstall or high farmstead) was an Anglo-Saxon settlement. Despite facing south to maximise the sun, farming was always a marginal activity on the Calder hillsides, and the inhabitants turned to cloth weaving to supplement their meagre incomes in early medieval times. At its peak, this dual economy of agriculture and cloth hand-weaving supported a population of 4000 in Heptonstall.

The village was a Parliamentary stronghold in the Civil War and was attacked in 1643 by Royalist troops based in Halifax coming up the steep buttress from Hebden Bridge. The first attack was repulsed, but when the Royalists returned, the Parliamentary forces had withdrawn to Burnley and Heptonstall was subjected to much damage.

With the coming of the Industrial Revolution, textile manufacture moved out of the home into the mill. Since Heptonstall had no water supply it was unable to make the transition, and there was a major migration from the village. This, however, has left Heptonstall today as a unique record of a pre-Industrial Revolution textile settlement.

It is not possible to do full justice to what is to be seen at Heptonstall in the space available here, but the many features of interest include:

- a large number of weavers' cottages with typical small upper windows (to give light to the looms),

- some fine homes of yeomen – the wealthy organisers of the cloth trade,

- Cloth Hall, built between 1545 and 1558, which is the earliest cloth trading hall in Yorkshire,

- the ruined 13th century church,

- the earliest Methodist church in continuous use in the world (established 1742).

At the church look for the grave of "King" David Hartley, a coin counterfeiter who was hanged in 1770 – it is 12 graves in front of the church porch and 2 to the left.

3.3 Lumbutts waterwheel tower

This waterwheel tower was built in the 1830s to supply the Lumbutts mill, owned by the Fieldens of Todmorden. The tower housed three 30 feet (9m) diameter waterwheels, arranged on top of each other, which were capable of generating 53 horse power. A particularly ingenious feature of the design was that the water was supplied by siphon from the upstream dams.

3.4 Piece Hall, Halifax

This magnificent Manufacturers' Hall was opened in 1779 to trade in cloth produced on hand looms and reflects the massive wealth of the clothier "middle-men". The 315 Merchant Rooms surrounding a cobbled courtyard and lawn became redundant early in the Industrial Revolution when buyers preferred to negotiate directly with the mills.

The hall served as a wholesale fruit and vegetable market, but by the 1960s was under threat of demolition. Saved by a single vote of the Halifax Town Council, Piece Hall is now a vibrant centre of specialist craft shops and an Industrial Museum and Art Gallery.

3.5 Stoodley Pike

The Napoleonic War caused great disruption to the export of cloth to the continent and there was great rejoicing in Calderdale when Napoleon was defeated. Standing on the Pennine Way at 1300 feet (394m), Stoodley Pike, the most prominent landmark in upper Calderdale, was erected in 1814 to celebrate the surrender of Paris and Napoleon's abdication.

The Pike was rebuilt in 1856, after a collapse in 1854, but there was another partial collapse in 1918. A staircase climbs the first 40 feet (12m) of the Pike, from where there are commanding views over the surrounding countryside.

3.6 Todmorden

Situated at the confluence of three valleys carved out of the gritstone during the Ice Age, much of what we see in Todmorden today was built around the turnpike, canal and railway during the one hundred years from 1770. The history of the development of the town is the history of one family: the Fieldens.

Joshua Fielden left Edge End Farm on the hillside above Todmorden in 1782. He moved to the valley bottom at just the right time. Cotton weaving was moving out of the home into the factory and was soon to become mechanised. At Millbrook House he built himself a house with a small factory for handloom weavers. When Joshua died in 1811, his five sons inherited the business and expanded it into one of Britain's greatest manufacturing concerns. (By 1846 they were producing 200,000 lbs of cotton a week.)

The Fieldens were not only entrepreneurs, but also social reformers and sponsors of public buildings. John Fielden MP is the most famous, making major contributions to the legal requirements for the protection of factory workers. (He sponsored the Factory Act of 1844, and the Ten Hours Act, 1847.) When he died in 1849, his funeral was attended by thousands of mill workers.

The Town Hall, Todmorden's most prominent building, and perhaps

Yorkshire's finest public building, was sponsored by the Fieldens. Built by John Gibson over the stream which was then the Lancashire/ Yorkshire border, it has an interesting roof level frieze depicting scenes from Lancashire and Yorkshire life. Lancashire is shown as industrial, whilst the Yorkshire end is more pastoral with farm labourers scything and shepherds with their flocks.

The one Fielden venture which was less than totally successful was the building of Dobroyd Castle. John Fielden, born in 1822, fell in love with one of his mill workers, Ruth Stansfield. She agreed to marry him only on the understanding that he would build her a castle on the hill. John Gibson was commissioned and a lavish castle was completed in 1869. Sadly, the marriage had failed; Ruth retreated to a chalet built for her in the grounds while John lived alone in the castle with his eight servants.

Todmorden is very rewarding for anyone interested in industrial archaeology, and perhaps deserves to be better known. In a distance of less than a mile down the Rochdale road from the town centre, it is possible to see in turn:

- the exquisite Town Hall,

- Todmorden Hall (on the right between Rise Lane and Hall Street),

- the Unitary Church (on the left, above Fielden Square), built by the Fieldens

- Dawson Weir (on the right on the corner of Dobroyd Road),

- Millbrook House (on the left),

- Gauxholme railway viaduct,

- Gauxholme Canal Warehouse, Bacup Road – both raw materials and finished products were transhipped here and it is said that it still houses an ice breaker.

Todmorden Hall is in outward appearance a 17th century hall with mullioned windows, but the stone cladding conceals a much older timber-framed building. Millbrook House was built by Joshua Fielden as a combined home and factory in 1782 when he left Edge Hill Farm to manufacture in the valley bottom. This mill's significance is that it predates the mechanisation which water and later steam power were to bring to manufacturing. I understand that Edge End Farm is still owned by the descendants of Joshua Fielden. Gauxholme railway viaduct was built by George Stephenson in 1840 and is the oldest cast iron railway bridge in Britain still in use.

Walk 4: River Dee (Dentdale)

Information Centre: Sedbergh: 015396 20125

Dentdale was settled by the Norse whose pastoral farming methods favoured the establishment of isolated farms, rather than the villages of the more arable Anglo-Saxon farmers. Over the centuries, Dentdale has largely retained its original settlement pattern, and Dent is the only village in the valley.

To apportion different qualities of land equally in this narrow valley, a large number of long narrow farms were created stretching up the hillside. A consequence of this apportionment, is that in some parts of the valley, the walker is faced with something of a steeple-chase in crossing the many stiles!

The dale has given its name to the section of the Pennine Fault which crosses the valley (this is best seen from the geology Nature Trail in adjoining Garsdale). In view of the many interesting rock exposures in Dentdale and its neighbouring dales, it is perhaps not surprising that Adam Sedgwick, Dent's most famous son, should become one of the founders of modern geology.

This delightful, intimate valley may easily be walked in one day, or shorter walks may be planned using the several car parks. The walk described progresses from the Dent Head Viaduct down the valley bottom to Dent. From Dent to Sedbergh, alternative valley bottom and hilltop routes are described.

Dent Head Viaduct to Sedbergh

Distance: 11 miles

Starting point: Dent Head Viaduct SD777843

Public transport: On schooldays there is an early bus from Sedbergh to Lea Yeat. The Settle to Carlisle railway stops at Dent station, just above Cowgill. I used a taxi to get from Sedbergh to Dent Head.

Maps: 4.1 and 4.2 plus Outdoor Leisure 2 and Landranger 98.

There is space to park a few cars under the Dent Head Viaduct. This is a fine structure built of dark limestone which is known as Dent Marble. Before setting off towards Sedbergh, it is worth following the road a little

The River Dee at Abbot Holme Bridge

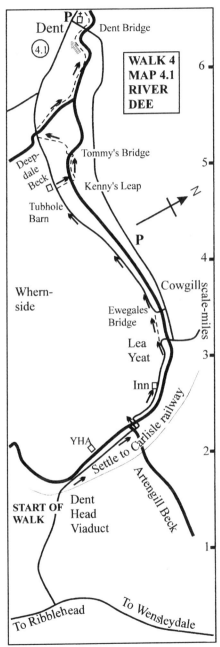

way above the railway line as there are extensive views looking down the valley.

From the viaduct, follow the road downstream, passing the Youth Hostel. Just after the Artengill Beck, the road crosses to the other side of the river. It was at Artengill that a young Newcastle solicitor named Armstrong saw a marble mill and carried out some calculations of its mechanical efficiency. This was so low that Armstrong conceived of the idea of the water turbine. He later founded the famous engineering company which bore his name.

Pass the Sportman's Arms to come to Lea Yeat, about 2 miles after leaving the viaduct. From Lea Yeat take the path down the south side of the river to Ewegales Bridge. This short section can be extremely floriferous, with a good show of orchids in July.

If you are keen on wall hopping, you could take the field path below Ewegales Bridge. The small road on the south of the river is, however, very quiet, and my preference is to take the road. In about 1½ miles you will come to Tubhole Barn. Take the path on the right here (from which there are good views of the valley to Dent and beyond) down to the river. Cross at Kenny's Leap.

At the next footbridge, Tommy's Bridge, recross the river and turn right. At the end of the second field after the bridge, cross a stile and take the path uphill. Pass a clump of trees on your way to the road.

At the road, cross Deepdale Beck and follow the beck down to its confluence with the Dee. Dent Bridge is now only just over half a mile downstream. The squat tower of the Norman church is to your left and if you wish to visit Dent, it is only two fields above you.

From Dent Bridge, follow the river downstream to Barth Bridge, about a mile away, only briefly touching the road on the way. There are two routes from Barth Bridge to Sedbergh, depending on whether you prefer to follow the river down the valley (probably the best stretch of the River Dee is to be seen near Abbot Holme Bridge) or to take the hilltop route across Long Moor (with its fine views). The hilltop route is only worthwhile when visibility is good.

Barth Bridge to Sedbergh, valley bottom route

From Barth Bridge, follow the riverbank downstream for about a mile, where you join the minor road running down the south side of the valley. This road is little used, as may be seen from the grass growing through the tarmac.

In about 1½ miles, you will pass a bridge over the river (Rash Bridge) and in another half mile, as the road bears left uphill away from the river, you take the footpath on the right. The path fol-

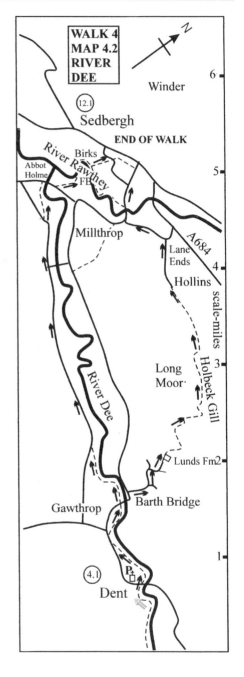

lows the edge of the first field above the river and then descends to a delightful stretch along the riverbank to Abbot Holme Bridge. As it tumbles downstream towards the Rawthey, the river here is a delightful sequence of pools and small falls.

Approaching the bridge, beware of flying balls! One of the greens of the Sedbergh Golf Club crosses the river here, as is attested by the good selection of balls lying on the riverbed. Cross the bridge, and in a short distance take the path on the left across the fields to a footbridge over the Rawthey at Birks. Pass through Birks, and take the footpath on the left which crosses the fields to Sedbergh.

Barth Bridge to Sedbergh, hilltop alternative

The hilltop path is reached by following the road downstream from Barth Bridge for only a very short distance and taking the first minor road on the right. Follow the metalled road which goes uphill, bears left for a short level section and then bears right, uphill again. Ignore farmtracks to the left (Rawridding) and to the right (Hining Hill) to come to a farmhouse at Lunds.

The path skirts to the left of Lunds and becomes a greenway between walls. When you reach a sheep pen where the walled road bears right, follow the line of the wall ahead. Ignore a sign to the left to Sedbergh,and carry on to the end of the wall-line, where you bear left to follow another wall to the highest point.

From here there is a splendid panorama which includes the Howgills, the Middleton Fells and, in the distance, the Lake District mountains. The route across the moorland is somewhat informal, but is sufficiently well walked for you to follow where others have gone before you. Skirt the left of Holebeck Gill and when you reach the first field wall, bear left away from the Gill. Cross the hillside to High Hollins where you take the lane to Lane Ends Rather than following the most direct route down the busy A684 into Sedbergh, turn left at Lane Ends to go through Millthrop.

Places of Interest in Dentdale

4.1 Dent

This is an attractive village of narrow, winding, cobbled streets which is made easy to access by its large car park. In the 17th and 18th centuries, Dent was one of the major centres of the knitting trade, its inhabitants being known as the Terrible Knitters of Dent.

The 12th century church of St Andrew's has some Jacobean pews and memorials to the Sedgwick family. Adam Sedgwick, son of an 18th century vicar of the village, was one of the founding fathers of modern geology. The granite stone in the centre of the village is his memorial.

Walk 5: Rivers Doe and Twiss

Information Centre: Ingleton 015242 41049

Towards the end of the Carboniferous period, about 280 million years ago, a massive vertical displacement took place along the western edge of the northern Pennines. In the Ingleton area this displacement (the Craven Fault) brought together Carboniferous rocks and previously deep lying Ordovician rocks. This juxtaposition of rocks of different hardness is ideal for the formation of waterfalls, and the area around Ingleton contains the highest concentration of spectacular waterfalls in England – the Pecca Falls, Thornton Force, Beezley Fall and Snow Falls.

These waterfalls lie along the Rivers Twiss and Doe, two rivers which descend respectively from the valleys of Kingsdale and Chapel-le-dale, both perched high above Ingleton. (At Ingleton the rivers combine to form the Greta, a tributary of the Lune.) In 1885, the Ingleton Scenery Company opened to the public a delightful 4 mile circular walk which visits all of these waterfalls. (A charge is made at the beginning of the walk.)

Although the path is well laid out, with steps crossing tricky areas, great care is needed during wet or icy conditions, when the paths can be very slippery. If possible, avoid week-ends and Bank Holidays, or start early.

The walk is well signposted, and the description given below is to explain the main features seen rather than for navigational purposes.

The waterfall walk

Distance: 4 miles
Starting point: Ingleton Scenery Company car park SD693733
Maps: 5.1 plus Outdoor Leisure 2 and Landranger 98.

Leaving the car park, you quickly pass from an area of soft coal measures into limestone. Here, the Swilla Glen is an impressive limestone gorge with a profusion of mosses, liverworts and lichens, some of which are rare.

At Manor Bridge, you reach the Craven Fault and for a short distance the river actually flows along the line of the fault. About 100 metres beyond the bridge, you will see on the other bank an inclined interface between limestone and Ordovician slate (see Fig. 5.1). The tunnel in the limestone just to the left of the interface was made by miners searching, unsuccessfully, for lead. End elevations of faults are quite common throughout the

Thornton Force

Pennines, such as Malham Cove and Attermire Scar (above Settle), but cross sections where different rocks are exposed adjacent to one another are rare.

After crossing the fault, you are now in an area where Ordovician slates and sandstones are tilted vertically. The sandstone is harder than the slate, and the river falls spectacularly over a staircase of five falls at Pecca Falls. The pools in the softer slate are said to be as deep as the falls themselves (see Fig. 5.2).

The next fall upstream is Thornton Force, one of the most important geological sites in Britain. Here the river falls some 50 feet (15m) over a cliff with a base of vertical layers of slate and a cap of carboniferous limestone (see Fig. 5.3). The base rocks were tilted and worn down before the limestones were deposited. The gap in geological time represented by the interface between these rocks is known as an unconformity.

Thornton Force is young in geological time, having been formed only after the last Ice Age, when a terminal moraine blocked the exit of Kingdale with boulder clay and diverted the river (see Fig. 5.4). As you walk upstream, it is possible to make out the pre-Ice Age river channel.

When you reach the footbridge at Raven Ray, cross it and follow the path which passes Twistleton Hall and Beezleys to the River Doe. From this path, there are excellent views of Ingleborough ahead and the Lune valley to the east. (The

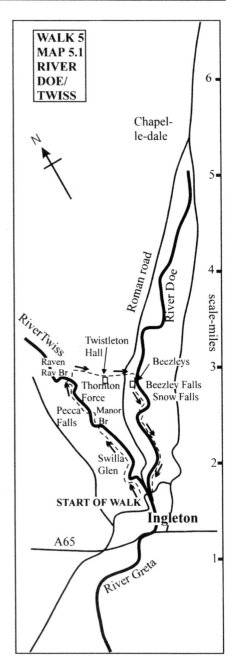

road you cross between Twistleton Hall and Beezleys was originally a Roman road built during the conquest of northern Britain by Agricola in around AD80. The other end of this road is seen on the River Ure walk, descending to the Roman fort at Bainbridge.)

On your way back to Ingleton you will follow the River Doe through Twistleton Glen. You will pass further spectacular falls at Beezley and Snow Falls and come out into Ingleton through a disused quarry.

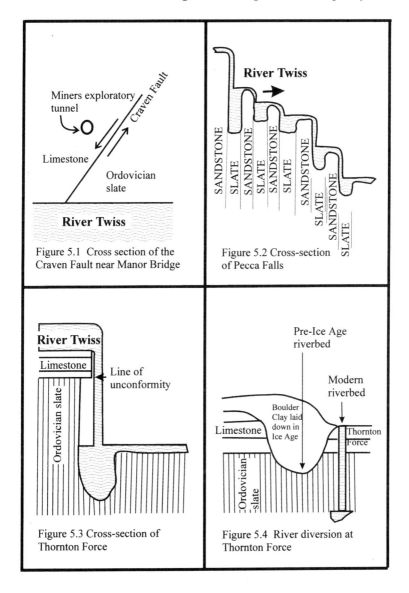

Figure 5.1 Cross section of the Craven Fault near Manor Bridge

Figure 5.2 Cross-section of Pecca Falls

Figure 5.3 Cross-section of Thornton Force

Figure 5.4 River diversion at Thornton Force

Walk 6: River Eden

Section 1: Garsdale Station to Kirkby Stephen, 13 miles
Section 2: Brough to Appleby, 10½ mile miles
Section 3: Lacy's Caves, Long Meg and her daughters, 5 miles
Section 4: Nunnery Walk, 2 miles
Section 5: Dry Beck to Wetheral, 6 miles
Information Centres: Kirkby Stephen: 017683 71199; Brough: 017683 41260; Appleby: 017683 51177; Carlisle: 01228 512444

The Eden rises in the remote Mallerstang Pass. It flows north until just past Kirkby Stephen, where it meets the massive wall of hills which lie along the line of the Pennine Fault. Here it turns to the north west and follows these hills towards Carlisle.

The upper reaches of the Eden lie in Carboniferous rocks which produce typical "Dales" scenery. In complete contrast, the lower Eden runs through younger red sandstone, laid down when the area was an arid desert. In places the Eden has cut deeply into these soft rocks, creating precipitous sandstone cliffs.

Being on a natural line of communication, the strategic importance of the Eden valley has led to an unusually high concentration of castles. Several are seen on the walks.

Although it is possible to walk the entire length of the valley from the river source to Carlisle, in some sections lack of public rights of way confines the walks to roads. These sections have been excluded, and the walks described have been limited to the best part of the "accessible" valley. What remains, however, is a tremendous variety of excellent walks.

You should allow yourself sufficient time to explore the attractive towns of Appleby and Kirkby Stephen. Although not on the walks, Carlisle, the main settlement in the Eden valley, is well worth a visit. The excellent Tullie Museum gives a comprehensive coverage of the history of the border region.

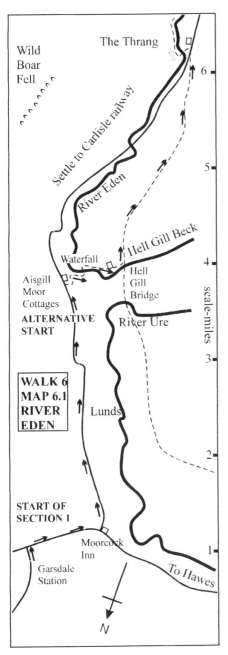

Wild
Boar
Fell

The Thrang

Settle to Carlisle railway

River Eden

Waterfall

Hell Gill Beck

Aisgill
Moor
Cottages
**ALTERNATIVE
START**

Hell
Gill
Bridge

River Ure

scale-miles

**WALK 6
MAP 6.1
RIVER
EDEN**

Lunds

**START OF
SECTION 1**

Moorcock
Inn

Garsdale
Station

To Hawes

N

6

5

4

3

2

1

Section 1: Garsdale Station to Kirkby Stephen

This is a wonderful walk down the remote valley of Mallerstang. In part, the walk follows the ancient green highway known as Lady Anne's Way, and two medieval castles and a medieval hall are passed on the way to the charming market town of Kirkby Stephen.

Distance: 13 miles (9½ miles from Aisgill Moor cottages)

Starting point: Garsdale station SD788918 (If using private transport, start at Aisgill Moor cottages 778963.)

Intermediate break points: Mallerstang is a quiet pass and you should be able to break this section almost anywhere along the line of the walk.

Public transport: A marvellous way to start this walk is to take the Settle to Carlisle railway from Kirkby Stephen to Garsdale.

Maps: 6.1 and 6.2 plus Landranger 98 and 91.

From Garsdale Station, descend to the Sedbergh to Hawes road where you turn right. Follow the road to The Moorcock Inn where you turn left towards Kirkby Stephen. About 3½ miles after leaving the station you reach Aisgill Moor cottages, your starting point if you are using the car.

Turn right at the cottages and cross the railway on the way to the waterfall at the bottom of Hell Gill.

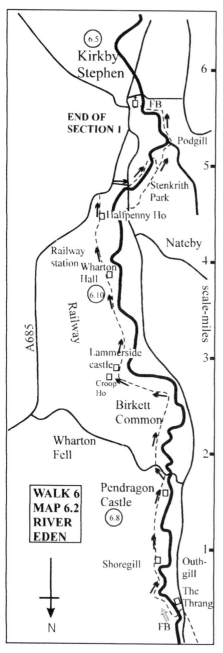

Follow the Eden upstream, passing a farmhouse to come to Hell Gill Bridge. Here you are on an ancient highway and an important drove road for Scottish cattle in the 17th and 18th centuries. It is better known, however, as the route taken by Lady Anne Clifford on her travels between her castles in Craven and Westmorland. It is for this reason that the highway is known as Lady Anne's Way.

Turn left at the bridge and follow the highway across a level plateau before descending the hillside towards the river at Thrang. In places the track is rutted and can be boggy. As you descend, there are wonderful open views down Mallerstang and across the valley to Wild Boar Fell.

Just before the Thrang Country Hotel, take the path past a limekiln down to and over a delightful packhorse bridge. The siting of the limekiln is typical of the many hundreds of derelict kilns which may still be seen throughout the Dales. It will have burnt local limestone using coal brought down Lady Anne's Way from the collieries above Garsdale. The resulting lime will have been used to reclaim adjacent moorland, which was then enclosed and used for pasturage by Scottish cattle being brought south to English markets.

Follow the path down the river to Shoregill. (On the other side of the river is the village of Outhgill where the father of Michael Fara-

Packhorse bridge at Thrang

day, one of the world's most eminent scientists, was the village blacksmith.)

At Shoregill the path goes into the fields on the west side of a row of cottages and Pendragon Castle is reached in about three-quarters of a mile.

At the road, bear left away from the river and climb uphill towards Wharton Fell. When you reach the last of the fields at the edge of the fells, turn right onto the track which crosses Birkett Common (signposted Wharton). Ahead of you, on the other side of the river you will see that the limestone rocks have been twisted almost to the vertical. You are now approaching the interface between two fault lines (the Pennine and Dent Faults) where the rocks have been massively distorted. Later in the walk, just as you enter Kirkby Stephen, you will see a further consequence of this meeting of the two faults.

At the north end of the Common, the track leads towards Croop House. On reaching the field before the house, go through the gate on the right to Lammerside Castle. The path passes immediately to the right of the castle, allowing you to look through the wall at the fine barrel roofing within.

From Lammerside, follow the stiles across the fields to Wharton Hall which is reached in just under a mile. Skirt to the left of Wharton Hall and follow the track past Half Penny House to the main road. If you are making for the Kirkby Stephen railway station, turn left here and follow the main road which climbs quite steeply for just over half a mile. If you are going into Kirkby Stephen, a more interesting route than going down the main road is to turn right at the first turning (Nateby Road) and then right at the T-junction to the bridge. (Steps down from the bridge allow you to go down to the river to see the Coopkarnel pot hole below.) Retrace your steps to the road and take the footpath down the west bank of the river into Stenkrith Park.

Follow the riverbank until you come to a footbridge which you cross. The path now doubles back somewhat, initially going away from Kirkby Stephen before turning left onto another path. This path takes you to Podgill where you cross a footbridge next to the river onto the meadow which takes you to Frank's Bridge. From the bridge a path leads uphill to the main square. Some of the stonework in the wall at the left of the path from the river up to the square is very interesting. If you look at it carefully, you will see that it is composed of two different types of rock – limestone particles embedded in a red sandstone matrix which is tens of millions of years younger. This unusual conglomerate, Bockram, is the building material used for many of the houses in the town, and is the result of the boundary between limestone and red sandstone rocks being at a point where two faults meet. Many millions of years ago, when the two faults were moving relative to one another, they subjected the local rocks to tremendous shearing stresses and produced a very effective "cake mixer".

Section 2: Brough to Appleby

This walk between the two Clifford castles of Brough and Appleby is along the Eden and its tributary the Swindale Beck. A feature of this part of the valley is the large number of drumlins laid down during the Ice Age. The walk crosses some of these drumlins, which give excellent views of the fells which follow the line of the Pennine Fault.

Distance: 10½ miles

Starting point: Brough Clock, NY795147

Intermediate break point: Warcop 4½ miles

Public transport: A bus service runs between Appleby and Brough

Maps: 6.3 and 6.4 plus Landranger 91.

From Brough Clock, take the Kirkby Stephen road under the A66 bridge and turn right into Church Brough. The ruined castle and the church are worth visiting, the latter having an inscribed stone from the Roman fort in the porch. Leave Church Brough along the sunken lane which runs between the church and the castle. As you climb the hill there are good views looking back of the castle and the Stainmore pass behind.

When the track you are on comes to an end at a barn, turn right along

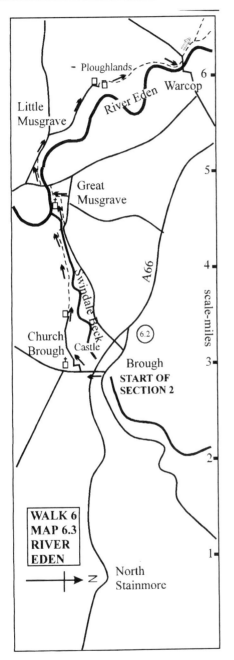

the field boundary taking you towards Great Musgrave. White paint on the top of a fence post marks the position of the stile at the other side of the field where you drop down to the river meadow. Cross the meadow to the next stile which takes you to Swindale Beck. Turn left here and follow the beck down to the bridge.

Cross the bridge and take the path into the field on the left. The path climbs uphill, crossing a system of particularly well developed strip lynchets. Again, as you climb the hill, it is worth looking back at the panorama of hills which spans the horizon.

At the top of the hill, skirt to the right of a white house to come to a lane. A little distance down this lane, take another lane to the left which will take you down to St Theobald's Church at the river's edge. Here turn to the right and follow the riverbank to the bridge. Cross the bridge and take the footpath on the right to Little Musgrave. Go through the village and just after Little Musgrave Farm, take the road to the right to Ploughlands – which you will reach in just under a mile.

Ploughlands is a settlement of two farms and you should take the stile to the left just before the second farm. Follow the small burn for the short distance to a gate. Here turn right, and follow the field edge up to another gate where you join a track coming up from Ploughlands. Follow the track to the river and then the riverbank to the bridge at Warcop. From the ribbing under the arches you can see that the bridge is of medieval design. This is the only remaining medieval bridge over the Eden, being the only bridge to survive centuries of high floods.

From the bridge, follow the road until it leaves the river. Here take the track ahead marked Blacksyke. When this splits into two, leave the metalled surface (going to Langford) and take the track ahead. Ignoring a turning to the left, in just under half a mile you will reach a gate. (During the Ice Age, the flow of ice was from the North West, and you are following the long axis of a drumlin formed under the ice).

After the gate, the track bears right, crosses the saddle of the drumlin and then bears right again before descending to Blacksyke. Although there is no notice to advise you of the fact, the track downhill is private. Go through the gate at the top of the hill (not signposted) and follow the hedge line which runs just to the left of the ridge of the drumlin, passing through several gates on the way to the bridge over the Eden at Blacksyke.

Stay on the south side of the river, pass the farmhouse by the river and climb the edge of the wood (not in the field). As you come over the crest of the hill, you get your first view of the top of Appleby Castle, nearly four miles away.

The path descends the hill and skirts round the left shoulder of the next hill before reaching first Little Ormside, and then Great Ormside. At Great Ormside, cross the road

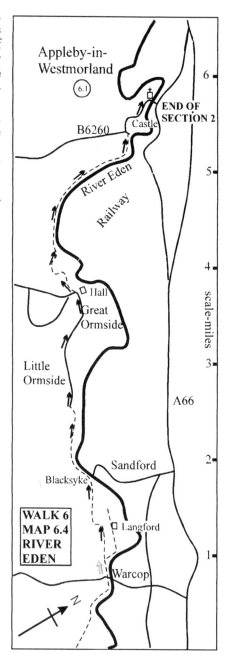

which leads to the Hall and the church and take the lane in front of you which goes under the railway. The path climbs to the left before bearing right downhill. It is important here to follow a small gully down to a stile which leads into the wood. If, as I did, you miss the stile, you will be confronted by a deep gully which you will not be able to cross.

The path now proceeds towards Appleby, sometimes on the top of the bank above the river, and sometimes at the river's edge. When you reach the outskirts of Appleby, a small road bears left up to the B6260 which, in turn, takes you to the top of Boroughgate. With the Castle behind you there is a splendid view down Boroughgate over the town below.

Section 3: Lacy's Caves, Long Meg and Her Daughters

This circular walk includes a fine stretch of the Eden, some 18th century man-made caves, a visit to a church with some interesting Anglo-Saxon and Viking artefacts, and to an important megalithic site.

Distance: 5 miles

Starting point: Little Salkeld, NY566362

Maps: 6.5 plus Landranger 90 and 91.

In Little Salkeld there is parking for a few cars on the green near the Hall. Take the road from the green towards the river (signed as a cul-de-sac). Just after Town End Farm, follow the sign on the right to Lacy's Caves.

The lane follows the Settle to Carlisle Railway with the river meandering below until some buildings are reached. These buildings were associated with the former Long Meg anhydrite mine. Just after the buildings, there is a road ahead which is private and the footpath bears left around an electricity sub-station and the railway marshalling yard. For a short distance the path is actually along the track of the former railway out of the mine. When you reach the river, an old corn mill, Force Mill, is on the opposite bank.

Follow the riverbank path until a short spur on the left is reached which leads to Lacy's Caves. Perched high above the river, the caves are named after Colonel Lacy, an 18th century owner of Salkeld Hall, who had them carved out of the sandstone rocks. It is thought that the caves were built as a fashionable folly rather than for any more utilitarian purpose.

After the caves, the path follows the river for just under a mile, sometimes high above the river and sometimes at river level, until you reach a bridge over Glassonby Beck. Somewhere in this vicinity, there was, until the 14th century, a village of Addingham. When the river changed its course, the village was flooded and disappeared. Anglo-Saxon and Norse artefacts from the church were rescued and moved to a new church which was built on higher ground and which will be seen later in the walk.

From the river, follow the minor road uphill to Glassonby. The name suggests a Norse origin, confirmed by the finding of a fragment of a Norse cross which is now on display in Carlisle Museum.

Turn right into Glassonby and walk through the village. At two stone barns bear right down to Addingham Church. Here you may see the artefacts rescued from the church inundated by the river – a fine Anglo-Saxon hammerhead cross in the churchyard, and a rare Norse hogsback gravestone in the church.

Leave the church in a southerly direction, crossing a field and a road before following the next field boundary towards a small wood. The path goes along the edge of the wood to Long Meg, one of the largest megalithic sites in the country.

Take the lane away from the circle towards Little Salkeld, but ignore the first turning to the left. Where the hedge line is broken there are wonderful views along both the Pennine Fault and over the Lake District mountains. The lane shortly joins the road from Glassonby which takes you to Little Salkeld. In the village, the 18th century water-powered cornmill now grinds organic flours, and tours of the mill are conducted during the summer months.

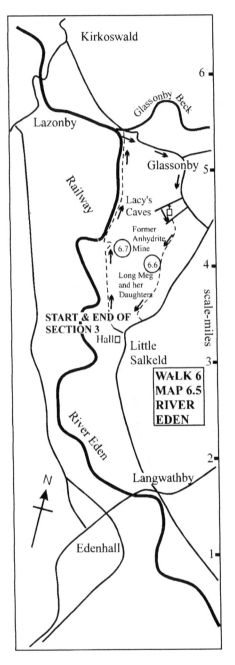

Section 4: Nunnery walk

In1775, Christopher Aglionby laid out this delightful short woodland walk along the banks of the Croglin Water and the Eden. In the 12th century there was a monastery here. The walk was a favourite of Wordsworth who penned a poem in its praise.

The walk is in the grounds of the Nunnery House Hotel, on the road between Armathwaite and Kirkoswald, and the hotel makes a charge for entry.

Distance: 2 miles

Starting point: Nunnery House Hotel, NY538478

Maps: N/A

There is a map in the grounds of the Nunnery House Hotel which shows the route and the main points of interest. The walk is straightforward and no further map is required here.

Signposts direct the walker in an anticlockwise circulation, and the outward section is high above the riverbank. In the summer there is only the occasional glimpse of the river below through the trees.

The return section is along the banks of the Eden until a ledge, cut into a red sandstone promontory by Christopher Aglionby, signals that you have reached the Croglin Water. The walk is now along the steep-sided ravine cut by the Croglin Water until a waterfall is reached which tumbles dramatically into a large circular pot. A water turbine produced electricity here until 1957.

On the way back to the hotel, you pass a summerhouse with several 14th century coats of arms built into the stonework. These are the only remnants of the original monastic foundation.

Section 5: Drybeck to Wetheral

This a most attractive walk down the lower reaches of the Eden. The river here is large and has cut a channel typically 100-150 feet (30-45m) below the hillside above, in places creating sandstone cliffs which drop precipitously to the river below.

Progress down the valley is mainly along the riverbank, with occasional detours to higher ground to circumnavigate steep hillsides and sandstone outcrops. In one such outcrop you will see Constantine's Cells, ancient caves of unknown age.

At Wetheral you will pass the site of a medieval priory with its salmon traps at the river's edge.

Although the first and last parts of the walk are relatively easy underfoot, some of the middle sections can be overgrown with creepers and brambles in late summer. Spring and early summer are probably the best times to tackle the whole walk.

Distance: 6 miles

Starting point: Drybeck, NY515485

Public transport: Wetheral and Armathwaite are both served by the railway, but are on different lines. An imaginative day's outing would be to combine the walk with a visit to Carlisle Museum. First take the train from Wetheral to Carlisle and then from Carlisle to Armathwaite, returning to Wetheral along the riverbank.

Maps: 6.6 plus Landranger 86.

The walk starts at the path adjacent to the river on the loop road off the Armathwaite to Wetheral road, but if you are starting the walk from Armathwaite station, take the road down into Armathwaite and turn left towards Wetheral. In about 2 miles turn right into the loop road, which passes Drybeck Farm. Here you join the main route.

Follow the river downstream for just under a mile, where you pass a large outcrop of red sandstone on the other bank and the path climbs uphill. The path stays above the river until you pass a farm on your left. In the next field, cross a stile into the wood.

Follow the river downstream for just under 2 miles until you come to Brocklewath on the other bank . Don't be misled as were some people I met on the walk who were making for Brocklewath to cross the river. Although the Ordnance Survey map shows a public right of way across the river, "Wath" is Norse for "ford". The only crossing here is a wet one!

After Brocklewath, cross the field to a stile into the woods near the river. When you come out of the wood, continue to follow the riverbank. Pass

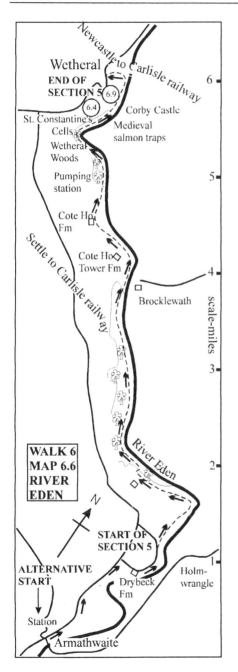

Cote House Tower Farm – the tower was built as a look out for salmon poachers.

At the end of the field, take the path up to Cote House Farm. Initially there seems nothing unusual about this house, but if you look carefully at the end wall, you will see that the left-hand section is composed of larger blocks of stone than the rest of the farm. This building was originally a bastle house, built in the 16th century to give much needed protection against the unsavoury marauders who were then all too active throughout the border regions.

From Cote House Farm, a track leads down to a pumping station where drinking water is extracted from the river. After the pumping station, you come to the National Trust property of Wetheral Woods, where the path climbs above the river cliff. From the top of the cliff, a path to the right leads to Constantine's Cells with their centuries of graffiti carved in the rock.

Rejoin the path and descend towards the river. On the other side of the river are the medieval salmon traps which belonged to the monks. The green, just before you enter Wetheral, is popular with both picnickers and swimmers in summer. From the green turn left up the lane and then right onto the small road to the viaduct of the Carlisle and Newcastle Railway line, built in 1830-4. When you reach the viaduct, a sign to the left advises you that there are 99 steps up to the railway station. At the station, you may take the path onto the viaduct for a bird's eye view of the River Eden below. The attractive village green is just up the road from the station.

Places of interest in the Eden valley

6.1 Appleby-in-Westmorland

Set in a loop of the River Eden, this former county town of Westmorland is a picturesque, bustling market town. The heart of the town is Boroughgate, the steeply sloping main street with its Norman castle at one end and St Lawrence's Church at the other.

Appleby's most famous citizen was the 17th century Lady Anne Clifford, High Sheriff of Westmorland. Lady Anne was passed over for her inheritance when her father died and fought with the "establishment" for decades before succeeding to her titles. Although by then at an advanced age, she was extremely energetic in travelling between and restoring her many castles, which had been ravaged during the Civil War. Her diaries, which have been recently published, give an interesting impression not only of this lady of steel and integrity, but also of the times in which she lived. She is buried in St Lawrence's Church and the almshouses she built may be seen on Boroughgate.

The high point of Appleby's year is the traditional Horse Fair in June. Travelling people converge on the town for the festival which centres on the display, buying and selling of horses.

6.2 Brough

The syncline, known as Stainmore, which runs eastwards across the Pennines from Brough has always been a strategically important transport corridor. Both the Romans and Normans built castles at Brough to guard the entrance to Stainmore. The castle, which is now a ruin, was one of many in the ownership of the Clifford family and is mentioned frequently in the diaries of Lady Anne.

6.3 Carlisle

Carlisle has been an important strategic centre for thousands of years, fought over by Romans, Vikings, English and Scots alike. Carlisle came permanently under English rule only in the reign of Henry III, having been part of the Kingdom of Strathclyde at the time of the Domesday survey. Even then, the countryside to the north and east of Carlisle was disputed for many centuries by the English and the Scots. This power vacuum allowed the reivers, bands of murderous cattle thieves, to terrorise the border counties of England and Scotland until the Union of the crowns in 1603.

During the Civil War, Carlisle was a royalist stronghold which surrendered only after a lengthy siege. In contrast, in 1745, Carlisle was easily taken during the Jacobite rebellion and Bonnie Prince Charlie was proclaimed King from Carlisle Cross.

In the 19th century, Carlisle became an important railway centre and today has good road and rail connections. Standing in the market square, you are as likely to hear Scots and Geordie as you are Cumbrian accents.

The history of both Carlisle and the North West region is excellently displayed in the Tullie House Museum.

6.4 Contantine's Cells, Wetheral

Mystery surrounds both the age of the cells and the person after whom they are named. It is thought that they may predate the Romans.

In medieval times the monks from the nearby Wetheral Priory used the cells as a hiding place for their belongings. Centuries of graffiti, including a quotation from a 9th century Welsh poet, are carved into the walls of the cells in the cliffs high above the Eden.

6.5 Kirkby Stephen

Kirkby Stephen is a town of much character set around the busy A685. The width of the main street and some interesting buildings compensate for the flow of traffic through the town.

The name of the town suggests that there was already a church when the Vikings arrived, and the church contains a rare 10th century Danish cross shaft, the Loki stone, depicting a devil in chains.

There is a riverside walk on the east of the town and upstream is the attractive limestone gorge in Stenkrith Park. Kirkby Stephen has free flying parrots, introduced by a local landowner who had previously tried free flying budgerigars. Whereas the budgerigars had been regarded as bounty by the sparrowhawks, the parrots are able to fend for themselves.

Just outside Kirkby Stephen at Waitby Greenriggs (757087), a nature reserve has been created on a disused railway line. Mid-June is probably the best time to see the wide variety of flowers, which include several varieties of orchid.

6.6 Long Meg and her daughters

Some sixty stones, standing in an almost circular formation 100 metres across, make this one of the largest stone circles in the country. Long Meg, at 15 feet (4.5m), is the largest of the stones, standing adjacent to her four daughters. Built between 3000 and 2000 BC, we can only guess at the original purpose of the circle. The ring and cup markings on Long Meg also intrigue and baffle interpretation. It is thought that the circle was named in the reign of Henry VIII after a very tall woman who lived in London.

6.7 Long Meg Anhydrite Mine

Some 200 million years ago, there were shallow lakes in the sandy region which was later to become the Eden valley. Evaporation of these lakes deposited anhydrite, a form of calcium sulphate.

Previously, anhydrite was an important feedstock for the production of both sulphuric acid and plasterboard, and several mines were worked in the Eden valley. Other more economic processes have since been developed for the manufacture of sulphuric acid and when plasterboard production was concentrated on more economic mines the Long Meg mine closed.

6.8 Pendragon Castle

By legend, Pendragon Castle was the home of Uther Pendragon, father of King Arthur. Sadly for the legend, the castle was probably built in the 12th century, several centuries after Arthur's death.

The castle had to be rebuilt several times after receiving too much attention from the Scots. The last rebuilding was by Lady Anne Clifford and the castle is mentioned many times in her diaries.

6.9 Wetheral Priory

Land at Wetheral was given by Ranulf de Meschine to the monks at St Mary's, York so that they could establish a Benedictine Priory. Today, all that remains of the Priory is the gatehouse (in the ownership of the National Trust) and the medieval salmon traps which are to be seen on the other side of the river, and are still used.

6.10 Wharton Hall

The earliest part of Wharton Hall was built in the 14th century in the classical **H** style favoured by the great families of the time (the **H** style is a main hall with two wings). Over the years the Hall has been considerably extended and the original simple layout is not obvious today.

The owners of the hall, the Whartons, were one of the most important families in the area for several centuries, and their family chapel is in Kirkby Stephen church.

Walk 7: River Greta

Information Centre: Barnard Castle 01833 690909

Perhaps less well known today than in earlier times, this delightful limestone valley captured the imaginations of many famous artists and writers including Turner, Cotman and Sir Walter Scott. The walk described has two contrasting sections:

- open countryside from Bowes to Rutherford Bridge (this section is not well waymarked);
- a gorge-like valley which is almost completely wooded with hardwood trees, from Rutherford Bridge to Greta Bridge.

Although the woodlands are very attractive, the two mile section between Brignall Mill and the ruined St Mary's Church has some clambering over fallen trees and scrambling over collapsed paths which may not be to everyone's taste. It is advisable to do the walk in dry weather in the spring or early summer before the undergrowth has become too established.

There is a fine Norman keep at Bowes (on the site of an earlier Roman fort) and Greta Bridge is also the site of a Roman fort. The fine Palladian mansion of Rokeby Park, at the confluence between the Tees and the Greta, is well worth a visit, as is the confuence itself. The latter is known as the "Meeting of the Waters", after the famous painting by Turner.

Bowes to Greta Bridge

Distance: 7 miles (11 miles if extended to Barnard Castle)

Starting point: Bowes castle, NY991135

Public transport: Although no public transport runs directly between the end points of the walk, there is a bus between Barnard Castle and Bowes. An alternative to the walk described, therefore, would be to use this bus and extend the walk from Greta Bridge to Barnard Castle (using a section of the Tees walk). Do, however, bear in mind that some sections of the Greta walk described can be slow (clambering over fallen trees), and the extended walk may seem longer than the measured 11 miles.

Maps: 7.1 plus Outdoor Leisure 30 and Landranger 92.

From the Norman fort at Bowes, follow the small lane to the east for a short distance before taking the path on the right which descends diagonally across two fields to the path along the riverbank.

Pass Gilmonby Bridge and follow the river until you reach a farm above you on the left (West Lowfields). The 2½ inch OS map shows the path going directly through the farm, but the path has been diverted to go round the left-hand side of the building.

The next stile is directly level (to the east) of the farm, but the right of way goes up to the road before doubling back to cross the stile. The path now passes a scar above the river on its way to Low Field Farm. Pass this farm a full field below the buildings (on the river side of the boundary).

At the next field boundary you must cross a small stream. There are no waymarks here, and the way ahead is most confusing. The 2½ inch OS map shows the path following the top side of the field boundaries down to the next farm. If you follow these directions you will end up in a field from which you are unable to exit! Ignoring the OS map, you should cross the stream directly below the wall under which the stream is passing. You must then keep to the river side of the field boundary to Mid Low Field.

Pass on the north side of Mid Low Field and the south side of East Lowfields Farm and Thackholme. ("Holme" is Norse for "water meadow", so it is no surprise to see a low-lying piece of flat ground here.)

At Hundah, walk through the farm, bearing right at the waymark to pass diagonally across the next field on your way to the Richmond to Barnard Castle road.

Cross the road above Rutherford

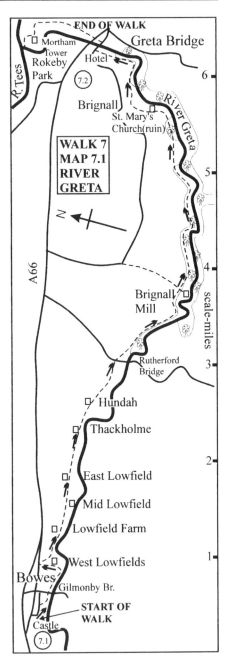

Bridge to access the next section of the walk – a delightful stretch on the terrace above a wooded valley. Pass Brignall Mill in the valley below. Shortly after crossing the track coming up from the mill, the path goes down into the woods. Some parts of the next two miles down to St Mary's Church can be fairly tough going – clambering over tree trunks which have fallen across the path, and working your way cautiously along parts of the path which have collapsed. Not all of this section is wooded, and in several places you emerge from the woods for short spells.

When you reach St Mary's Church, abandoned in 1833 and now a ruin, the path climbs upwards. Cross the gully leading down from Brignall and make for the top edge of the wood. There is now no further tangled undergrowth to fight, and the path takes you along the top of the terrace to Greta Bridge.

As you approach Greta Bridge, the undulations in the field in front of The Morritt Arms are the outlines of a Roman fort. The fort has never been properly excavated, but the hotel has a collection of Roman artefacts found on the site, just inside its front door. The bridge itself is very elegant and was made famous by Cotman's painting "Greta Bridge". (Although I have been an admirer of this painting for many years, I had not appreciated that the subject still existed.)

If you wish to visit the confluence of the Tees and the Greta (made famous by Turner's painting " The Meeting of the Waters"), take the path on the east side of the bridge. This goes under the A66 and passes Mortham Tower (a 14th century peel).

Should you decide to extend your walk to Barnard Castle, bear left at the confluence and follow the river to the town (see Tees walk for directions).

Places of interest in the Greta valley

7.1 Bowes

For thousands of years, Stainmore has been a strategically important transport corridor between Scotland and England. The Romans built a fort at Bowes, and in the 12th century the Normans built a keep on the same site to defend an area claimed by both England and Scotland. The imposing square keep is unique among Norman castles, standing alone with no adjacent buildings.

In more peaceable times, Stainmore became an important turnpike road. In 1838 Charles Dickens travelled this road by coach and stayed at the Unicorn Inn in Bowes. While there he met William Shaw, owner of The Academy. Dickens incorporated both Shaw and The Academy into his novel "Nicholas Nickleby": The Academy as Dotheboys Hall and William Shaw as the unscrupulous and sadistic Wackford Squeers.

Two miles to the west of Bowes, a natural bridge takes the Pennine Way across the Greta. In medieval times such natural phenomena were regarded with some awe, and the bridge is known as God's Bridge (there is a similarly named bridge at the top of the Ribble walk). In the 18th century, God's Bridge was used by the drovers bringing cattle from Scotland to English markets, as was Gilmonby Bridge at Bowes.

7.2 Rokeby Park (see Tees walk)

Walk 8: River Irthing

Section 1: Gilsland, Roman bridge abutment and Walter Scott's popping stone, 5 miles
Section 2: Hadrian's Wall and Lanercost Priory circular, 7 miles
Information Centre: Brampton: 016977 3433

This relatively little known river rises in the wastes which were home to cattle thieves known as the reivers, and later became Britain's rocket testing site (Spadeadam). After flowing through a gorge which was popular with the Victorians, the Irthing enters the valley which takes it to its confluence with the Eden.

Similar to the Tyne further east, the Romans used the northern side of the Irthing valley as a foundation for Hadrian's Wall. Unlike the Tyne, the first wall here was of turf rather than stone.

Access to the valley is somewhat limited and it is not possible to plan a continuous walk. Two separate circular walks are described. Not directly on the walks, but well worth a visit if you have the time, are Birdoswald Roman Fort and Bewcastle Cross (probably the finest remaining Anglo-Saxon cross; this is in the churchyard at Bewcastle, about 6 miles north of the Irthing).

Section 1: Gilsland, Roman bridge abutment and Walter Scott's popping stone

This walk first follows Hadrian's Wall to visit the Willowford Roman bridge abutment and then goes up the Irthing gorge to see Walter Scott's popping stone before returning to Gilsland via Gilsland Spa.

Distance: 5 miles

Starting point: Samson Inn, Gilsland. NY637663

Maps: 8.1 plus Landranger 86.

From the Inn (next to the railway line), follow the sign to milecastle 48. This Roman milecastle is unusual in that it has the remains of an oven used by the Roman soldiers.

Follow the path along the railway, cross where indicated and there should now be a stretch of wall below you. Cross the field, keeping to the left of the houses to come to a road. Cross the road and follow the wall towards Willowford Farm.

Just before the farmhouse, notice a Roman commemorative plaque built into a farm outbuilding. It was the practice of Roman centurions to commemorate a stretch of the wall built by their troops, and this plaque commemorates the work of centurion Gellius Philipus.

When you reach the farm, a small fee is payable to visit the bridge abutment which is in the field below. The river has moved since Roman times, and the bridge abutment is now some distance from the river. The Roman fort of Birdoswald is on the hilltop on the other side of the river.

Retrace your steps to the road and turn left down to the Post Office. Here, take the path which goes up the eastern bank of the river. Pass some stepping stones, which you will cross on the return journey, and pass to the left of Irthing House before climbing steeply up the field to join the road.

Take the drive on the left to Wardrew House, but just before the house, a path bears left to take you down to the bottom of the gorge. Cross the second footbridge you come to and turn right to follow the path which will take you up to Walter Scott's "popping stone".

Retrace your steps, but do not cross the footbridge this time. Climb up the gorge to the hotel. From above, there are good views looking down on the gorge below. Follow the road round the hotel and go down to the church, where you turn left. Cross the fields to the stepping stones – cross, and then turn right to return to Gilsland.

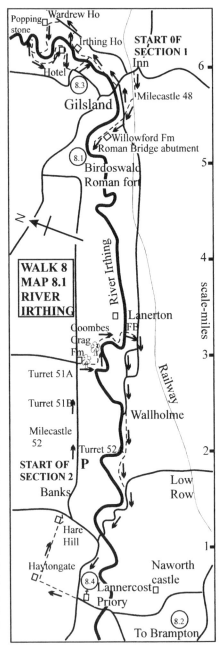

Section 2: Hadrian's Wall and Lanercost Priory circular

This circular walk starts with a fine stretch of Hadrian's Wall on the northern side of the Irthing valley before descending a steep, wooded hillside to the valley below and then proceeding along the valley bottom to Lanercost Priory

Distance: 7 miles

Starting point: Banks car park, NY575647

Maps: 8.1 plus Landranger 86.

From the car park, the first 1½ miles of the walk are along the road, following the line of Hadrian's Wall. You will pass turret 52A, milecastle 52, turrets 51B and 51A.

On reaching a farm at Coombe Crag, take the footpath on the right in front of the farm, signed Lanerton. A local farmer told me that in Victorian times these woods were part of a large estate, the paths being laid out as carriage drives. Today the paths are overgrown and something of a maze. Care is necessary if you are to avoid becoming lost. From the farm, the overgrown path will lead you through the woods to a sandstone exposure which was a Roman quarry. The graffiti is more recent, with a marked deterioration in the quality of the carving since the wood-warden left his mark in 1850.

Several paths leave the quarry and it is here that you need to be careful with the directions. Ignore the path on the right (which is a cul-de-sac down to the river) and after crossing the line of the sandstone outcrop you will see two paths ahead. Ignore the path which bends to the left, and take the other path (at about 2 o'clock) which descends in a zigzag to the bottom of the quarry.

You should not now be far above the river, but the slope is steep and the path crosses this slope for some distance before finally reaching the river's edge at another disused quarry. (It should have taken you about 10 minutes from the top of the first quarry.) Although the path is not difficult, there are a few places where there are substantial drops so be particularly careful not to slip.

The lower quarry is directly adjacent to the river, and a short section of concrete has been emplaced which should considerably help your progress. Follow the riverbank to a suspension bridge, which you cross.

From the bridge, follow the track uphill, and pass some houses onto the road. Follow the road to the right for only a short distance before turning right to follow a metalled road to the bridge at Wallholme.

Here follow the south side of the river. When you come to a house high above you, follow an old trackway at the bottom of a field. This touches the river and then follows the bottom of the hill until the road coming down from Low Row is reached. Turn right here, pass a picnic site and when you cross a bridge, Lanercost Priory is just over half a mile away.

From the road T-junction just to the north of the priory, take the track directly ahead which climbs steeply up the hillside to Haytongate. Here turn right and follow the wall line to Hares Hill, which you skirt on the right to come to a road. At the road, turn right downhill and then take the left turn up to Banks and your car park.

Places of interest in the Irthing valley

8.1 Birdoswald

The Romans occupied the fort of Birdoswald for some 300 years and no other point on Hadrian's Wall has such a complete collection of components of the Roman frontier system: fort, original turf wall, later stone wall, granaries, mile castle, and bridge abutment (on the other side of the river, accessible from Gilsland).

Birdoswald continued to be occupied after the departure of the Romans and may have seen continuous occupation down to the present day.

8.2 Brampton

The Anglo-Saxons first settled Brampton in the 7th century, but the early growth of the town was the result of the establishment of a market in 1252.

Brampton played a part in the Civil War with Cromwell keeping 40 prisoners in the Moot Hall in 1648 (now the Tourist Information Centre).

A century later, the town played a role in the Jacobite rebellion. In 1745, Bonnie Prince Charlie stayed in the oldest house in Brampton (Prince Charlie's House) while his troops besieged Carlisle castle. The mayor of Carlisle acknowledged defeat by presenting the keys of the city to the Prince outside the house.

Indirectly, the rebellion led to Brampton's greatest period of prosperity when most of the buildings we now see in Brampton were constructed. During the rebellion, General Wade found himself unable to transport troops from Newcastle to Carlisle. After the crushing of the rebellion, he built the Newcastle to Carlisle Military Road. Although built for military purposes, this turnpike between two cities which were undergoing rapid expansion at the beginning of the Industrial Revolution led to considerable trade passing through Brampton.

8.3 Gilsland

Gilsland has been known as a spa since Roman times, but for many centuries was too unruly to attract visitors. A centre of the "reiving" trade, a euphemism for rustling, Gilsland was said still to be a "nest of freebooters" long after the Union of the Crowns of England and Scotland. Only in the late 18th century was the rule of law finally established.

Sir Walter Scott, himself of a famous reiving family, did much to popularise Gilsland. On a visit in 1797, he met his future wife and proposed to her at the famous "popping" stone on the banks of the Irthing. He also used Gilsland as a setting for his novel "Guy Mannering".

The coincidence of the Victorian craze for spa towns and the opening of the railway in 1835 brought Gilsland's greatest period of prosperity. The main interest of the stretch of Hadrian's Wall which runs through Gilsland is the Willowford Roman Bridge abutment.

8.4 Lanercost priory

This Augustinian priory, idyllically situated in the Irthing valley, was founded in 1169 on land given by the Vaux family of Norfolk. It was visited by both sides in the Anglo-Scottish wars – three times by Edward I, and once by William Wallace and Robert Bruce.

After Henry VIII's Dissolution of the Monasteries, Lanercost passed into the hands of the Dacres, a local landowning family. The Dacres converted the west range and Prior's tower into a residence which they occupied until 1716, when the family died out.

In 1740 the north aisle was reroofed and converted into a parish church.

Walk 9: River Kent

Section 1: Kentmere and Kentmere reservoir circular, 6 miles
Section 2: Staveley and Kentmere circular, 9 miles
Section 3: Staveley to Kendal, 6 miles
Section 4: Kendal to Levens Hall, 5½ miles
Information Centre: Kendal 01539 725758

On the short journey from its source above Kentmere to the sea, the Kent runs through three different types of rocks. Each produces its own distinct scenery, giving a valley of great variety.

The remote upper valley is particularly attractive, isolation being guaranteed by the very limited amount of parking. To ease the problem of access, the walks described above Staveley are circular. In contrast, the valley below Staveley is very accessible, with both public transport and parking making it easy to carry out the linear walks described.

Scenery is not the only attraction of the Kent valley. Historic Kendal, which is directly on the line of the walk, is an interesting town (and would be even more so if it could do something about its traffic). Levens Hall, at the end of the walk, is a magnificent Elizabethan manor house built around an early medieval pele tower. It has a unique 17th century topiary garden.

The upper Kent valley

Section 1: Kentmere and Kentmere reservoir circular

This is the only walk in this book where the rocks are predominantly volcanic. The result is rugged lakeland crags on the hilltops.

The splendid walk is around the bed of a post-glacial lake in a remote and narrow valley. There is only limited roadside parking, just to the west of the church in Kentmere (12-15 cars), and this is not a walk to be attempted at popular times, unless you are willing to start early. If you are one of the lucky few, the lack of parking does have the benefit that you will not see hordes of other people on the walk.

An alternative way of getting round the parking problem, which I used when first researching this walk for the book, is to park in Staveley and combine this and the next walk. The resulting 14 miles make an excellent full day's walk.

Distance: 6 miles

Starting point: Kentmere Church, NY455042

Maps: 9.1 plus Outdoor Leisure 7 and Landranger 90.

From the car park just beyond the church, follow the road away from Kentmere. When you reach a house on the left, take the gated road opposite, towards Hartrigg. You are now crossing from an area of sedimentary Silurian rocks into volcanics. As you climb upwards, you can see a very clear delineation between the two rock types on the opposite side of the valley where the craggy volcanic outcrops abut the more rounded sedimentary rocks.

Follow the road round the base of Ravens and Calfhowe Crags, with the bed of a post-glacial lake to your right. In just over a mile from Kentmere, you will reach Hartrigg.

When Turner visited Kentmere in 1816, he sketched the valley from just above Hartrigg. The view we see today is almost indistinguishable from that sketched by Turner, even to the line of the wall descending from the fell to Tongue House, the only habitation in view. (We shall visit Tongue House, now a ruin, later in the walk.)

Take the track which climbs to the left of Hartrigg and then follows the contour towards the reservoir. The streams coming down from the fells on your left can be quite impressive in wet weather. The side of the track is boggy and supports a good population of that lovely, blue-flowered insectivorous plant, the Butterwort (so named because of its use in former times as a butter preservative).

Pass Reservoir cottage and the spoil heap of a slate quarry to come to the reservoir which was built to supply downstream mills. The cwm behind, formed by Mardale and Kentmere Common, is most impressive. The Roman road known as High Street followed the skyline to the left of you.

The path from the reservoir crosses the footbridge over the overflow channel and then the river. In wet weather the river is not fordable, and you will need to cross the reservoir dam wall.

Follow the river downstream, passing further quarry spoil to come to a ruin at Tongue House, the building sketched by Turner from the other side of the valley. (Immediately before Tongue House, the semicircular disturbance in the field is the site of an ancient settlement.)

About a mile after Tongue House, you will come to Overend, where you meet a path coming down from Mardale. Two tracks leave Overend, and you should take the lower one through the gate at the back of the farm. Cross a footbridge and follow the track down the valley. When you reach the end of the glacial lake bed, you will hear the river on your right as it cascades some 200 feet (61m) over several waterfalls to reach the flood plain below.

The track joins a small road. Shortly, you turn to the right and go down to the bridge and then pass the church back to the car park.

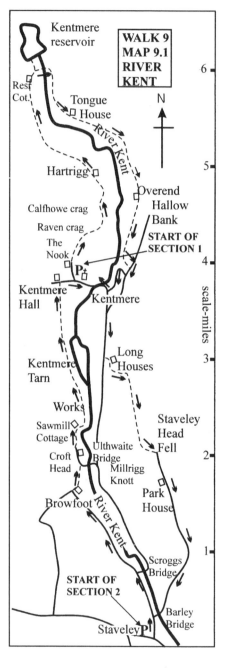

Section 2: Staveley to Kentmere circular

This walk is similar to the first walk in that it also goes along both sides of a narrow valley which encloses the bed of a post-glacial lake. Here though, the remnant of the lake still remains at Kentmere Tarn.

In contrast to the volcanic rocks above Kentmere, the rocks in this part of the valley are sedimentary. The hills, while still lofty, have weathered to a more rounded profile, reminiscent of the Howgills of Sedbergh rather than the lakeland fells.

The return journey from Kentmere to Staveley includes a climb over Staveley Head Fell.

Distance: 9 miles

Starting point: Staveley, NY470985

Maps: 9.1 plus Outdoor Leisure 7, Landranger 90 and 97.

From the centre of Staveley, take the road up the valley towards Kentmere. Pass Barley Bridge and Scroggs Bridge to come to Browfoot in just under 2 miles from Staveley.

At Browfoot, pass the drive going down to the farm, but take the next track on the right which passes behind the farm. A green road, sunken in places, takes you from Browfoot to Ulthwaite Bridge, where you follow a metalled road to Croft Head. About 100 metres after Croft Head, take the path on the right. A footbridge over a beck takes you to Sawmill Cottage, delightfully situated above a bend in the river.

You now cross the glacial deposits which were responsible for the blocking of the valley and the formation of the tarn. The public right of way goes through a mineral factory and you are then on the former bed of a post-glacial lake. Sediments have filled much of Kentmere Tarn, which is a fraction of its former size. As you pass the tarn, notice the buildings on the opposite side of the valley at Long Houses. On your return journey, this is where you will climb up to cross Staveley Head Fell.

About 1½ miles after leaving the factory, you will come to Kentmere Hall, a 14th century pele tower with a house added in more peaceable times.

Follow the road through Kentmere and round to Long Houses, where you bear left and climb the hill. In about a third of a mile, take the path on the right which follows a line of blue markers across the moorland. With Millrigg Knott on your right, you bear slightly left after a wall to descend to a track which follows Hall Beck to Park House. The road is now metalled, and will take you to Staveley in just under 2 miles.

Section 3: Staveley to Kendal

Despite being between the conurbations of Staveley and Kendal, and passing through an industrial site at Burnside, this walk contains some fine stretches of riverbank, perhaps the best being between Sandyhill and Cowen Head.

Distance: 6 miles

Starting point: Staveley. NY4709985

Public transport: Kendal and Staveley are connected by both bus and train.

Maps: 9.2 plus Outdoor Leisure 7 and Landranger 97.

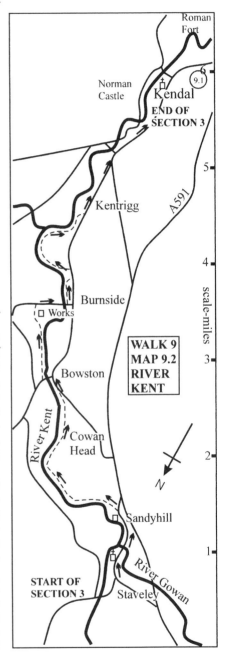

From the centre of Staveley, follow the road which passes the remains of a 14th century chapel to the river. At Sandyhill the river leaves the road, bearing left. Formerly the path followed the riverbank here, but has now been diverted a further 250 metres down the road towards Kendal. Turn left at the footpath sign and follow the track to the river.

The next section of just over a mile down to Cowen Head is a delightful stretch along a typical dales riverbank. At Cowen Head, the former mill complex is undergoing a facelift and conversion to living accommodation.

At Bowston, cross the bridge and follow the path down the opposite bank to Burnside. A large, modern factory complex is reached at Burnside and here, the path skirts the left of the mill. Turn right at the road and go down to the river.

Immediately after the river, take the minor road on the left. A short section across a field and about 200 metres along a narrow road bring you to a path along the riverbank to Kentrigg. As you approach Kentrigg, country meets town. Here there is the rather incongruous sight of trout rising to the fly and cattle drinking in the river against a backdrop of large modern factories.

At Kentrigg, the path goes between the river and some houses and then climbs up to the road which will take you into the centre of Kendal.

Section 4: Kendal to Levens Hall

This section of the walk is through limestone country, the limestone being exposed in several places where the river has cut gorges through it. The shortness of the walk should leave you plenty of time to visit Kendal, at the beginning of the walk, and the delightful Levens Hall and 17th century deer park at the end of the walk.

An alternative to the path described on the east side of the river through Levens Park is the path on the west bank (shown on the map but not described). Using the bridge just to the north of the A590 to link the two paths, it is possible to make a short circular walk through the park, starting at Levens Hall.

Distance: 5½ miles

Starting point: Kendal Centre, NY515925

Public transport: There is a bus from Kendal to Levens Hall

Maps: 9.3 plus Landranger 97.

From the centre of Kendal, follow the path down the west side of the river. High above you on the other bank is the 13th century Norman castle which was the birthplace of Katherine Parr, Henry VIII's last wife. On your right you will pass the splendid parish church which is well worth a visit.

Cross Nether bridge to the east side of the river. Pass the K shoe factory and factory shop which, judging by the number of coaches in the car park, is a popular place to visit. Recross to the west bank, and follow the path downstream, passing the sewerage works. As you go round a large loop in the river, the slight undulations in the field on the other bank indicate the site of the Roman fort of Watercrook.

At the end of the loop, cross a small road and take the first gate on the right into the fields. This cuts across two bends in the river before following the riverbank down to Natlands bridge. At the bridge, cross to the east bank and follow the river downstream. The river here cuts gorges through the limestone and is a popular salmon stretch.

Just before Sedgwick, join a small road and follow this down and over the A590 before taking the path into Levens park. The parkland was laid out in the 17th century and the path follows a line of ancient oak trees. When you reach the A6, the splendid Levens Hall is ahead of you.

Places of interest in the Kent valley

9.1 Kendal

In the bend of the river at the southern perimeter of the present town, the Romans established the fort we know as Watercrook. Little is to be seen at the site, but many finds are housed in the Museum of Natural History and Archaeology. Analysis of pottery finds from Watercrook suggest that the site was several times abandoned, only to be later reoccupied.

The Normans built their motte and bailey a mile to the north of the Roman fort in the 11th century, and upgraded it to a stone castle in the 13th century. Henry VIII's last wife, Katherine Parr, was born in the castle around 1510. Today the castle is a prominent ruin above the town.

By the 13th century, Kendal had already established itself as one of the most prominent wool towns in the country. This prosperity may be judged by the size and splendour of the parish church. Flemish weavers settled in Kendal in the 14th century,

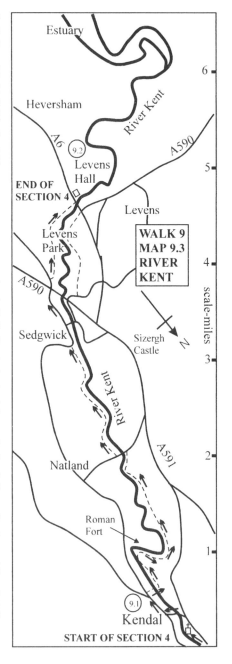

further extending its prominence as a wool centre.

By the end of the 18th century, Kendal was differentiating itself from other woollen centres by knitting expensive fine stockings, most of which were sent for sale in London by packhorse. The trade was on such a scale that it kept 350 packhorses busy. With the coming of the Keighley to Kendal turnpike in 1753, and the Liverpool to Kendal canal in 1818, Kendal became the most prominent town in Westmorland, even though the administrative centre remained at Appleby.

There are two museums in Kendal:

- the Museum of Lakeland Life and Industry, housed in the Abbott Hall (built in 1759);
- the Kendal Museum of Natural History and Archaeology.

9.2 Levens Hall

Predominantly an Elizabethan hall, Levens is built around a 14th century pele tower. The site has been in the ownership of a single family for some 700 years, but was "won" by the current line of the family in 1688 in a game of cards. This event is celebrated in the "ace of hearts" insignia to be seen on the drainpipes.

Although the house is brimming with artefacts of historic interest accumulated over the centuries, and would be worth visiting for these alone, it is perhaps for the gardens which Levens is best known. In the 17th century the gardens were reconstructed by Guillaume Beaumont, gardener to James II. Partly through benign neglect, the garden has retained its original design. The topiary is said to be the finest in the world.

Just to the north of the hall, Beaumont laid out Levens Park with its splendid avenue of oaks. Footpaths allow the park to be walked on both sides of the river. Look out here for the black fallow deer and the rare Bagot goats.

Walk 10: River Lune

Section 1: Tebay to Sedbergh, 11½ miles
Section 2: Sedbergh to Kirkby Lonsdale, 16½ miles
Section 3: Kirkby Lonsdale to Caton, 12½ miles
Section 4: Caton to Lancaster, 4 miles
Information Centres: Kirkby Lonsdale 015242 71437;
Sedbergh 015396 20125; Lancaster 01524 32878

Few of the thousands speeding daily up the M6 motorway can have any knowledge of the marvellous river below them in the Lune gorge; a river of deep pools and late medieval bridges. Nor perhaps do they realise that the narrow track they see on the other side of the valley was established by the Romans, almost two millennia ago, during the campaign to conquer northern Britain. Only on foot is it possible to appreciate this wonderful valley.

Scenically, the Lune is a river valley of two halves. From Tebay to Kirkby Lonsdale, the river flows through Silurian rocks more characteristic of the Lake District than the Dales. These "basement" rocks, which were considerably twisted and tilted during periods of mountain building, produce high fells and exposures of jagged "teeth" in the riverbed. These "teeth" form deep salmon holding pools (known by the Norse name of "dubs") and provide the foundations for a number of medieval bridges. From Kirkby Lonsdale to the sea, the river flows through younger Carboniferous rocks. Here the fells are lower and the river meanders across a wide alluvial plain.

Although historically the Lune has been an important transport corridor – the Romans and the Normans built forts to control the transport routes and, more recently, the railway and motorway have used the upper reaches of the valley – significant population centres never developed above Lancaster. This leaves the Lune as one of England's most unspoilt waterways and best salmon rivers.

Almost the whole of the river is covered in the 45 miles of excellent walking between Tebay and Lancaster. Only the section above Tebay has been excluded on the grounds that the walking is rather uninteresting.

The walk is divided into four sections, the first having two alternative end points. Although most of the walking is along the valley bottom, the second section takes to the hills and provides what must be some of the finest panoramas in northern England.

The Howgills from the Crook of Lune

Section 1: Tebay to Sedbergh

This section of the walk is along the western edge of the Howgills, passing spectacular pools in the river. Towards Sedbergh, there are marvellous views along the Lune valley down to the distant Bowland Fells.

Although salmon enter the Lune in early summer, it is late autumn before the fish and the fishermen arrive in this section in any numbers. Particularly when there are floods in autumn, you will see fishermen on the water, and there is then some pressure on the few car parking places next to the bridges.

Although the standard walk ends at Sedbergh, a route is described at the end of the section which takes you from Hole House farm to an alternative end point at Killington bridge.

Distance: 11½ miles

Starting point: B6260, north of Tebay. NY619055

Intermediate break point: Crook of Lune bridge (620963) 7 miles

Public transport: Not available.

Maps: 10.1 and 10.2 plus Landranger 91 and 97.

It is possible to park a car about 100 metres south of the river Lune on the Tebay to Orton road, B6260. Cross the river and take the path to the left, which passes Bybeck Farm. Pass under the M6 and over the Birk Beck. If you look towards the river Lune, you will see Castle Howe, the site of a Norman motte, immediately adjacent to the motorway slip road.

As the track bears to the right to a farm, leave it, and bear left towards the river. Pass successively under the M6, the railway and then the M6 again to reach Roundthwaite. From Roundthwaite, the path goes down the beck towards the M6 motorway. The start of the path is somewhat indistinct, and it is best to follow the road uphill for about 100 metres before descending across the hillside to the beck.

Go under the motorway then after going under the railway, turn right and then left onto Lune's Bridge. The bridge is built on one of the many outcrops of highly tilted ordovician-silurian rocks you will see on your way down the valley. This now redundant 17th century bridge over a spectacular gorge was on an important drove road, bringing Scottish cattle to English markets.

The A685 is now in front of you. Cross the road and take the track down to Brockholes. The path is not signposted at Brockholes, but is round the right-hand edge of the farm buildings, from where you follow the river down to Low Borrowbridge.

(Over the bridge at Low Borrowbridge, between the farm and the railway, is the site of a Roman fort. This was an important strategic site for the

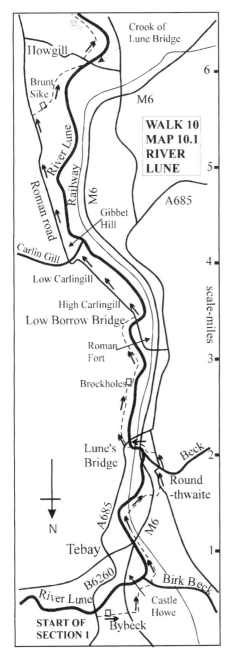

Romans on the road linking Manchester and Carlisle, and was occupied throughout the period of Roman rule. Finds from the site are to be seen in the Kendal Museum.)

Do not cross the bridge, but take the minor road down the east side of the river towards Sedbergh. Pass High Carlingill and Low Carlingill to come to Carlin Gill itself. The gill was formerly the Westmorland and Yorkshire county border, and a gallows was sited at Gibbet Hill, 624994.

For the next mile the road (an old Roman road) crosses open moorland. There are fine views of the river below which is like a stream in contrast to the deep pools seen at Lune's Bridge. There are also good views of the motorway and railway on the other side of the valley.

After leaving the moorland, you could take any of the farm tracks on the right to go down to the river. Probably the most direct is to take the fourth farm track to Brunt Sike (now derelict). Pass to the right of the farm buildings and in the field ahead bear slightly left. Cross the beck but do not descend to the river's edge. Keep above the trees and descend to the river bank at Crook of Lune Bridge. If you wish to finish your walk here, there is a small car parking area on the other side of the bridge.

At the bridge, take the road away from the river uphill to the first corner and go through the gate onto a path. Follow the river downstream for about 1½ miles, passing through some delightful wood-lands on the way. Cross Chapel Beck and when you reach Smithy Beck, the path leaves the riverbank to go up to Hole House farm. Hole House was reputed to have been the birthplace of Roger Lupton, founder of Sedbergh school. Later, the house belonged to a Lancaster slave trader and is said to be haunted by the owner's wife and a negro slave he murdered.

If you wish to proceed down the river to Killington bridge rather than detouring to Sedbergh, jump to the description of this part of the walk at the end of the section.

If you wish to finish the walk in Sedbergh, go through Hole House Farm and follow the track up to the road between Low Borrowbridge and Sedbergh. Turn right and follow this road to Sedbergh about two miles away, passing Nab Fell and Winder on the way. Although narrow, the road is quiet and as height is gained, gives some excellent views down the valley to the Bowland Fells (some 20 miles away).

Alternative ending, Hole House farm to Killington bridge.

Go through the small gate on the right of the path immediately before Hole House farm (not signposted). Skirt round the right-hand side of the farm buildings and climb up to the top of the small field where you will find an old track going along the hedge line.

Go through the first gate on the left, and cross two fields to Nether Bainbridge. Bear right into a walled greenway and in about 0.4 of a mile you will come to the next building down the valley, Bramaskew. Pass to the right of Bramaskew and bear right along a lane marked "Dalesway", which will take you to Low Branthwaite.

At Low Branthwaite you may proceed down either side of the beck to the river. The right-hand side has the advantage that it takes you under the impressive Lune viaduct, but requires you to ford a beck. The beck is not wide and in normal conditions is easy to hop. However, if there has been heavy rain, it is probably wiser to cross the beck next to the farm and proceed down the left bank of the beck, taking the railway underpass, and missing out on the viaduct.

Follow the river down to Lincoln's Inn Bridge. After the bridge, the path initially follows the riverbank, but then leaves it to go to Luneside. Pass to the left of Luneside and in about 0.4 of a mile bear sharp right towards the river. The next section, down to Killington Bridge, is on a bank high above the river. Below are deep salmon pools.

Section 2: Sedbergh to Kirkby Lonsdale

Although it is possible to walk this section along the valley bottom, there is little direct access to the riverbank. An outstanding alternative is this moderately strenuous walk with a height gain of some 2000 feet (606m) over the Middleton Fells.

From the hilltops, there are some of the finest panoramic views in northern England, and this is one of the best places to view the geological faults which stretch along the western edge of the northern Pennines.

Distance: 16½ miles from Sedbergh, or 13 from Middleton Bridge

Starting point: New Bridge, Sedbergh SD662913 or Middleton Bridge SD630898.(From Killington Bridge, the alternative end point of the previous section, Middleton Bridge is about one mile down the B6256.)

Public transport: There is a single bus each day between Sedbergh and Kirkby Lonsdale, Monday to Saturday.

Maps: 10.2 and 10.3 plus Landranger 97.

The first part of the walk, between Sedbergh and Middleton Bridge, is described in the last section of the Rawthey walk. You may shorten the walk by starting at Middleton Bridge where there is a small space for car parking.

From Middleton Bridge, go through the gate and take the path which climbs through the woods. Cross the line of the disused railway to reach Jordan Lane, a little used country lane with grass growing through the tarmac (a former Roman road). Follow Jordan Lane southwards until you reach the A683. Here take the minor road on the left which climbs uphill. Pass between farm buildings at Fellside. In about two miles the track meets a wall which you follow.

As you climb higher, magnificent views open up of the Lune, Rawthey and Dee valleys below. As the path goes to the south east, Dentdale is below, but when it swings to the south west, you will be above Barbondale.

About 4½ miles and a climb of some 1750 feet (530m) from the valley below brings you to the trig point on Calf Top, the highest point on the walk. On a clear day there are magnificent views and you should be able to see:

- almost the whole of the Lune valley, from around Tebay down to Lancaster;

- the Langdales in the Lake District, the Howgills, Ingleborough, the Dufton and Bowland Fells;

- Morecambe Bay with the Heysham Nuclear Power Stations and Barrow shipyard;

- on the far horizon, some 50 miles away, Blackpool Tower.

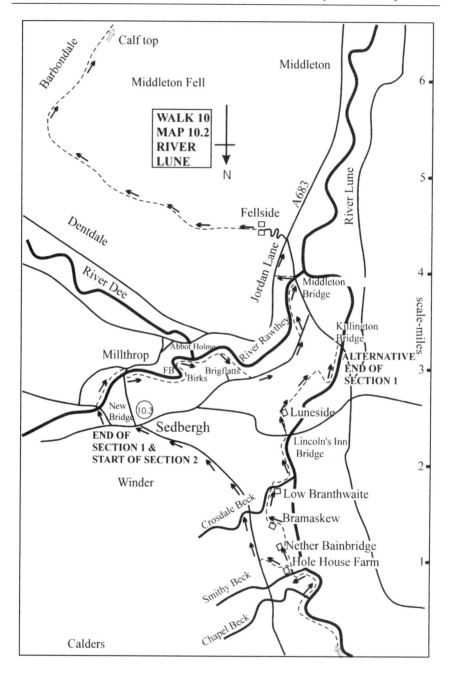

Calf top

Barbondale

Middleton

Middleton Fell

Middleton

**WALK 10
MAP 10.2
RIVER
LUNE**

N

Fellside

A683

River Lune

6

5

Dentdale

River Dee

Jordan Lane

River Rawthey

Middleton
Bridge

4

Killington
Bridge

scale-miles

Millthrop

Abbot Holme

FB   Brigflatts
Birks

**ALTERNATIVE
END OF
SECTION 1**

3

New
Bridge   10.3   Sedbergh

Luneside

**END OF
SECTION 1 &
START OF SECTION 2**

Lincoln's Inn
Bridge

Winder

Crosdale Beck

Low Branthwaite

Bramaskew

2

Nether Bainbridge
Hole House Farm

1

Smithy Beck

Chapel Beck

Calders

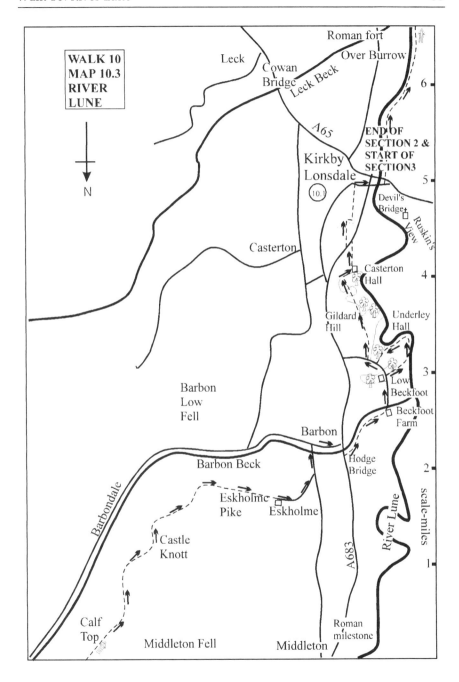

WALK 10
MAP 10.3
RIVER
LUNE

N

Roman fort
Over Burrow
Leck
Cowan
Bridge
Leck Beck
A65
END OF
SECTION 2 &
START OF
SECTION 3
Kirkby
Lonsdale
10.1
Devil's
Bridge
Ruskin's View
Casterton
Casterton
Hall
Gildard
Hill
Underley
Hall
Low
Beckfoot
Barbon
Low
Fell
Beckfoot
Farm
Barbon
Barbon Beck
Hodge
Bridge
Barbondale
Eskholme
Pike
Eskholme
River Lune
scale-miles
Castle
Knott
A683
Calf
Top
Middleton Fell
Middleton
Roman
milestone

6

5

4

3

2

1

From the wall material you can see that the local rocks are Silurian, but if you look cautiously over the steep slope down to Barbondale below, you will see much younger outcrops of carboniferous limestone. The Dent Fault, a geological slippage of several thousand vertical feet (i.e. many hundreds of metres!), runs down the valley. The Dent Fault is only part of a continuous line of faults around the northern Pennines which were created when the Pennines tilted. From here, the Dent Fault runs to the north west and links with the Pennine Fault which runs along the base of the Dufton Fells (which you should just be able to see in the distance.)

From the Calf Top, the path descends only to climb again up to Castle Knott. If anything, there are even better views along the length of the Lune valley from here. Your destination at Kirkby Lonsdale is now in sight, and to the south, just peeping over the top of the Bowland Fells, is Pendle Hill on the other side of the Ribble valley.

The path descending from Castle Knott passes a cairn at Eskholme Pike before descending steeply to Eskholme. In summer, the hillside here is covered with Tormentill, the diminutive yellow-flowered member of the rose family.

Go through Eskholme onto the lane down to Barbon, cross the Barbon Beck and follow the road on the right to Hodge Bridge. Cross the bridge and follow the beck through a golf course to Beckfoot Farm. Cross the beck (there is a delightful, very narrow packhorse bridge here) and in about a quarter of a mile you will reach some buildings on the left at Low Beckfoot.

Turn right here, just before a small wood. When the track you are on bears left, leave it and proceed directly ahead to the river. Follow the river for about half a mile, passing some excellent salmon pools and Underley Bridge. Bear left up the edge of the wood to rejoin the road next to a small cottage. Turn right onto the road, but in a short distance take the path to the right towards Casterton. The path makes towards the top edge of a wood under Gildard Hill before passing into the wood.

The path leaves the wood, but then re-enters it. When you re-emerge, follow the edge of the wood to the right to Casterton Hall. The path goes through the courtyard of the hall and then across the fields to the road.

Kirkby Lonsdale is only about half a mile down the road on the right. However, the road is narrow and can be busy. To minimise road walking, it is better to turn left than right. In about 200 metres, take the path on the right, Laitha Lane, just in front of the golf club. Follow this path until it splits, and then take the right branch, signed Kirkby Lonsdale. Pass a caravan site, and at the end of the lane bear right onto the minor road, which will take you down to Devil's Bridge.

Section 3: Kirkby Lonsdale to Caton

This section compensates for lack of access to the riverbank of the previous section. Almost the whole of the section is across an ancient lakebed, and the valley bottom is still liable to flooding. In winter it is a good place to observe migrant waterbirds, and in the late autumn you may see salmon making their way upstream to spawn.

Distance: 12½ miles

Starting point: Devil's Bridge car park, Kirkby Lonsdale SD617782

Intermediate break point: Loyn Bridge 6½ miles

Public transport: The Ingleton to Lancaster bus stops at Caton and Hornby, and can be used for the section of the walk between Loyn Bridge and Caton

Maps: 10.3, 10.4 and 10.5 plus Landranger 97.

From the car park, cross Devil's Bridge, a bridge of great antiquity. Notice the ribbed arches, a style of building which went out of fashion after the Dissolution of the Monasteries. Cross the Kendal to Skipton road, and follow the riverbank downstream. In about 1½ miles, the Leck Beck joins the Lune on the other side of the river.

Although there is nothing that you can see, just up the Leck Beck from the confluence at Over Burrow, the Romans had an important fort which they occupied throughout the period when Britain was part of the Roman Empire.

Your Ordnance Survey map will not show a public right of way down the river from here, but a concessionary path has recently been established.

About a mile below the Leck Beck, the path detours somewhat away from the river, and about half a mile along the detour, the path crosses a footbridge over the Whittington Beck. This footbridge was replaced by the Lancashire County Council in 1995, the previous bridge having been washed away in the 1994 winter floods. Cross a stile and follow the course of an old stream which has now been truncated.

As you pass a farm on the terrace above the river, the Greta joins the Lune on your left (having come from Ingleton – see Doe and Twiss walk). Ahead, on the skyline, you should be able to see a wind farm.

After a stile and a footbridge, take the track up to a farm. Go through the yard and follow the path to the railway. Go under the railway bridge and take the track which follows a loop to Arkholme. As you enter Arkholme, you pass immediately to the right of a motte and bailey which has commanding views over the valley.

Arkholme is a delightful village with many charming 17th century cottages which greatly benefit from not being on the main road. It is set at right angles to the river, and at one time there was a ferry crossing here. From the river end of the village, drop down to the flood plain.

Loyn Bridge is now about 1½ miles further down the river, and if you wish to terminate your walk at Hornby, you should cross the bridge. Over the other side of the river is a fine Norman motte and bailey site.

The confluence with the Wenning is reached about a mile below Loyn Bridge. Hornby is across the flood plain and Ingleborough is behind.

In a further half a mile you will come to a fishing hut raised on stilts. During the summer this may seem a long way above the river level, but in the winter of 1994 the water level came to within a few inches of the bottom of the hut, showing that the builders had not been overcautious.

Just after the fishing hut, the path bears right away from the river towards the Snab. When you reach the hillside, take the path to the left. As you pass a cottage, the path is to the left, almost hidden. In wet weather the first part of this track can be very muddy and you may need to detour a little up the hillside. The path through Wild Carr woods is somewhat undulating.

Pass through another wood. Shortly, Aughton will be above you. Bear left when you join a farm track coming down from Aughton and follow this to a barn which is situated in a large bow in the river.

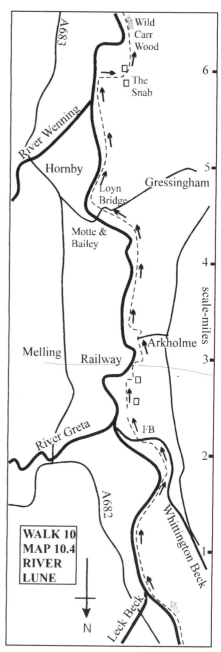

WALK 10
MAP 10.4
RIVER
LUNE

N

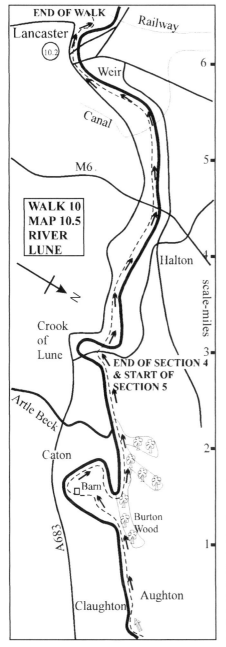

After the barn, follow the riverbank round in a great curve. At one point the river has turned through a full 180 degrees, and you are actually walking back towards Kirkby Lonsdale!

At Burton Wood the river runs below a steep bank, and the path has to climb to some elevation before returning to the river flood plain. When you come out of the wood you are only about a mile from the car park at Crook of Lune.

Section 4: Crook of Lune to Lancaster

This is an easy walk along the track of the former Lancaster to Wenning railway line and takes you into the heart of the historic city of Lancaster. The walk ends on the hilltop which was once the site of several Roman forts, a Norman fort and a Benedictine monastery.

Distance: 4 miles

Starting point: Car park, Crook of Lune SD522647

Public transport: The Lancaster to Ingleton bus stops at Caton.

Maps: 10.5 plus Landranger 97.

From the car park, drop down onto the disused railway track – now a footpath. In about a mile, you will see Halton on the other bank of the river. In Anglo-Saxon times Halton was much more important than Lancaster and was the administrative capital of this region.

After the M6 you will pass the Post House Hotel on your left and an army training camp on the other bank of the river. Industrial buildings now start to crowd the left bank of the river. In earlier days, a linoleum factory here was the biggest employer in Lancaster.

The first bridge reached takes the Lancaster canal over the river, and when the weir is reached, it signals the upper limit of tidal water. Next pass under Skerton Bridge, said to be the first bridge in England to have been built with a level profile.

An underpass takes you under the modern road to Morecambe and you then come into an open space which was the site of a former railway station. Follow the old railway line along the river until a sign to the castle and church is reached. If you wish to see the old docks, keep straight on here, but otherwise climb the hill to the top, passing the old Roman bathhouse on the way.

When you reach the hilltop, which both dominates the lowest fording point of the Lune and gives a good view across Morecambe Bay (the old route to Scotland), you will appreciate why the Romans, and later the Normans, decided to fortify this site.

Places of interest in the Lune valley

10.1 Kirkby Lonsdale

Kirkby Lonsdale is an attractive town of winding lanes and hostelries, some dating back to the 16th and 17th centuries. It is sited at a natural crossing point of the Lune. A weekly market is held in the square, a market having been held in the town since 1272.

The name of the town indicates that there was a church in pre-Norman times. The oldest part of the present church is 12th century (some fine Norman arches) and most of the building fabric is 13th century.

Turner visited Kirkby Lonsdale and produced a famous picture of the view from the churchyard. Stimulated by Turner's picture, Ruskin visited the town and wrote, "I do not know in all my country, still less in France or Italy, a place more naturally divine... " Clearly, the pen is mightier than the paintbrush, for today the view is known as Ruskin's View.

The Devil's Bridge, a very fine early medieval bridge spans the Lune. Its age is not known, but is thought to be 13th century, possibly a monastic bridge built by Fountains Abbey. The caravan at the east end of the bridge is famous for its "egg and bacon butties". It is firmly on the motor cyclists' circuit and at week-ends ranks of expensive, gleaming machines are to be seen.

10.2 Lancaster

Lancaster is an attractive city where the visitor can see much of historical interest in a compact area.

During his conquest of northern Britain, Agricola built the first of three Roman forts in Lancaster on the hilltop site overlooking the lowest fording point of the Lune. Recent excavations have revealed a Roman bathhouse on the hillside.

In Anglo-Saxon times, the capitol of the area was at Halton, five miles further up the Lune. However, the Normans re-established Lancaster's pre-eminence because of its strategic position on the route from Scotland.

There are no visible remains of the first Norman castle built by Roger de Poitou in 1093. Perhaps the most magnificent part of the castle is John O'Gaunt's gatehouse, built in around 1400. We now know that the gatehouse was wrongly attributed and was actually built by John O'Gaunt's son, the future Henry IV.

When Henry became King, the estates of the Duchy of Lancaster passed to the Crown, where they have remained to this day. This explains why the Lancastrian response to the Royal Toast is not the standard, "The Queen," but rather, "The Queen, Duke of Lancaster."

The castle has been a prison for many centuries and remains so today. It has the gruesome record of having seen more people condemned to death than any other place in Britain. Those executed include the ten Lancashire witches, and many condemned because of their religious beliefs.

In medieval times, Lancaster was one of the most important ports in the country, being particularly strongly involved in the slave trade. Its downfall was the shallowness of the river and trade ceased when larger ships were unable to berth. Many of the old dock buildings may still be seen on the riverfront. The Maritime Museum, housed in the old Customs House, has an interesting display of the history of the port.

10.3 Sedbergh (see River Rawthey walk 12.1)

Walk 11: River Nidd

Section 1: Tor Dike to Scar House Reservoir, 5½ miles
Section 2: Scar House Reservoir and Lofthouse circular, 9 miles
Section 3: Lofthouse to Pateley Bridge, 6½ miles
Information Centre: Pateley Bridge 01423 711147

Although outside the National Park, and less well known than many of the other dales, Nidderdale provides some excellent walking.

This is a mainly gritstone valley, with moorlands on the hilltops and pasture in valley bottoms. Upper Nidderdale is primarily a sheep farming area, as it has been back since Norman times. (In medieval times, almost the entire valley was owned by Fountains and Bylands Abbeys; the monks raising large flocks of sheep at their many granges.)

At the end of the Ice Age, glacial debris blocked the valley at Wath, forming a lake which lay roughly between Wath and Lofthouse. In the early 20th century, this lake was recreated to supply water to Bradford. With its pastoral surroundings, mudflats and reed-beds, Gouthwaite is more like a natural lake than the man-made reservoirs further up the valley, and considerably enhances the amenity of the valley.

Limestone may be seen in the riverbed above Lofthouse (where the river goes underground), and in its tributary, the How Stean Beck. The limestone exposure in the How Stean Gorge is a popular tourist attraction.

The only reminder of a once prosperous flax manufacturing industry around Pateley Bridge is the 34ft waterwheel at Foster Beck Mill.

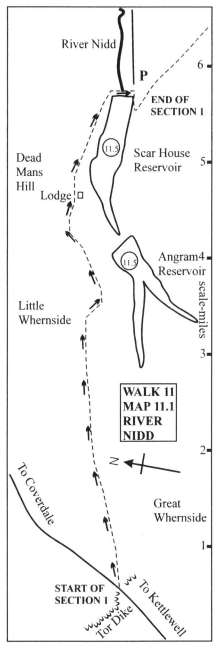

River Nidd

P

END OF SECTION 1

Dead Mans Hill

Lodge □

Scar House Reservoir

Angram Reservoir

Little Whernside

scale-miles

WALK 11
MAP 11.1
RIVER
NIDD

N

To Coverdale

Great Whernside

START OF SECTION 1

To Kettlewell

Tor Dike

Section 1: Tor Dike to Scar House

This delightful walk enters Nidderdale from Tor Dike, an ancient fortification thought to have been erected by the Brigantians as a defence against the Romans. The saddle between Great Whernside and Little Whernside is crossed, and an ancient packhorse route is followed down to Lodge and then to Scar House Reservoir. There are some fine views looking down Coverdale to Wensleydale.

There is informal roadside parking at Tor Dike and a proper car park at the reservoir. The latter is reached from Lofthouse by taking the toll road up the west bank of the Nidd (small fee payable on entering the toll road).

Distance: 5.5miles

Starting point: Tor Dike SD986757

Public transport: Not available. Unless you intend to return to your starting point, this is a walk that can only be completed with transport at both ends. Because of the isolation of upper Nidderdale, the end points of the walk are actually 28 miles apart by road!

Maps: 11.1 plus Outdoor Leisure 30, Landranger 98 and 99.

At Tor Dike, follow the path signed to Lodge 4. This path can be seen climbing diagonally across the flank of Great Whernside. The bridleway is used by bikers and is somewhat churned in places, with boggy patches that can be difficult to cross in wet weather.

As you climb upwards, there are very attractive views on your left, looking down Coverdale towards Leyburn in Wensleydale. When you reach a wall on the skyline, bear left to follow the line of the wall. At the saddle between Great Whernside and Little Whernside, follow the posts to the right which traverse Little Whernside. Pass Angram reservoir to come to a derelict inn at Lodge. The origin of the name is thought to be an ancient hunting lodge in the Norman forest of upper Nidderdale.

Dead Man's Hill, the name of the hill above Lodge, commemorates a gruesome event in 1728 when three decapitated Scottish pedlars were discovered. From Lodge, follow the path to the dam of Scar House Reservoir. Cross this to reach the car park.

Section 2: Scar House Reservoir and Lofthouse circular

This circular walk from Scar House Reservoir to Lofthouse takes in the limestone exposures in both the Nidd and How Stean beck. The high level sections of the walk provide splendid views up and down the valley.

The starting point for the walk is the Scar House Reservoir car park, accessible from Lofthouse by taking the toll road up the west side of the Nidd (a small fee is payable on entry to the toll road).

Distance: 9 miles

Starting point: Scar House Reservoir car park, SE068766

Public transport: On Sundays and Bank Holidays in the summer, there is a bus up the valley to How Stean Gorge from Pateley Bridge

Maps: 11.2 plus Outdoor Leisure 30 and Landranger 99.

From the car park, take the path down to and across the reservoir dam. Climb up the hill for a short distance and when the path divides, take the right fork marked Calderdale Way. The path climbs gently upwards to a moorland, which can be boggy in places. From the moorland, there are delightful views of the U-shaped valley below.

At a small woodland, the path begins to descend towards two small streams, which it crosses just above their confluence. After the streams, the path climbs steeply upwards. Before reaching a small building, follow a line of white-topped posts across the bracken on your right. After a gate in the wall in front of you, join a track and follow this downhill. The track bears left to pass a number of farms on the moor's edge and in just over a mile bears right, following a change in direction of the valley. You now

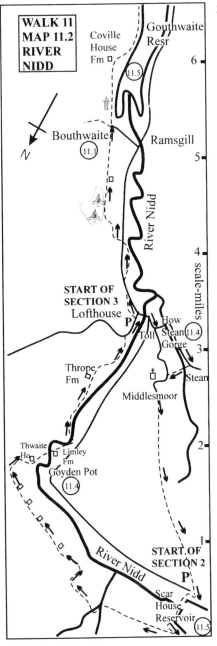

WALK 11
MAP 11.2
RIVER
NIDD

Coville
House
Fm

Gouthwaite
Resr

11.5

Bouthwaite
11.1

Ramsgill

River Nidd

scale-miles

START OF
SECTION 3
Lofthouse
P

How
Stean 11.4
Stean
Gorge

Thrope
Fm

Middlesmoor

Thwaite
Ho   Limley
Fm
Goyden Pot
11.4

River Nidd

START OF
SECTION 2
P

Scar
House
Reservoir
11.5

have some excellent views looking back up the valley towards the reservoirs.

Continue along this path to Thwaite House, then take the path on the right, which zigzags down to the river. When you reach the river, you will find the riverbed dry (under normal conditions), the river having gone down Goyden Pot just upstream. Cross the river, walk through Limley Farm and follow the riverbed downstream for a short distance until the path recrosses the river to the other bank.

The path now pulls away from the riverbank towards Thrope Farm and then follows Thrope Lane for about a mile to join the road from Masham just outside Lofthouse. In Lofthouse, pass the village fountain, with its exhortation to drink water, and the public house.

When you reach the road coming up from Pateley Bridge, turn right and cross the river. Pass the entrance to the toll road to the reservoirs, ignore the turning to Middlesmoor and come to the How Stean Beck. The road follows the beck upstream and gives a good view of the gorge below. If you wish to descend into the gorge, you may purchase a ticket at the cafe.

Follow the road towards Stean, but just before the village, take the footpath on the right down to and across the beck. Follow the line of stiles up towards Middlesmoor.

The path comes out onto the road just below Middlesmoor, and it is worth leaving the road through the village to see the view down the valley from the churchyard. Rejoin the road and pass through the village square with its pub. The road terminates just above the village where it becomes an ancient trackway up to the moorland. This takes you back to the car park at Scar House Reservoir, some 2½ miles away. Whilst on this path, do look back occasionally, for there are some excellent panoramas down the valley to Gouthwaite reservoir and beyond.

Section 3: Lofthouse to Pateley Bridge

This delightful pastoral walk is almost entirely along the valley bottom, following the river and Gouthwaite reservoir. Although man-made, with its mudflats and reed beds the Gouthwaite reservoir resembles a natural lake and, particularly during winter, attracts a wide range of waterfowl.

Distance: 6½ miles

Starting point: Lofthouse Institute, SE101734. There is a small car park at the Lofthouse Memorial Institute.

Public transport: On Sundays and Bank Holidays in the summer, a bus service runs between Pateley Bridge and Lofthouse

Maps: 11.2 and 11.3 plus Landranger 99.

Gouthwaite reservoir

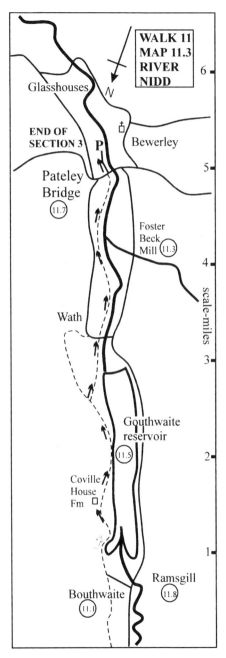

Cross the stile into the field at the back of the Institute, and follow the line of the wall. About half-way across the field, take the stile over the wall. Pass through some squeeze posts and cross the next field diagonally to the road. Bear left and follow the road for no more than 400 metres before taking the path into the fields on the right.

When this footpath meets the road again, cross the road into the field on the other side of the road. Initially, the path follows the line of the dismantled railway, but then climbs to the bottom of the wood above.

Follow the path along the bottom edge of the wood and at the end of the wood, pass on the uphill side of a farm. The path then goes along the hillside to Bouthwaite.

Although Bouthwaite was a monastic grange only until the Dissolution of the Monasteries, you will see on your right a later building of 1613 which has retained the title of grange.

Cross the road from Ramsgill (this was a road used by the monks to go to the market at Kirkby Malzead) and follow the track down to Gouthwaite reservoir. The track touches the edge of the reservoir before making a detour to Coville House Farm. This is a typical early Dales settlement situated on the banks of a beck above the flood plain.

If you wish to walk through Wath, follow the track all the way from Coville House Farm. If you wish to visit the dam, descend from the track just before it reaches the line of the dam. Whichever route you choose, the path downstream from Wath starts at Wath Bridge.

This was originally a monastic bridge. If you look underneath you will see that the original bridge was even narrower than the present bridge (being built for packhorses rather than wheeled vehicles). It is said that farmers had to take the wheels off their carts and to roll the axles along the bridge parapets! The rolling hillocks around Wath are the moraines deposited in the last Ice Age, which blocked the valley, forming a natural lake on the site of the present reservoir.

From Wath Bridge, take the path across the field to a stile in the wall and then make for the dismantled railway line. The path to Pateley Bridge is across a flat alluvial plain, in some places following the dismantled railway line, and in others the riverbank. The river is tree-lined, and slightly below the level of the alluvial plain. This is a good stretch to watch trout rising to feed on the insects which descend to them from the canopy above.

You reach Pateley Bridge at the road bridge. If you cross the road and proceed directly ahead, you will come to a large car park.

Places of interest in the Nidd Valley

11.1 Bouthwaite

In monastic times, Bouthwaite was a grange belonging to Fountains Abbey. At the Dissolution of the Monasteries, the Inman family purchased Bouthwaite. A macabre Inman heirloom was a dagger which one of the Inmans, Bold Robin, used to execute thieves.

The present Bouthwaite Grange was built in the 17th century. The road leading east from Bouthwaite was used by the granges at Bouthwaite and Ramsgill to take their produce to market at Kirkby Malzead.

11.2 Brimham Rocks

Three miles to the east of Pateley Bridge are the spectacular Brimham Rocks. Here, hard gritstone on softer rocks has led to wind, frost and rain eroding the rocks into fantastic shapes. The rocks give good views over the Nidd valley to the west and the Vale of York to the east. Entry to the popular National Trust site is from a large car park.

11.3 Foster Beck Mill

In the 18th century Nidderdale was an important textile centre. Foster Beck mill was the last remnant of that industry. Erected in 1904, the mill had a 34ft overshot waterwheel and produced yarn until 1966.

The wheel remains in working order, but the mill has been converted into a pub and restaurant.

11.4 How Stean Gorge and Goyden Pot

Although Nidderdale is predominantly a gritstone valley, above Lofthouse, in both the main river and in How Stean beck, glaciers have cut through the gritstone into the limestone basement.

In the Nidd, the river disappears underground at Goyden Pot (in normal river conditions) to resurface two miles downstream, below Lofthouse. Goyden Pot may be reached by paying a small toll fee to take the water authority road up the west side of the Nidd to Lofthouse.

The spectacular 80ft deep How Stean Gorge may be seen by walking up the road at the side of the beck, or by paying a fee at the cafe, which allows access to the bottom of the gorge.

11.5 Nidderdale reservoirs

Although many shallow lakes were created in the Yorkshire Dales at the end of the Ice Age, most of the rocks are permeable and are not suitable for building commercial reservoirs. (The only natural lakes in the Dales are Malham Tarn and Semer Water.)

Nidderdale, however, has a mainly gritstone foundation and is eminently suitable for water collection. This fact did not escape the attention of the Victorian water engineers looking for a source of water for Bradford.

Gouthwaite was the first reservoir to be opened in 1901, and this was followed by Angram (1919) and Scar House (1939). Underground aqueducts take the water to Bradford some 30 miles away.

Gouthwaite is used as a compensation reservoir, which leads to less violent swings in level than for a direct water supply reservoir. Angram and Scar House reservoirs are rather austere moorland reservoirs. Gouthwaite, however, with fields running down to the water's edge and mudflats and reedbeds, is more like a natural lake. Indeed, Gouthwaite is largely the recreation of a natural lake formed by moraines across the valley at Wath at the end of the Ice Age. Gouthwaite is an important wildlife and nature reserve, with large numbers of waterfowl visiting it in winter months. It is best viewed from the footpath running down the eastern edge.

11.6 Nidderdale Valley Light Railway

The railway was built to provide a freight service during the construction of the Scar House Reservoir, and also provided a passenger service to Lofthouse. Owned by the Bradford Corporation, the railway was opened in 1907 and closed only in 1936 on completion of the reservoirs.

The rolling stock was second hand, bought from the London Metropolitan Line when that line was electrified. Much of the line of the former railway may still be traced, and some sections have become footpaths which are included in the walks.

11.7 Pateley Bridge

From Roman times until the 19th century, lead mining flourished on Greenhow Hill just to the west of Pateley Bridge (two Roman lead ingots have been found and may be dated to AD81-2 and 97-117 respectively).

In the early years of the Industrial Revolution, water power made Pateley Bridge an important centre for the manufacture of linen. Today, the prosperity of this attractive town is based on agriculture and tourism.

11.8 Ramsgill

Ramsgill's position is typical of so many settlements in the Yorkshire Dales; built on a beck just above the flood plain of a glacial lake. Ramsgill was part of an endowment of 27,000 acres of land, given by the Mowbray family of Kirkby Malzead to the Cistercian foundation of Bylands Abbey. The abbey built a grange and a chapel at Ramsgill. (A gable of the monastic chapel may still be seen at the back of the church.)

Following the Dissolution of the Monasteries, the Yorke family bought the monastic estate from the Crown and established themselves in Gouthwaite Hall. The hall was flooded when the reservoir was built.

Today, this very picturesque village of two greens is dominated by The Yorke Arms, built in 1843.

Walk 12: River Rawthey

Section 1: Waterfalls circular, 4½ miles
Section 2: Cautley Spout, Howgills and Sedbergh circular, 10½ miles
Section 3: Sedbergh to River Lune circular, 6½ miles
Information Centre: Sedbergh 015396 20125

The area around Sedbergh, where several river valleys come together, provides some of the most attractive walking in northern England. In large measure the attractiveness is a result of the Dent Fault which runs along the Rawthey valley, leading to a mixture of different rock types. To the west of the river are the hard Silurian rocks which have weathered to the smooth, steep hillsides of the Howgills. In contrast, the Yoredale rocks on the east of the valley produce scenery more typical of the Yorkshire Dales.

A striking feature of the 40 or so square miles of the Howgills is the almost total absence of walls. It is only possible to farm sheep on these open fells because of the remarkably territorial nature of the type of sheep raised. A sheep will spend its life on the patch of hillside on which it was born. In turn, one of its daughters will inherit the same territory.

The three walks described are circular, cover nearly the entire length of the valley, include riverbank sections and hilltop sections which provide some breathtaking views. Several waterfalls are seen, including Cautley Spout, a succession of waterfalls tumbling 700 feet (212m), and more modest falls in the Yoredale rocks at the top of the valley.

Sedbergh itself is a most attractive town and is well worth a visit. The Tourist Information Centre has a useful leaflet describing a circular walk around the town which takes in the places of historical interest.

Walking towards Cautley Spout

Section 1: Waterfall walk

This is a mainly level walk to visit some modest waterfalls in the Yoredale rock formations, returning across open moorland with good views of the Howgill Fells.

Distance: 4½ miles

Starting point: Rawthey bridge, SD713978

Maps: 12.1 plus Landranger 98

Park near the bridge and follow the "greenway", known as The Street, from near the bridge (signed Uldale and Bluecaster).

When you reach the brow of the hill in about 0.4 miles, the path crosses a gully and you should take the path to the left. This path, which can be boggy in places, crosses almost level ground to reach the river in about 1½ miles, just below Needle House. The river here is most attractive with a series of small waterfalls tumbling across exposures of Yoredale rocks.

Do not take the footbridge across the river here, but proceed upstream to an old quarry. Much of the stone used to build Sedbergh came from here.

Beyond the quarry the path proceeds to the much more impressive waterfall of Uldale Force, but this section is only recommended to those who are sure of foot. The path is narrow with precipitous drops to the river below!

From the quarry (or the waterfall) retrace your footsteps to the footbridge below Needle House. Cross the river and pass Needle House to the small road above. When you reach level ground there is ahead of you a pleasant mile of road across open moorland with good views of the Howgills.

You will rejoin The Street at a T-junction where limestone is exposed and there is evidence of former lead mining activity. Turn left here to return to your starting point in just over half a mile.

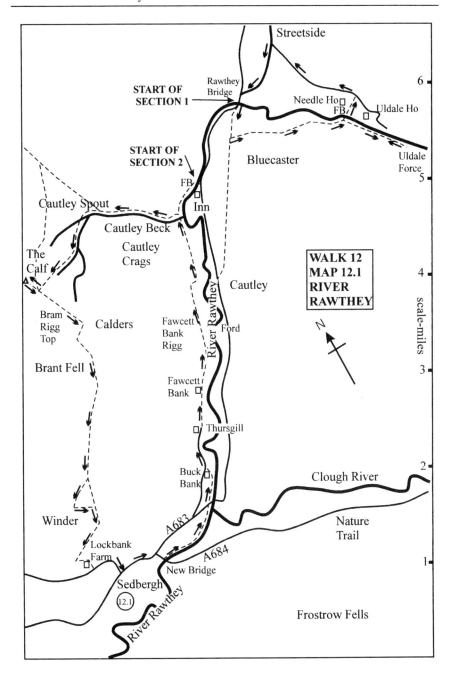

Section 2: Cautley Spout, Howgill and Sedbergh circular

This exhilarating circular walk starts with a steep climb beside the 700 feet (212m) fall of Cautley Spout. It then follows the top of the Howgills to Sedbergh, with some outstanding views, and returns along the river Rawthey.

Although it requires no more than a scramble, the path adjacent to Cautley Spout is moderately steep. If it is beyond your capability, there is an easier path to the right, just before the Spout, which will add about a mile to your journey.

Distance: 10½ miles

Starting point: Cross Keys Inn. SD698969

Public transport: An infrequent bus service (timetable at the car park next to the inn) from Sedbergh to Cautley allows you to split this circular walk into two linear walks.

Maps: 12.1 plus Landranger 98

From the 18th century Inn, descend to the river. Cross the footbridge and follow the Rawthey down to the Cautley Beck, which you follow upstream towards Cautley Spout. For just over half a mile you cross almost level ground and as you approach Cautley Spout, the rock face in front of you looks almost impossibly steep. This is an optical illusion – it is merely steep!

If you feel the path beside the Spout is too steep for you, take the easier route up the small valley on the right at the bottom of the Spout.

Climb up the right-hand side of the Spout. This path up the Spout is not actually marked on the map as a public right of way, as is the case with many well-used paths on the Howgills. As you gain height, there are some excellent views looking back at the beck snaking away into the distance.

Above the Spout, the beck divides, and you should follow the track along the left beck, Red Gill. When this in turn divides, take the right branch and follow this to and beyond its source. When you reach the skyline, you are on the path between Calders and The Calf. Turn right to reach The Calf, where there are extensive views over the rolling hills that make up the Howgill Fells and the Lune Valley to the west. Sedbergh is out of sight.

From The Calf take the path to Calders, just under a mile away, passing Bram Rigg Top on the way. From Calders take a dog leg right , initially following a fence line. Winder, the last hilltop along the ridge, is some 2 miles away. Although there are excellent views from the path to Winder, as you walk parallel to the Rawthey, the best views are from Winder itself. Here you can see several valleys – Rawthey, Dentdale, Garsdale and Lunedale – and Morecambe Bay.

Lune is an early British word meaning full or healthy river. Looking at the sheer size of the Lune catchment area, it is easy to appreciate why it has a much larger flow than many rivers of the same length.

From Winder, there are many paths down the hillside towards Sedbergh. You could take the path to the left which heads in the direction of Garsdale, and follow this until you meet a track coming down from the left. Join this, and it will take you to Sedbergh, passing Lockbank Farm.

Walk through the attractive, narrow main street of Sedbergh and follow the A684 to New Bridge.

Take the path on the left which follows the west bank upstream. In about three quarters of a mile, the Clough river tumbles into the Rawthey on the other bank, having crossed the Dent Fault only a little way upstream in Garsdale.

Shortly after the confluence, you will reach the A683 at Straight Bridge. If you look upstream over the parapet, you will notice that the river is now in a ravine below the surrounding countryside. As you progress upstream, the ravine will become deeper and for the next couple of miles the river will only be briefly glimpsed below you. From the bridge, the path initially follows the riverbank, but then climbs to join the minor farm road running up the valley at Buck Bank. At Thursgill, the metalled road gives way to a gravel track, and at Fawcett Bank becomes a green way.

Above Fawcett Bank the path is sometimes an ancient hollow-way between gnarled hawthorn bushes, and sometimes merely a sheep track. The stretches which most intrigue me are some flat, well-engineered sections reminiscent of minor Roman roads in the Peak District. Although there are no fully authenticated Roman roads in the upper Rawthey valley, it is almost inconceivable that the Romans did not use the valley to travel between their camps on Stainmore and in the Lune valley. It has long been suggested that the straight track running over Bluecaster Side is a Roman road (both Bluecaster and Street, which is just beyond, are names which suggest a Roman origin). Since the engineered sections are directly in line with the track crossing Bluecaster, it is tempting to surmise that a Roman road crossed the Rawthey at or near the present ford below Fawcett Bank Rigg.

About 1½ miles beyond Fawcett Bank, as you approach Cautley Beck, you will meet a wall on your left. Go through the gate and follow the wall line to the Beck, which you cross to return to your starting point.

Section 3: Sedbergh to River Lune circular

The outward journey of this circular walk is mainly along the riverbank, where fractured and tilted rocks result in attractive pools and rapids. The return along the south side of the valley reaches sufficient elevation at Holme Fell to give splendid views along several valleys.

Distance: 6½ miles

Starting point: Sedbergh centre SD660920

Maps: 12.2 plus Landranger 97.

From the centre of Sedbergh, take the A684 to the New Bridge, which you cross before taking the riverside path down to Millthrop. At Millthrop, recross the river. Ignore the first lane on the left to Millthrop Mill, but immediately afterwards, take the footpath signed Birks. The path passes through an attractive wood on a promontory above the river. Do not take the circular path in the woods, but leave the woods at the northern edge.

Descend to the river and after skirting a playing field, climb up to Birks.

The riverbank walk from Birks passes a footbridge over the Rawthey before reaching the confluence with the River Dee (coming down from Dentdale). Pass the old railway bridge and Brigflatts (on the right) to come to the A683.

(Brigflatts is famous for its delightful, very early Quaker Meeting House. Although Brigflatts is adjacent to the riverbank, sadly there is no public right of way from the path. If you wish to visit Brigflatts, double back along the Sedbergh road. The detour will add less than a mile to your journey.)

Turn left at the road, which you follow for nearly a mile. Just after a small parking area, take the footpath to the left into the fields. Go diagonally across the field to a stile and footbridge over a stream. Climb up to a terrace above the river and follow this to Middleton Bridge. From the bridge the confluence with the Lune may be seen downstream. Cross the bridge and take the gate on the left. Follow the path as it climbs through the wood, cross the disused railway line and turn left onto Jordan's Lane, a former Roman road.

When the lane reaches the disused railway line, go through the gate on the right into the field. The path follows an old hollow-way, the walls of which are in a state of disrepair, and then joins the track coming up from Holme.

Here, you are at a sufficient elevation for there to be good views over Sedbergh and four valleys – the Lune, Rawthey, Garsdale and Dentdale.

Follow the track to Abbot Holme bridge. Upstream from the bridge is a most attractive stretch of the River Dee as it tumbles down towards the Rawthey. One of the greens of the local golf club crosses the river here, and there is a good selection of golf balls on the riverbed.

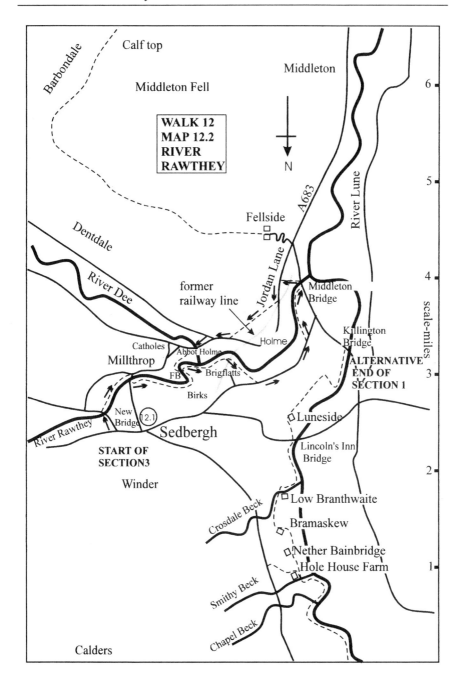

WALK 12
MAP 12.2
RIVER
RAWTHEY

Barbondale

Calf top

Middleton

Middleton Fell

N

6

A683

Fellside

River Lune

5

Dentdale

Jordan Lane

River Dee

former
railway line

Middleton
Bridge

4

Holme

Killington
Bridge

Catholes

Abbot Holme

**ALTERNATIVE
END OF
SECTION 1**

Millthrop

FB

Brigflatts

3

Birks

New
Bridge

(12.1)

Luneside

River Rawthey

Sedbergh

Lincoln's Inn
Bridge

scale-miles

**START OF
SECTION3**

Winder

2

Crosdale Beck

Low Branthwaite

Bramaskew

Nether Bainbridge

Smithy Beck

Hole House Farm

1

Calders

Chapel Beck

Just after the bridge, a footpath on the left will take you to the footbridge over the Rawthey at Birks, from where you retrace your footsteps along the riverbank to New Bridge and Sedbergh.

Places of interest in the Rawthey valley

12.1 Sedbergh

This very attractive town nestling beneath the Howgill Fells is the largest town in the Yorkshire Dales National Park and is the only settlement in the Rawthey valley. Originally settled by the Danes, Sedbergh was the most northerly Lancashire town to feature in the Domesday survey, land to the north being held by King Malcolm of Scotland. Its church has Norman origins.

A market town since 1251, Sedbergh was a major centre of the knitting trade in the 17th and 18th centuries. Spinning was carried out in galleries in the upper storeys of the houses. Today, only one gallery survives – at Railton's Yard.

During his flight northwards in 1745, after his failed attempt to seize the Crown, Bonnie Prince Charlie is said to have hidden in the chimney breast of the 17th century house in Main Street which is now the Webster's Chemists shop. The chimney breast may be seen behind the shop in Weavers Yard. The Prince escaped in disguise with packhorses carrying wool produced in the Yard.

Sedbergh has strong associations with the founders of Quakerism, and the earliest Meeting House in the north is to be seen at Brigflatts, two miles away. In the grounds of the Meeting House there is the top section of the 16th century Sedbergh Market Cross which was broken up in the 19th century.

Sedbergh is perhaps best known for its Public School. Founded as a chantry school in 1525 by Thomas Lupton, native of Sedbergh and Provost of Eton, it became a Grammar School in 1552 and a Public School in 1874. It was rebuilt in 1716, and the oldest fabric of the school is from that period – the library and museum on Dent Road.

Before the advent of the railways, Sedbergh was on the Lancaster to Newcastle coaching route. The stage coach changed horses in the main square at 7.30am (having started from Lancaster at 4am) and the return journey came through the square the following afternoon. The former coaching inn is now a coffee shop, The Posthorn. Only the very strong willed are able to pass its doors without calling in for one of its wonderful range of coffees!

Walk 13: River Ribble

Section 1: Ribblehead to Horton-in-Ribblesdale, 6 miles
Section 2: Horton-in-Ribblesdale to Settle, 7 miles
Section 3: Stainforth to Settle via Victoria Cave, 4 miles
Section 4: Settle to Gisburn, 13 miles
Section 5: Settle to Long Preston, 4 miles
Section 6: Gisburn to Sawley, 4½ miles
Section 7: Sawley to Clitheroe, 5 miles
Section 8: Higher Hodder Bridge to Ribchester, 8½ miles
Information Centres: Settle: 01729 825192; Clitheroe: 01200 25566

Packhorse bridge across Thorns Gill

The Ribble rises in the high, barren triangle formed by Ingleborough, Whernside and Penyghent (The Three Peaks). On the way to its tidal reaches at Preston, the river passes through countryside which has considerable scenic variety, and almost throughout its length the valley is a popular walking area. In addition to its scenic beauty, there is much of historical interest:

- a cave which yielded important prehistoric remains (Victoria Cave),

- a Roman fort (Ribchester),

- a Norman fort (Clitheroe),

- two Cistercian abbeys (Sawley and Whalley),

- the attractive town of Settle with its 17th and 18th century buildings and medieval bridge over the Ribble.

The bottom section of the River

Hodder, an attractive tributary of the Ribble, is included in the walk, which is almost continuous from Ribblehead to Ribchester. Only a short section from Clitheroe to the Hodder is omitted, in the interest of avoiding road walking. The sections immediately above and below Settle have hill top and valley bottom alternatives which may be combined into wonderful circular walks.

The railway stops at four places in the upper Ribble valley (Long Preston, Settle, Horton-in-Ribblesdale and Ribblehead), greatly facilitating the planning of linear walks in this part of the valley.

Section 1: Ribble Head to Horton-in-Ribblesdale

This is a fine walk across a drumlin field and then along the limestone terraces on the east side of the upper Ribble valley. The scenery is beautifully austere, dominated by limestone outcrops, the Three Peaks of Ingleborough, Penyghent and Whernside, and the impressive Ribblehead Viaduct.

Distance: 6 miles

Starting point: Ribble Head SD776797

Public transport: The Settle to Carlisle Railway stops at Horton and Ribblehead. The ideal way to carry out this walk is to take the Settle to Carlisle Railway from Horton-in-Ribblesdale to Ribblehead, and then to walk back to your car at Horton-in-Ribblesdale station.

Maps: 13.1 plus Outdoor Leisure 2 and Landranger 98.

There are several access points to the Gayle Beck, the primary tributary of the Ribble, from the B6255. The Ribble Way starts from Gearstones, a former drovers' inn, but we shall start about a quarter of mile to the west of Gearstones, at a footpath signed Nether Lodge 1¾. The reason for this choice is to see the lovely packhorse bridge at Thorns Gill.

To your right you will see the Ribblehead Viaduct and the characteristically stepped outline of Ingleborough. Ahead is Penyghent and a valley filled with drumlins. Follow the line of the wall over a drumlin towards Gayle Beck. Cross the beautifully simple packhorse bridge at Thorns Gill and skirt to the left of the hill ahead to come to the deserted hamlet of Thorns, set in a small copse.

On the way up from the beck you will pass some interesting glacial erratics – rocks brought here from elsewhere by ice, and perched on basement rock. These are typically 0.5m above the current ground level, and are an indication of the amount of surface erosion that has taken place in the Craven district since the Ice Age.

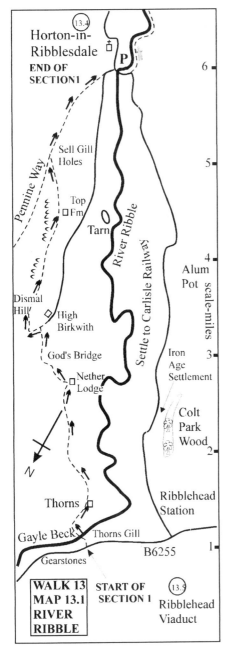

Horton-in-
Ribblesdale
**END OF
SECTION 1**

Sell Gill
Holes

Pennine Way

Top
Fm

Tarn

River Ribble

Settle to Carlisle Railway

Dismal
Hill

High
Birkwith

God's Bridge

Nether
Lodge

N

Thorns

Gayle Beck   Thorns Gill

Gearstones

Alum
Pot

Iron
Age
Settlement

Colt
Park
Wood

Ribblehead
Station

B6255

**WALK 13
MAP 13.1
RIVER
RIBBLE**

START OF
SECTION 1

6
5
4
3
2
1

scale-miles

Ribblehead
Viaduct

At Thorns, you meet the Ribble Way coming from Gearstones and bear right at the sign to Nether Lodge 1¼. There should be no difficulty following the path over the rolling drumlin field to Nether Lodge as it is well-worn.

On your way to Nether Lodge you should be able to see Colt Park Wood running along the limestone scar on the other side of the valley. Below this wood there is the remains of a Celtic settlement of 7 stone huts in some 70 acres. The Iron Age people grew crops in the small fields – the outlines of which can still be seen. As at the glacial erratics in Thorns Gill, there has been considerable soil erosion. Colt Park would, in Iron Age times, have been much more fertile than it is today.

At Nether Lodge, cross the stream and bear left, following the track signposted to High Birkwith. In about a quarter of a mile from Nether Lodge, you will pass over God's Bridge, a natural bridge over the Brow Gill Beck. About 600 metres beyond God's Bridge, you will come to a T-junction just above High Birkwith. Bear left, away from High Birkwith, and when you reach the wall above, bear right. The path goes through a gate and crosses the top of a wooded gully before entering a terrace between limestone outcrops below Dismal Hill.

At the end of the terrace, descend from the limestone outcrops on your right to cross a stile over a gully. The gully is steep, and the stile remains hidden from view until you are almost upon it. (When there is snow on the ground you may find the gully too steep to descend in safety. You should then detour to the left, cross a stile and skirt a small hillock before rejoining the path.)

Follow the path for about a mile across terraces and over stiles until you come to a farm, Top Farm, on your right. Below the farm you will see a tarn. Just out of sight, between the tarn and the river, there is a remarkable spring at Turn Dub. The water from the famous cascade at Alum Pot on the other side of the valley travels underground for about 24 hours to reach Turn Dub. Before emerging at Turn Dub, the water flows under the riverbed!

From Top Farm the path follows the hillside for about a third of a mile before joining the Pennine Way at Sell Gill Holes. You may have noticed gateposts and watertroughs made of slate. This is the first indication of the Silurian rocks to be seen further down the valley. From Sell Gill Holes, follow the Pennine Way down into Horton-in-Ribblesdale.

Section 2: Horton-in-Ribblesdale to Settle

Much of this walk is along the riverbank. At Stainforth, there is an attractive 17th century packhorse bridge and a waterfall where salmon may be seen making their way upstream in autumn.

Distance: 7 miles

Starting point: Horton-in-Ribblesdale station, SD803727

Public transport: As for the last section, use the Settle to Carlisle Railway. Park at Settle and take the train to Horton-in-Ribblesdale.

Maps: 13.2 plus Outdoor Leisure 2 and Landranger 98.

If you go down the road to the centre of Horton, do not fall into the same trap that I did of thinking that you can carry on down the east side of the river. The right of way across the river marked on the Ordnance Survey map is a ford rather than a bridge! Cross the river at the north end of Horton-in-Ribblesdale and follow the riverbank downstream.

In about 1½ miles from Horton-in-Ribblesdale, you will pass a footbridge leading to Studfold. During the monastic period, the monks of Jervaulx Abbey (Wensleydale) raised horses here, and today's racing stables at Middleham are a direct descendent of this activity.

Go under the railway bridge and bear left to go down to Helwith Bridge. Cross the river at Helwith Bridge. Join, and then almost immediately leave, the main road, taking the steep path uphill. In about a quarter of a mile, this lane divides. The path to the left is to Penyghent, but you should take the right fork onto Moorhead Lane, an old monastic road used by

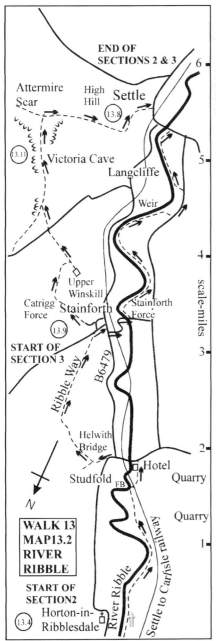

END OF
SECTIONS 2 & 3

Attermire
Scar

High
Hill

Settle

13.8

13.11

Victoria Cave

Langcliffe

Weir

Upper
Winskill

Catrigg
Force

Stainforth

Stainforth
Force

13.9

START OF
SECTION 3

Ribble Way

B6479

scale-miles

Helwith
Bridge

Hotel

Studfold

FB

Quarry

N

Quarry

WALK 13
MAP 13.2
RIVER
RIBBLE

Settle to Carlisle railway

River Ribble

START OF
SECTION 2

Horton-in-
Ribblesdale

13.4

Fountains Abbey to bring its sheep eastwards from the abbey granges in Cumberland. About half a mile along Moorhead Lane, turn right again to follow the Ribble Way down into Stainforth. There are good views from the highest point over both the valley and The Three Peaks.

In Stainforth, walk northward along the B6479 for a very short distance only before taking the turning on the left which leads to the attractive Stainforth packhorse bridge. Before the coming of the turnpikes in the 18th century, this was an important river crossing on the Lancaster to York road.

Turn left after crossing the bridge and pass Stainforth Force. The area around the bridge and the waterfall is popular with tourists in summer and can be crowded. In late autumn it is a good place to watch salmon making their way over the falls to spawn further upstream.

In just over a mile downstream from Stainforth Force, you will come to a weir and fish-ladder at Langcliffe. Salmon are caught here and stripped of their eggs for breeding, before being returned to the river.

Bear right at the weir and when the road is reached, turn left. Follow the road for about a quarter of a mile. A path on the left then takes you across the fields to Settle, about a mile away. Notice that the upstream side of the bridge in Settle is of the "ribbed arch" design, indicating that it is over 400 years old.

Section 3: Stainforth to Settle via Victoria Cave

This is a marvellous high-level alternative to the riverbank walk between Stainforth and Settle. It passes Catrigg Force, an impressive waterfall which was a favourite of Elgar's, and Victoria Cave which has yielded much valuable information about the prehistory of the area.

The return to Settle is along the Craven Fault, and there are marvellous views not only of the town, but also of the valley up to Ribblehead.

This high-level walk may be combined with the riverside walk between Stainton and Settle described in section 2 to give an excellent circular walk of about 7 miles.

Distance: 4 miles

Starting point: Stainforth SD822673

Maps: 13.2 plus Outdoor Leisure 2 and Landranger 98.

Take the road through Stainforth to the Thwaites's public house. Here turn left up the small road (marked as a cul de sac).This becomes a gravel track between limestone walls which climbs steeply up from the village, reaching Catrigg Force in just over half a mile. To reach the force, you take the signed path to the left, descending steeply into the ravine. As you descend, there are good views of Penyghent in front of you.

Returning to the path, you are now at the end of the walled track. Here you bear right, following the path to the small hamlet of Upper Winskill.

On reaching Upper Winskill, take the road leading out of the hamlet to the Settle road. This is sparse limestone countryside. On your left you will pass an "erratic", an anomalous rock brought here by glaciers during the Ice Age.

On meeting the Settle road, bear right, cross a cattle grid and then immediately turn left onto a well-worn track. This will take you to a stile which brings you to the line of the scar limestone. After crossing a field, the path bears left and takes you to a gate where you turn right, joining a track coming down from the left. Victoria Cave is about a quarter of mile further down this path, above the path on the left. (See entry at the beginning of the history appendix for the significance of the finds from Victoria Cave.)

Leaving Victoria Cave, follow the path along the line of the Attermire Scar. When the path begins to descend, you have reached the line of the Craven Fault. Turn right here and follow the path which follows the scar running towards the west.

The hill on your left, High Hill, is not the scar limestone seen in all the local outcrops, but is the most westerly of a series of some 15 reef knolls which follow the southern edge of the Craven Fault to the Wharfe. A more impressive aspect of High Hill is seen just after leaving Settle on section 4

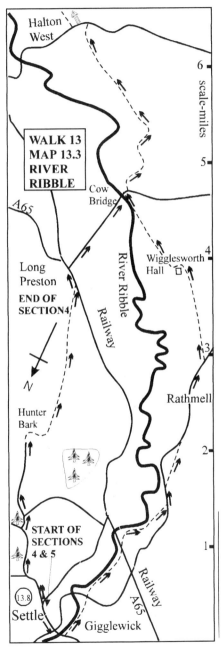

WALK 13
MAP 13.3
RIVER
RIBBLE

Halton West

scale-miles

6

5

A65

Cow Bridge

River Ribble

Railway

Wigglesworth Hall 4

Long Preston

END OF SECTION 4

3

N

Rathmell

Hunter Bark

2

START OF SECTIONS 4 & 5

1

13.8

Settle

Railway

A65

Giggleswick

of the walk. The descent towards Settle again gives excellent views. Bear left onto a somewhat stony track which eventually leads you down Constitution Hill into the main square in Settle.

Section 4: Settle to Gisburn

Starting with the backdrop of the limestone hills above Settle, this walk first crosses the bed of a large post-glacial lake, and then the rolling countryside of a field of drumlins. As the walk nears Gisburn, the flat-topped Pendle Hill begins to dominate the skyline.

Distance: 13 miles

Starting point: Settle centre, SD820635

Intermediate break point: Long Preston, 6½ miles

Maps: 13.3 and 13.4 plus Landranger 98 and 103.

From the centre of Settle, follow the main road under the railway line to the bridge over the river. Cross the bridge and take the path down the west side of the river. On the outskirts of the town, the path temporarily leaves the riverbank to pass through a housing estate before rejoining the river.

Cross a small beck and go under the Settle bypass (A65). When the path leaves the river, it crosses the fields to meet the Giggleswick to Rathmell road.

You are now on the bed of an old

glacial lake which covered an area of some 5 square miles. This is one of the lakes that the Middle Stone Age owner of the harpoon found in the Victoria Cave would have fished. The valley is still liable to flooding, and you will see that there are no habitations on the flood plain.

Stay on the road only until you reach a path on the right. Follow the line of stiles and rejoin the road just below Rathmell. Climb up to Rathmell.

About half a mile after leaving Rathmell, and shortly after passing the end of a farm road to Far Coppleside, follow the Ribble Way sign to the left.

As you follow the hillside contour to Wigglesworth Hall, there are good views back up the valley over the alluvial plain to Ingleborough, Penyghent and the copper dome of Giggleswick School chapel.

Ahead, the angular outline of Sharp Haw in the Aire Valley may just be seen. Before the Ice Age, the Ribble flowed eastwards down the Aire valley, and it was only the deposition of the drumlin field between here and Skipton which diverted the river westwards.

The path goes round the right-hand side of Wigglesworth Hall. In medieval times the Hamertons of Wigglesworth Hall were one of the most powerful families in the area and were said to be able to ride on their own land from here to York. The Hamertons were one of the many families in the north which came to an untimely end when

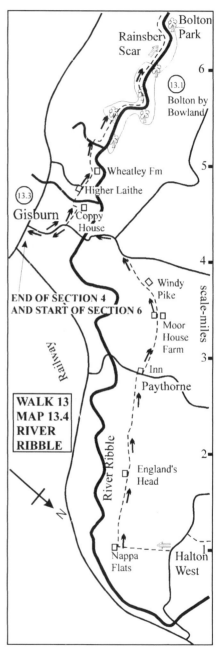

they challenged Henry VIII by joining the Pilgimage of Grace. From the hall, follow the beck down to the Ribble and then the riverbank to Cow Bridge.

If you are breaking your walk at Long Preston, bear left over Cow Bridge. Otherwise, bear right and then immediately left to follow a track. In about a mile, just after a wooded ravine, follow a Ribble Way sign on the left.

The path leads to a stile, almost equidistant between the ravine and a farmhouse on the right. Another stile leads you forward to two farms, which you pass on the right. At the second farm, Low Scale, you join a farm track which takes you to Halton West.

Turn left in Halton West and at the last building on the right as you leave the village, take the stile into the fields (not signposted). Make for the left edge of a small wood, cross the beck by footbridge, and then aim for a building ahead (Nappa Flats).

At Nappa Flats bear right, and follow the right edge of a hedge. This apparently little used path follows an ancient hollow-way which must have been a heavily used roadway in medieval times. Pass England's Head on your left and then join a farm track which will take you to Paythorne. Here, cross the road and follow the footpath sign behind the Buck Inn which indicates Windy Pike.

The path from the Buck Inn can be confusing as there is no obvious single way across the fields. It is important to climb slightly to reach the footbridge across a gully which blocks your way. The footbridge is not easily seen, but is not far below a caravan park.

Cross the gully and proceed to Moor House Farm where you take the track which bears slightly left. Pendle Hill should now be ahead of you.

Pass Windy Pike, a white 17th century building, and when you reach Carters Lane, bear left. Bear left onto a larger road at a kennels and descend to the river. Climb up the steep hill from the river and pass Gisburn Park to come into Gisburn.

Section 5: Settle to Long Preston (via Hunter Bark)

This high-level alternative to the walk down the valley bottom from Settle follows an ancient road over Hunter Bark. ("Bark" is Old English for "hill")

There are wonderful views over the valley bottom and the distant hill-tops, and the line of the Craven Fault is seen as it approaches Settle.

This section may be combined with the first part of section 3 to provide an excellent circular walk of just over 10 miles.

Distance: 4 miles

Starting point: Settle centre SD820635

Public transport: A few Leeds to Carlisle trains stop at Long Preston, as does the regular bus service between Settle and Skipton.

Maps: 13.3 plus Landranger 98 and 103.

From the Shambles in the centre of Settle, take the road to Upper Settle. Before the building of the turnpike in 1743, this was the main route from Settle down the valley. Afterwards, it was extensively used as a droving road. The drovers bringing Scottish cattle to the English markets, used this road to avoid paying tolls on the new roads.

Shortly you will pass on your left, Settle's finest building. The Folly was built in the 1670s by a wealthy tanner, its name reflecting the fact that its extravagance is reputed to have bankrupted the owner.

When you reach the top of the first brow, leave the Kirkby Malham road by taking the road on the right which makes for the bottom of a small wood before again climbing. On the hillside to your right there is much evidence of medieval strip farming. Only with the coming of the lucrative droving trade were the fields enclosed, and pastoral farming replaced 1000 years of arable farming.

When the road reaches the corner of a wood, it splits. Take the right fork and follow the edge of the wood. In another mile, on Hunter Bark, you will reach the highest point of the walk at just over 1000 ft (300m).

The top of the hill is just off the path, on the right, and it is well worth the slight detour to see the tremendous panoramic view. Here you can see for miles, the skyline being dominated by hilltops – Ingleborough, Pendle and Sharp Haw (the sharp pointed hill in the Aire valley between Gargrave and Skipton). Penyghent is not in view, being masked behind High Hill with Attermire Scar behind.

Attermire Scar is on the line of the Craven Fault (Malham Cove is just 4 miles to the east) and High Hill is geologically very interesting. It is the first of a line of reef knolls which follow the Craven Fault between the Ribble and the Wharfe. In Carboniferous times, there was a reef belt, similar to today's Great Barrier reef off the Australian coast, which was subsequently eroded to a series of isolated reef knolls (see map in geology introduction).

From Hunter Bark, the road descends across the hillside to Long Preston in just under 2 miles. The gravelled way becomes metalled part way down the hillside. As you descend, the river snakes sinuously below you across what was once a great post-glacial lake. (The owner of a primitive harpoon found in Victoria Cave will have fished this lake.) The riverside meadows were only finally drained and enclosed by Parliamentary Act in 1799, and the valley bottom is still liable to serious flooding in wet weather.

To your left, the rounded drumlins fill the valley. It was these remnants of the Ice Age which diverted the river from its former channel down Airedale to its present westward route. In some places, the track is considerably hollowed, confirming its ancient usage. In Long Preston, there was a Roman marching camp or fort on the site of the present church, and it is possible that the track you have been following over Hunter Bark, which we know to be medieval, is considerably older. (The alignment of the Roman road from Ribchester to Long Preston may be seen to the west of the river between Bolton-by-Bowland and Long Preston.)

In Long Preston, turn left along the main road and then right down the minor road to Wigglesworth. Pass the railway station on your left (trains to Settle and Giggleswick) and in just under a mile you will join the path down the west side of the valley at Cow Bridge.

Section 6: Gisburn to Sawley

This section follows a most attractive stretch of the Ribble as it flows through a deeply wooded gorge.

Distance: 4½ miles

Starting point: Gisburn cattle market, SD833489

Maps: 13.4 and 13.5 plus Landranger 103.

Gisburn can be busy with passing traffic, but it is usually possible to park either at the east end of the village or at the west end next to the cattle market. From the cattle market, take the road towards Bolton-by Bowland. After crossing the railway line, you will come to a bridleway on the left, opposite Deerhouse Farm.

Take the bridleway towards Coppy House. Pass on the left of Coppice Cottages and cross the field to a gate, where you enter a small wood. Descend to and cross Wheatley Beck, and then bear right up to Higher Laithe. Here join a macadamed road which takes you to Wheatley Farm.

Take the stile to the left of the farm and follow the field edge to a barn, where you cross a stile.

Continue to a small stream then follow the sign towards the river. At the next stile, woodland is reached. Bear left to follow the river, which is flowing some 100 feet (30m) below in a wooded ravine. The next section is well signed. When you reach the end of the terrace, the path descends to the riverbank. Cross the stile at the river's edge. There are steep woodlands to your left with bluebells, primroses, wood anemone and celandine in springtime. As the river bears right, the path is forced to higher ground before again dropping to river level.

As the path leaves the ravine, there is a limestone cliff, Rainsber Scar, on the other side of the river. This is the site of Sir William Pudsay's famous leap (see Places of Interest, Bolton-by-Bowland).

At the end of the wood, the scenery changes and you are now on a former lake bed. The path leaves the river's edge and after the terrace above the river, follows an old mill leat towards Sawley. Below Sawley Lodge, cross a stile to give access to the road from the lodge to Sawley.

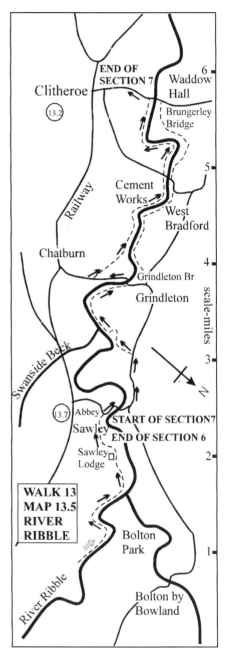

WALK 13
MAP 13.5
RIVER
RIBBLE

Section 7: Sawley to Clitheroe

The attractive walk between Sawley and Clitheroe is mainly adjacent to the riverbank. Between Grindleton and Brungerley Bridges there are footpaths down both sides of the river. This section is popular with people seeking short, circular riverside walks.

Distance: 5 miles

Starting point: Sawley bridge, SD776466

Maps: 13.5 plus Landranger 103.

From the west side of the Sawley river bridge, follow the road towards Grindleton and Waddington. In about half a mile, take the footpath to the left, which crosses the fields to join the river opposite the Swanside Beck.

Follow the flood defence down the river, and when the first bridge is reached, cross the river. Follow the road along the south riverbank for a short distance and after climbing up a hill, take the footpath on the right. Follow the wooded hill edge until you rejoin the riverbank.

Follow the river downstream to the next bridge (the Clitheroe Cement works is to your left). At the bridge, cross the road, staying on the same side of the river. In about another mile you reach Brungerley Bridge where the road on the left will take you into Clitheroe. With the exception of the first section uphill from the bridge, the road has a footpath.

The Ribble in Winter

Section 8:
Higher Hodder Bridge to Ribchester

This walk is through attractive countryside along the banks of the Ribble and its tributary the Hodder.

Ribchester has some interesting weavers' cottages. The Ribchester Museum, with its Roman artefacts from the fort (which include a replica of a cavalryman's exquisite helmet), is well worth a visit.

Distance: 8½ miles

Starting point: Higher Hodder Bridge SD698412

Maps: 13.6 plus Landranger 103.

There are spaces for a few cars to park at the roadside on the east side of the Higher Hodder Bridge. Cross the bridge and follow the path down the west bank of the river. The path is at some elevation above the river and there are some good views down to the river below. As you progress down the river to Lower Hodder Bridge, it is necessary to scramble across tree roots in one or two places.

As you cross Lower Hodder Bridge, you will notice the attractive ruined Cromwell's Bridge just downstream. Here, in 1648, Cromwell took the decision to march westwards to Preston to meet the Scots in what was to be one of the most important battles

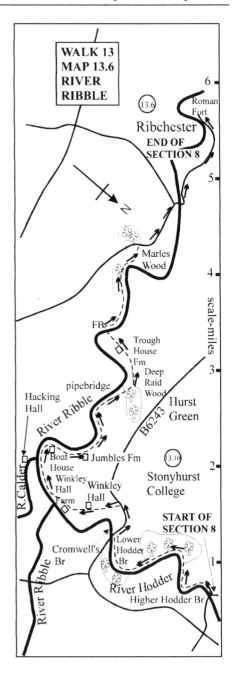

in the Civil War (see history appendix).

From the bridge, follow the B6243. In nearly half a mile, just opposite a bus shelter, take the path to the left over a stile, and climb up to the edge of a wood. If you look back here, Stonyhurst College dominates the skyline. Follow the edge of the field and cross another field to come to Winkley Hall. Pass to the left of the hall down to Winkley Hall Farm, where the Ribble and the Hodder meet.

Half a mile downstream you come to the confluence with the Calder. On the opposite bank is the splendid Hacking Hall of 1607. With its gables and mullioned windows, it is typical of so many of the halls built throughout the north at that time. The next building downstream is the Hacking Boat House which operated a ferry across the river from the 18th century until the 1950s. It is sad that there is no river crossing here today as Whalley Abbey is less than two miles up the river Calder. As you walk towards Jumbles Farm, Stonyhurst College is now in front of you.

In just under a mile, pass a pipebridge taking water pipes across the river and then climb up into Deep Raid Wood. The Ordnance Survey map shows the need to go up into Hurst Green here, but a concessionary path allows you to follow the top edge of the wood before descending to Trough House Farm. From Trough House Farm take the path down to the river, cross the Dinkley footbridge and turn right towards Marles Wood.

The scenery here is most attractive, but there has been a noticeable deterioration in the quality of the river water since the confluence with the River Calder. As potentially one of the most attractive stretches of water in northern England, this ought to be high on the water regulator's list for improvement.

At the end of the wood, as the river bears right, take the footbridge over a ravine up to a small, quiet road which takes you to Ribchester Bridge. The road from Ribchester Bridge into Ribchester is much busier, but there is now a footpath.

Places of interest in the Ribble valley

13.1 Bolton-by-Bowland

Just to the north of the Ribble is the charming little village of Bolton-by Bowland. After his defeat at Hexham, Henry VI was hidden in Bolton Hall by Sir Ralph Pudsay. Sir Ralph's tomb, which displays his three wives and 25 children, may be seen in the church.

The once powerful Pudsays were one of the many families in the north which suffered for being of the wrong religious persuasion. A penurious descendant of Sir Ralph, William Pudsey, took to counterfeiting, but was discovered. The story tells of his escape from those coming to arrest him by leaping over Rainsber Scar on his horse and riding to London where he was pardoned by his godmother (Queen Elizabeth I). The walk passes below Rainsber Scar, known colloquially as Pudsay's Leap, and you will be able to make up your own mind about the likelihood of anyone surviving such a leap. Although it is generally believed that the story is far-fetched, it must be remembered that in 1606 Robert Willance survived a more spectacular leap on his horse from a cliff to the west of Richmond (see Swale walk).

13.2 Clitheroe

A castle with the smallest Norman keep in England dominates the skyline of this busy market town. The castle was irrecoverably damaged in the Civil War, and is now a ruin.

Clitheroe's biggest industry is cement, which is manufactured just to the north-east of the town.

13.3 Gisburn

The manor of Gisburn was held by the Lister family from 1312 until the family died out in 1925. The family was ennobled to the Lordship of Ribblesdale in 1797 when Thomas Lister raised an army in response to Napoleon's invasion threat. Thomas Lister is perhaps best remembered as a forester, planting over a million trees on the banks of the Ribble.

Until the end of the 19th century, a herd of wild, white cattle roamed Gisburn Park, reputedly descendants of animals owned by the monks of Whalley Abbey. The deer which range the Bowland Fells are later escapees from the park.

The busy village is a popular stopping place for travellers from industrial Yorkshire making for the Lancashire coast.

13.4 Horton-in-Ribblesdale

Horton is one of the few places in the Yorkshire Dales where carboniferous rocks have been sufficiently eroded to expose older basement rocks beneath. Silurian slates are to be seen between Horton and Stainforth. In earlier times, the ability of these rocks to cleave made them highly prized as slates and slabs. Today the output of the massive Maughton quarry goes into road building.

Horton has a Norman church, and it is said that the scratch markings on the porch door were left there by medieval archers sharpening their arrows. Horton slates may be seen in the church paving and the roof of the lychgate.

The Penyghent cafe in Horton is one of the favoured starting points for the gruelling 24 mile Three Peaks Walk. Completion of the walk inside 12 hours qualifies the walker for membership of the Three Peaks Club.

13.5 Ribblehead viaduct and the Settle to Carlisle Railway

The Settle to Carlisle Railway runs through some of the most dramatic scenery in England. The 100ft, 24 arch viaduct is the most striking feature of this feat of Victorian engineering. Built between 1870 and 1876 in an area with an average rainfall of over 70 inches a year, the viaduct involved some 2000 people in its construction. The 20,000 bricks which were required each day were made on site from the boulder clay recovered from the drumlins which cover the Ribblehead area.

Despite frequent attempts by British Rail to close this costly service, the line still runs a regular service between Leeds and Carlisle. This service greatly facilitates the planning of linear walks in the Ribble and Eden valleys.

13.6 Ribchester

Agricola chose this site for his fort of Brementennacum during ∙s campaign in the AD80s to conquer Brigantia and Scotland. The fort, which was built to house 500 cavalrymen,was strategically placed on the Roman road from Manchester to the Tyne, and also to receive ships from the legionary fort at Chester.

Work continues to excavate the site, and there is an excellent display of the history of the site and many Roman artefacts at the Museum adjacent to the fort. Among the musuem's collection is the replica of a Roman cavalryman's exquisite parade helmet, found in 1796 by a 13-year-old Ribchester boy digging in his garden (the original is in the British Museum).

The road leading to the Roman site has some attractive weavers' cottages, and The White Bull public house has some most unusual pillars – columns which were originally in the Roman fort and were later recovered from the bed of the river.

It is interesting to compare the weavers' cottages with those seen on the Calder valley walk at Heptonstall. In both villages the handloom weavers worked at home, but whereas the Heptonstall weavers worked in the attic, the Ribchester weavers worked in the cellar. (Two cellar workshops are to be seen near The White Bull Inn at the centre of the village.) The reason for the difference is that while the Calderdale weavers were working with wool, those in Ribchester were working with cotton. Only in the cellars could the humidity be created which avoided breakage of the more fragile cotton thread.

13.7 Sawley Abbey

This Cistercian abbey, founded in 1147, seems to have had more than its fair share of woes:

• its crops rotted because of the wet weather,

- it was raided by the Scots,
- it was in several disputes with the more successful nearby Cistercian foundation at Whalley,
- its last abbot was executed for taking part in the Pilgrimage of Grace.

Although there are some ruins to be seen at Sawley, a much better understanding of the operations of the Cistercians may be gained by visiting the nearby Cistercian abbey at Whalley.

13.8 Settle and Giggleswick

Settle's market, established in 1249, flourished on the trade between the livestock farmers of upper Ribblesdale (limestone) and the arable farmers of the Bowland Fells (gritstone). Perhaps its greatest period of prosperity was in the 17th and 18th centuries, and it benefited greatly from its position on the Kendal to Keighley turnpike of 1743 (one of the earliest turnpikes to cross the dales).

A planned canal did not come to Settle, and other towns such as Skipton overtook Settle in the race to industrialise in the 19th century. However, this now leaves Settle as a most attractive market town, with many fine 17th and 18th century buildings including:

- the group of shops known as the Shambles;
- The Naked Man Inn, a 17th century protest against the excessive fashion of the day;
- The Folly, a fine Tudor style hall on the road to upper Settle which is reputed to have bankrupted its builder.

The river bridge is even older. Although widened to take the turnpike, the 15th century "ribbed arch" design is still to be seen on the northern side of the bridge.

13.9 Stainforth

The name reflects the fact that there was once a rocky ford here on the road from Lancaster to York. Samuel Watson built the elegant packhorse bridge at the ford in the 1670s, at the same time that he built himself Stainforth Hall. Owners of the hall were responsible for the maintenance of the bridge until it passed into the ownership of the National Trust.

Below the bridge, the river falls into a deep pool at Stainforth Force. The Force is a good place to see salmon jumping the falls as they make their way up to the spawning grounds in late autumn.

Elgar was a frequent visitor to Catrigg Force, above the village on the Stainforth Beck

13.10 Stonyhurst

When this school for English Catholics was founded in 1593, it was set up on the continent because the regime of Elizabeth I was oppressive to Catholics. In 1794, the French Revolution forced a move, and the school came to the Tudor country house at Stonyhurst. The journey from the Low Countries was itself eventful, including the newly opened section of the canal from Leeds to Skipton, followed by an 18 mile walk.

13.11 Victoria Cave (see history appendix)

13.12 Whalley Abbey

The Cistercian abbey at Whalley was built in 1330-80. Following the Dissolution of the Monasteries, part of the abbey was converted into a manor house and remained a private property until 1923 when ownership reverted to the church. The Abbey has some interesting ruins and there is an instructive Visitors' Centre on site.

Whalley parish church is one of the finest in the north. It has choir stalls which were made for the abbey, and three Anglo-Saxon crosses.

Walk 14: River Skell

Information Centre: Ripon 01765 604625

The Skell, a tributary of the Ure, runs through Fountains Abbey and close to Ripon Cathedral. This walk gives excellent approaches to these two famous ecclesiastical buildings and, in my view, is one of the most pleasant ways of visiting them.

Fountains Abbey, in a perfect riverside setting, has the finest Cistercian remains in the country, while Ripon has the earliest complete Anglo-Saxon crypt. Not to be overlooked, is the very fine 16th century Fountains Hall, which is adjacent to Fountains Abbey.

In addition to the famous 18th century garden setting at Fountains, the walk has some delightful woodland sections. These are at their best in spring and early summer, when there is a good display of woodland flowers.

Fountains Abbey is now owned by the National Trust, and for those who are not members, an entrance fee is charged for the middle section of the walk.

Distance: 6½ miles

Starting point: B6265 river crossing (Grantley Hall), SE249693

Public transport: not available

Maps: 14.1 plus Landranger 99.

There is a limited space for parking just to the north of the point where the B6265 (Pateley Bridge to Ripon road) crosses the River Skell. I left my car in Ripon, and took a taxi from the Market Square to the starting point.

Take the path into Spa Gill Wood, just to the north of the bridge. This delightful woodland path follows the Skell as it winds its way down the valley to Fountains Abbey about 1½ miles away. In the spring, there is a profusion of woodland flowers and, on a warm day, butterflies.

You will come out of the woodlands next to a small bridge. Here the path climbs away from the river to meet the road. Down the road you enter the Fountains estate, now owned by the National Trust, at the magnificent Fountains Hall. Those who are not members of the National Trust will have to pay a fee to enter the estate.

You can explore the hall, abbey and splendid grounds as you progress down either side of the river.

After passing the Half Moon Pond and the Lake, you will come to the

The River Skell at Fountains Abbey

Seven Bridges Walk. Here the riverbed is limestone, and the river has a tendency to go underground during dry weather.

Leaving the estate, you are now back on a quiet woodland walk. Just before reaching the first cultivated field, cross a bridge and follow the path to the top of a gully. Turn left, following the sign to Ripon. Follow a line of hawthorn trees towards the road. At the crest of the hill, Ripon comes into view with the cathedral standing out majestically against a backdrop of the Cleveland Hills. If you are really lucky, the sun will be on the tower!

At the road bear left, passing Whitcliffe Hall. Follow the road to the outskirts of the built-up area, but when the first houses are reached, bear left. Before reaching the river, there is a single building on the left. Here you should take the path to the right.

A pleasant path now takes you through woods into the city, passing the confluence with the River Laver on the way. Keep as close as you can to the river, and it will take you to the cathedral.

Places of interest in the Skell valley

14.1 Fountains Abbey, Hall and Gardens

A dispute at the Benedictine house of St Mary's, York, in 1132 led to a group of monks breaking away to search for a more austere life.

They were encouraged by Thur-

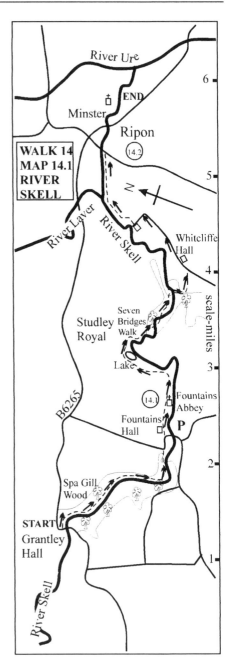

stan, Archbishop of York, who sheltered them at Ripon and gave them land three miles up the Skell. Here they established their abbey of St Mary of Fountains.

The abbey was initially not a great success, and the monks appealed to the Cistercian order in France for help. The Cistercians were sympathetic, having themselves been founded by a similar breakaway group. Fountains Abbey was admitted to the Cistercian order in 1135. The aim of the Cistercians was to create a network of sister abbeys which would support the Pope in his fight for supremacy over secular rulers on ecclesiastical matters. The Cistercians were a highly centralised order. Abbeys had similar physical layouts to engender cohesion, and their abbots were required to travel to the mother foundation, at Citeaux in France, every year to discuss general policy.

Initially, at least, the life in a Cistercian abbey was harsh. The monks wore undyed sheep's wool (hence their description as White monks), they were committed to silence, the diet was barely above subsistence and the architecture of their buildings was severe and unadorned.

The success of Fountains Abbey sprang from its decision to establish an order of lay monks to do all the day-to-day manual work. This enabled Fountains Abbey to flourish in the 13th century, controlling vast interests in mining, quarrying and agriculture across the north of England. The biggest business was sheep, with great flocks as far away as the Lake District.

If the abbey was at its most successful in the 13th century, the 14th century was a disaster. This was due to a combination of the effects of the Black Death, Scottish raids, bad harvests, financial mismanagement and overcommitment to grandiose projects.

Salvation was achieved by a radical revision of the running of the abbey's estates. The lay monks were disbanded and the monastic granges previously run by them were let out to tenant farmers. This 14th century form of privatisation was a success, and from then on the abbey would live on the rents, rather than manage the estates directly.

There was a considerable revival of the abbey's fortunes under Abbot Huby (1495-1525). The great Perpendicular Tower was built, and the number of monks greatly expanded. However, this was the lull before the storm. In 1539, a hard up Henry VIII dissolved Fountains Abbey and raised capital by selling the abbey and 500 acres to Richard Graham in 1540.

The lands were later sold to Stephen Proctor for £4500. Stephen Proctor came from a family which had served the abbey for generations, but rose to great power and wealth by hunting down and dispossessing rich Catholic families. Proctor's wealth allowed him to build first, the lovely small mansion of Friar's Head (seen on the Aire walk) and next, between 1598 and 1611, the magnificent Fountains Hall (largely with stone taken from Fountains Abbey).

Proctor's methods must have been unscrupulous, even by the lax standards of the time, for his meteoric rise to wealth and power was followed by an equally meteoric fall. He was successfully prosecuted for "bribery, legal abuse, malicious prosecution and slander" and died in 1619 in poverty. His wife was forced to make a distress sale of the hall for £7000.

The grounds of Fountains Abbey were later developed by the Aislabie family. The 18th century garden is one of the few to have remained largely in its original form.

14.2 Ripon

An attractive, small city with many fine 18th and 19th century buildings. Ripon developed both as an important ecclesiastical centre and as a market town. A monastery was first established in 655, and St Wilfred completed his famous church in 672. Although this was razed by the Vikings in the 9th century, the crypt survived and is the oldest complete crypt in the country.

The magnificent cathedral we see today is the result of building over many centuries including:

- the 7th century crypt,
- the 12th century Norman transitional church,
- the 13th century Early English west front,
- the 16th century Perpendicular nave.

Ripon's growth as a market town was a result of a favourable position near the big trading abbeys of Fountains and Jervaulx in the early medieval period, and between the pastoral areas of the Pennines and the arable areas of the Vale of York. This was later important when agriculture started to become more specialised, needing markets to trade the larger volumes of agricultural products then being produced.

Walk 15: River Swale

Section 1: Keld to Reeth, 11½ miles
Section 2: Reeth to Richmond, 11 miles
Information Centre: Richmond 01748 850252

This intimate dale is one of my favourites, and two excellent walks will take you from Keld and Richmond.

Farming throughout the mainly gritstone valley is pastoral, and there is much evidence of former lead mining activity, particularly in the side valleys to the north of the river.

A characteristic of Swaledale is its fine stone barns, stone cottages and Georgian houses. The barns were mainly built in the 17th and 18th centuries, when the fields were enclosed and the dale moved from arable to pastoral farming. The cottages and Georgian houses were built at a time when lead mining brought considerable prosperity to the valley

Section 1: Keld to Reeth

This wonderful walk mainly follows a river of much variety. There are waterfalls near Keld, a streamy section between Keld and Muker (a torrent in heavy rain) and a more sedate sequence of pools from Muker to Reeth.

Farming is traditional, a late cutting of the hay producing beautiful meadows in early summer.

An alternative to the linear walk described is to use one of the other paths shown on the maps between Muker and Keld to produce a circular walk.

Distance: 11½ miles

Starting point: Keld. NY892010

Public transport: A bus runs up the valley as far as Keld on Tuesdays and Saturdays, allowing you to choose any length of the walk described.

Maps: 15.1 and 15.2 plus Outdoor Leisure 30 and Landranger 91 and 98.

In Keld, take the road down towards the river and then the footpath signposted to Muker. The river channel is relatively new here. Until the last Ice Age, the Swale flowed to the west of Kisdon Hill. It was only the blocking of the former channel with boulder clay which diverted the river eastwards.

In a short distance, you will reach the Pennine Way. Ignore the path to the left, which crosses the river, but if you wish to see Kisdon Force, take the next turning to the left. There is no way downstream from the waterfall, so you must retrace you steps to the path above. Shortly, bear left again (the path ahead also goes down the valley to Muker, but at a higher elevation) and go down to the riverbank again.

As you come out of the wood, there is much evidence of former lead mining activity on the other side of the river. Approaching Swinnner Gill, Crackpot Hall is high above you. Now a ruin, the hall was inhabited until the 1950s. Many of the barns and cottages in this area are also in a ruinous state.

The riverbed down from here to Ramps Holme Bridge is streamy with boulders, and is a torrent in wet weather. Only as you approach the bridge are there pools which are deep enough throughout the year to hold trout. Unless you wish to terminate your walk at Muker, which is just across the fields, cross the bridge and follow the sign which reads Gunnerside via Ivelet. At Ivelet, you will come to an exquisite 17th century packhorse bridge. Without any doubt, Ivelet Bridge is the most beautiful in Swaledale.

Take the road up from the bridge into Ivelet, where you turn right to follow the path across the meadows to Gunnerside. In Gun-

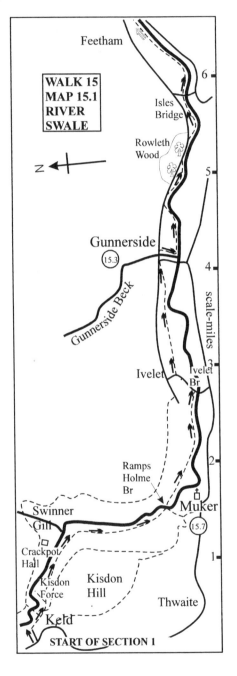

WALK 15
MAP 15.1
RIVER
SWALE

Feetham

Isles Bridge

Rowleth Wood

Gunnerside

Gunnerside Beck

Ivelet   Ivelet Br

Ramps Holme Br

Swinner Gill

Crackpot Hall

Kisdon Force   Kisdon Hill

Keld

Muker

Thwaite

scale-miles

START OF SECTION 1

Packhorse bridge at Ivelet

nerside, cross the beck, turn right in front of the public house and then left at the public conveniences. Here the path divides. Take the path to the right down to Gunnerside New Bridge, where you turn left to follow the river-bank.

Gunnerside was a major centre of the lead mining industry, so it is no surprise to see the delicate, white, five-petalled spring sandworth in the sandy patches by the riverbank. The flower is lead tolerant and normally an indication of lead in the soil.

Follow the path along the riverbank until the river meets the road. Go onto the road, but almost immediately leave it again for the riverbank.

When the road next meets the river at Rowleth Wood, you must follow it for perhaps 400 metres before taking the gate into the field on the right. (Rowleth Woods is one of the few really ancient woodlands in Swaledale. A footpath goes through the wood, but this may only be accessed from above).

Follow the track from the gate across the field, go through a stile in the wall and pass in front of the house before following a line of squeeze posts across the fields to Isles Bridge. At the bridge there is a signpost to Reeth 3½ miles.

The path follows the flood defence along the riverbank. For a length, this is on the top of a fairly high wall. Although adequately wide, it can be interesting when you meet others coming the other way (there are trees adjacent to the wall for one party to hold onto while the other passes). If these aerial gymnastics give you cause for concern, the alternative is to cross the river at Isles Bridge and follow the track to the next bridge.

The hillside is now much more densely populated than higher up the valley, with Low Row and Feetham being almost a continuous linear village along the roadside. The inn you see at Feetham is The Punch Bowl. In earlier times this was a stopping point for funeral corteges carrying the dead from the upper valley down the Corpse Way for burial at Grinton.

Before reaching the road, you will come to a boggy stretch where there are attractive groups of yellow monkey flower, a member of the figwort family. When you reach the road at Feetham, there is a 1 mile stretch of road walking before you rejoin the riverbank at a sign which advises you that Reeth is 1¾ miles. (To minimise the road walking, you could take a path on the left which climbs up from Feetham Wood to Healaugh, and then take the path back down to the river.)

Whichever of the routes you choose, about half a mile after Healaugh, the path leaves the riverbank at a bend in the river and you enter Reeth across a field of medieval strip lynchets. These are a reminder that although the valley is now entirely pastoral, from the first settlement by the Angles to the field enclosures in late medieval times, arable farming was practised in Swaledale. As you enter Reeth, you should be able to see the outline of Marrick Priory further down the valley.

Section 2: Reeth to Richmond

The second half of the Swale walk continues down a sinuous, narrow valley to Richmond. The river and woods provide fine views, and there are good views of Richmond as you descend towards the plain. Although the farming is still pastoral, it is more intensive than further up the valley, and this section does not have the same floral diversity as the first walk.

Distance: 11 miles

Starting point: Reeth Green, SE038993

Public transport: There are buses each day from Richmond to Reeth.

Maps: 15.2 and 15.3 plus Outdoor Leisure 30 and Landranger 92, 98 and 99.

From Reeth Green, take the road downhill and cross the Arkle Beck. Built in 1773, this is one of many fine bridges by John Carr of York.

Follow the road through Low Fremington to Grinton Bridge. At Grinton Bridge, bear left along the riverbank. In about half a mile, join the track from Low Fremington to Marrick Priory. When Turner visited the Swale in

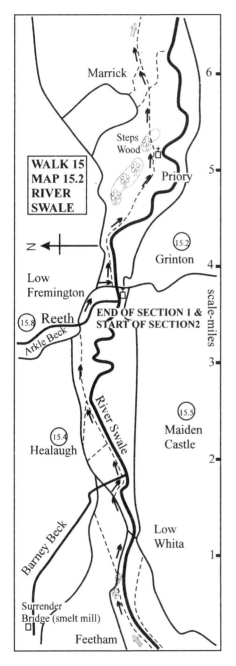

WALK 15
MAP 15.2
RIVER
SWALE

Marrick

Steps
Wood

Priory

Grinton

Low
Fremington

Reeth

END OF SECTION 1 &
START OF SECTION2

Healaugh

Maiden
Castle

Low
Whita

Surrender
Bridge (smelt mill)

Feetham

scale-miles

1816, he sketched the Priory and later developed a masterpiece from the sketch. After the Priory, take the path up through Steps Wood to Marrick. There are some 300 steps. They predate the Dissolution of the Monasteries and would have been used by the nuns from the Priory.

Just before Marrick, turn right at a barn and follow the path to the bottom of the village. From here, take the path ahead, ignoring several paths to both left and right. In about 2 miles from Marrick, you will reach the riverbank. Follow this down to a small road and bear right down to Downholme Bridge. Taking the path into the field on the left of the bridge, you will see the Hutton Monument on the skyline.

For the first two fields from the bridge, follow the riverbank, but then cut diagonally across the next two fields to join the road to Marske at a right-angled bend. Follow the road through Marske, passing the hall and crossing the bridge over the Marske Beck. This is the oldest bridge in Swaledale, and is of the medieval ribbed arch design.

About half a mile after crossing Marske Beck, take the field path on the right. This crosses the meadow to a footbridge before climbing up the hillside to a white cairn beneath Applegarth Scar. Follow the path, which passes several farmhouses, including West Applegarth and East Applegarth (a family named

Applegarth lived here in medieval times).

At East Applegarth, Robert
Willance jumped over the scar
above you on his horse when out
hunting in 1606. Miraculously,
he survived the fall. His horse did
not, nor did his leg. Willance had
his leg buried in St Mary's
churchyard Richmond, so that
he could be reunited with it
when he died. The site of the
accident is known as Willance's
Leap.

When you cross the next wall,
which is in some disrepair, there
are the outlines of walls and foot-
ings just above you, under Whitcliffe Scar. The site has been
excavated, and has been found to
have been occupied from the
Iron Age to the end of the Celtic
period (7th century).

The path now takes you
through Whitcliffe Wood. After
the wood, you climb gently to the
hillcrest, where there are good
views of Richmond, its castle, the
plain and the Hambledon Hills
beyond. From the woods, the
centre of Richmond is just over
1½ miles down the track.

Places of interest in the Swale valley

15.1 Easby Abbey and church

A mile down the riverbank from
Richmond, and accessible by
footpath, is the Premonstratensian Easby Abbey, founded in
1152 by Roald, Constable of

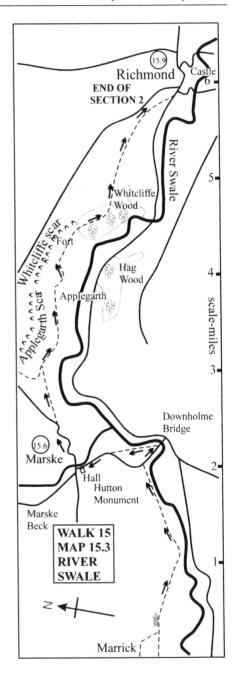

Richmond Castle. Although not as wealthy as some of the Cistercian foundations such as Fountains Abbey, Easby was a considerable landowner and at one time owned 9 granges.

The 14th century was a turbulent period for the north and, in common with many other abbeys, Easby suffered at the hands of marauding Scots. It was also badly damaged by a "friendly" English army! After the Dissolution of the Monasteries, the magnificent choir stalls were taken to St Mary's Church, Richmond, and the carved oak screen to Wensley Church. They may be seen today in these locations.

Near the abbey is St Agathas Church, a foundation which predates the abbey. The church has extensive 13th century wall paintings and a cast of the beautifully sculpted, 7th century Easby Cross (the original is in the Victoria and Albert museum).

15.2 Grinton

Now upstaged by Reeth over the other side of the valley, Grinton was, at one time, the centre of a parish which stretched to the Westmorland border. The church is of Norman origin, and has additions through to the 16th century. It has many interesting features including a Norman window and font, and grooves in the porch where medieval archers sharpened their arrows.

15.3 Gunnerside

Originally a summer pasture of a Norseman named Gunnar, Gunnerside ("Gunnar saetr") later became one of the major centres of the Swaledale lead mining industry. The potential rewards from mining may be judged by the £120,000 raised from the Blakethwaite mine by one man in the early 19th century.

The search for this mineral wealth led to the creation of something akin to a lunar landscape in the gill behind Gunnerside. This is particularly so towards the top of the gill where "hushing" (the release of large volumes of water down the hillside) was used as a way of uncovering the ore body.

Gunnerside is surrounded by a patchwork of small fields, the result of 16th century enclosure. The stone barns built to overwinter 3 or 4 cattle are a strong feature of the landscape.

15.4 Healaugh

Healaugh was originally an Anglian settlement ("helah" meaning a clearing in the forest), and was probably the furthest the Angles penetrated up the dale. In medieval times, Healaugh was much more important than Reeth, and was one of the three manors of upper Swaledale (the others being Muker and Grinton).

At the Dissolution of the Monasteries, Healaugh was owned by Sir

Francis Bigod who suffered the same fate as many northern landowners who supported the Pilgrimage of Grace – he was executed. The estate, which included the north side of the valley between Muker and Arkengarthdale, passed to the Wharton family of Wharton Hall, Westmorland (see Eden walk). They then became central players in the development of the Swaledale lead mining industry.

About 1½ miles up the Barney Beck from Healaugh are the remains of Surrender Bridge Smelting Mill, one of about 40 such mills in the dale when the lead mining industry was at its peak.

15.5 Maiden Castle

Until recently, it had been accepted that Swaledale was little settled in the Bronze and Iron Ages. Recent finds of early house bases and field patterns are causing this theory to be revised. The most visible evidence of man's early presence in the valley is the massive (approximately 100 metres by 100 metres) monument on Harkerside known as Maiden Castle, and the apparently associated linear earthworks on both sides of the valley around Reeth. Unfortunately, no evidence has come to light to allow these earthworks to be dated. Finds of Roman military equipment near Reeth support the possibility of the earthworks being erected by the Brigantians in their fight against Roman domination. It is equally likely, however, that they were earlier Iron Age structures.

More is known about the fort, which the walk passes further down the valley under Whitcliffe Scar. This has been shown to be an Iron Age site which continued to be occupied until about the 7th century.

15.6 Marske

Marske is a small village situated at the foot of a small glacial valley where it meets the Swale. There is a small church which has some Norman fabric, but the village is dominated by Marske Hall which was built by John Carr of York for the Hutton family in 1750.

During their 400 year ownership of Marske, the Hutton family provided an Archbishop of York (1594) and an Archbishop of Canterbury (1757). Early archbishops did more than say their prayers, and while Matthew Hutton was Archbishop of Canterbury, he owned several mills in Richmond.

The obelisk known as The Hutton Memorial, which stands above Marske, commemorates another Matthew Hutton who died in 1814. Marske Bridge (over the Markse Beck) is the oldest bridge in Swaledale, is of the medieval ribbed arch design, and is probably of the 15th century. The Huttons had the Downholme Bridge built over the Swale in 1684. This was destroyed by the floods of 1771 and was rebuilt by John Carr in 1773.

15.7 Muker

Originally a Norse settlement, the earliest reference is to Meuhaker – a cultivated enclosure – in 1274.

The building of the church at Muker in 1580 brought to an end the need to carry the dead from upper Swaledale to Grinton for burial, a journey which could take 2 days. Restoration earlier this century uncovered a possible earlier church. This may explain why the 13th century bells considerably predate the church. An alternative explanation is that they came from a dissolved monastery.

Muker was a centre of the lead mining industry. Traditional meadowland farming is still practised between Muker and Reeth, and explains the spectacular show of meadowland flowers in June and early July.

15.8 Reeth

With its attractive houses round a large green, and superb situation between Calva Hill and the confluence of the Swale and Arkle Beck, Reeth is a popular tourist centre. Originally an Anglian centre, Reeth was a slow starter, achieving a market charter only in 1695. It became prosperous in the Georgian period as a centre of both lead mining and hand knitting. This prosperity is reflected in the many fine buildings.

Following the failure of the lead mining industry, Reeth's population fell to a quarter of its early 19th century level.

15.9 Richmond

Only six years after fighting in the Battle of Hastings, Alan Rufus built Richmond Castle to defend the north for the Normans against possible Danish incursion. The seriousness of the threat may be judged by the fact that the castle is stone built, at a time when most castles were of the motte and bailey construction. The massive keep, from which there are splendid views, was built a century later. The town grew up under the protection of the castle.

By the 14th century, Richmond was well within striking range of the Scots who were raiding the north of England with impunity, and Swaledale lead was taxed to pay for the building of a town wall. Fragments of the medieval wall survive.

By the 16th century, Richmond had become a major knitting centre, with some 1000 knitters employed in the trade. Its peak prosperity, however, was to be as the result of the lead mining industry in the late 18th and early 19th century. This prosperity is reflected in the many fine Georgian houses in the town. (The Georgian Theatre of 1788 is the oldest theatre in the country in its original form.)

Frances I'Anson , who lived in Hill House, Frenchgate, was immortalised by Leonard McNally who wrote "Lass of Richmond Hill". The song had the desired effect and they were married in 1787!

In common with many other towns throughout the north, Richmond lost its bridge in a massive flood in 1771. The bridge was jointly owned by the North Riding and Richmond Corporation. The North Riding commissioned John Carr of York to design a new bridge, but the Corporation were very reluctant to rebuild, being compelled only by the threat of legal action. Piqued, the Corporation gave only minimal co-operation and insisted on building their half of the bridge with a separate contractor. Carr's bridge still stands today!

Walk 16: River Tees

Section 1: Cow Green to High Cup Nick and return, 13 miles

Section 2: Cow Green to Langdon Beck circular, 7 miles

Section 3: Langdon Beck to Middleton in Teesdale, 9 miles

Section 4: Middleton in Teesdale to Barnard Castle, 11 miles

Section 5: Barnard Castle to Winston, 8 miles

Section 6: Winston to Piercebridge, 5 miles

**Information Centres: Middleton in Teesdale 01833 40400;
Barnard Castle 01833 690909**

With its magnificent waterfalls, attractive villages and profusion of flowers, Teesdale offers some of the most scenic walking in northern England.

High Force

Meadowlands on many Teesdale farms are deliberately cut late to encourage flowers, and in the upper valley there are rare flowers which are remnants of the last Ice Age. For those interested in the plants, a visit to the Bowlees Visitors' Centre is strongly recommended. Here there are natural history displays and an excellent publication on plant localities may be purchased ("Plants of Upper Teesdale" by Christopher Lowe).

An impressive Norman castle dominates the riverbank at the bustling market town of Barnard Castle. "Barney", as it is known locally, is recognised as one of the most historically and architecturally important towns in Britain, and has largely escaped 20th century improvement.

Piercebridge, a village on the

site of a Roman fort, is conventionally regarded as the eastern end of Teesdale, and the walks described are continuous from Cow Green down to Piercebridge. Also included is a walk along Maize Beck, a tributary of the Tees, to High Cup Nick, one of the classical views of English landscape.

Bus services run along the valley from Langdon Beck to Piercebridge, allowing linear walks of almost any length to be planned throughout the dale.

At the time of researching this book a waymarked walk, the Teesdale Way, was being extended along the valley. Not all the sections of this walk were previously rights of way, and it would be worth checking with the Tourist Information Centres to see whether any additional access has been achieved.

Section 1: Cow Green to High Cup Nick return

There is no public right of way from Cow Green to the source of the Tees on Cross Fell. As an alternative starting point, this section follows the Maize Beck, a tributary of the Tees, from Cow Green to High Cup Nick.

High Cup Nick, one of the classical views of English landscape, is a glacial valley which cuts through an outcrop of whinsill (dolerite) on the line of the Pennine Fault. (An alternative route to High Cup Nick is from Dufton in the Eden valley. The Youth Hostels at Dufton and Langdon Beck are ideally situated to take in High Cup Nick on a linear walk).

Distance: 13 miles

Starting point: Weelhead Sike car park, Cow Green, NY810309

Maps: 16.1 plus Outdoor Leisure 31 and Landranger 91.

From the Weelhead Sike car park, follow the nature trail to the bottom of the reservoir. Take the footbridge over the Tees, just before the top of Cauldron Snout. Follow the track through the farm at Birkdale, shortly after which the path climbs to reach the boundary of an army range. The range keeps the path away from the Maize Beck for about 2 miles, and over this distance the path climbs gently some 400 feet (120m) over the edge of Dufton Fell.

After rejoining the Maize Beck, follow it upstream to reach a Pennine Way signpost indicating a ford across the beck. There is a slightly easier fording place a little upstream, but if the height of the water makes neither of these passable, you should go further upstream to 749270 where there is a footbridge.

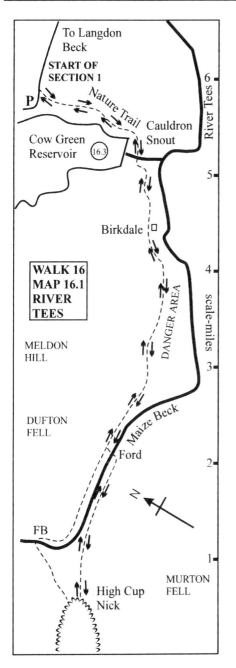

After crossing the beck go across the plateau to High Cup Nick where you can look down the glacial valley towards Appleby and the Eden valley. A particular feature of the valley is the exposure of the whinsill around its rim. The whinsill (dolerite) is a plate of solidified magma which underlies much of the northern Pennines, but is only locally exposed.

Follow the same route back to Cow Green. On the day I walked this route (second Saturday in July), I was enveloped on the return journey by a single great flock of sheep being driven by a number of farmers and sheepdogs down from the fells to Dufton for clipping. The only modern feature of this impressive centuries old sight was a Japanese four wheel drive runabout! It was more than a little eerie to complete the walk across the fells with not a sheep in sight.

Section 2: Cow Green to Langdon Beck circular

This circular walk includes Cauldron Snout, England's most spectacular cascade, and the Widdybank Fell nature trail. On the trail, the juxtaposition of limestone and volcanic rock has caused the formation of sugar limestone which supports a unique collection of alpine plants. Some of the plants, such as the Spring Gentian, are rare remnants of the Ice Age.

Distance: 7 miles

Starting point: Weelhead Sike car park. NY810309

Maps: 16.2 plus Outdoor Leisure 31 and Landranger 91.

Display boards near the car park illustrate the geology of the locality and list the plants to be seen, some of which are rare.

From the car park, follow the road towards Langdon Beck for a few metres before turning right onto the nature trail. Shortly after the reservoir dam you will come to Cauldron Snout, the most magnificent water cascade in England. Some care is needed in clambering down the rocks at the side of the Snout, particularly in wet weather when the rocks will be slippery.

From the bottom of Cauldron Snout the walk passes under Falcon Clints. The area is boggy and must previously have been difficult to negotiate. However, much has been done here to help the

walker by laying of stone slabs and wooden stepping boards.

Further along the path you will come to a field of boulders. Progress will be much slower until you reach the flat pastureland of Holmwath. Pass Widdy Bank Farm, which offers refreshments, and follow the farm road towards Langdon Beck. As the road rises, there are good views down the valley of the white farmhouses of the Raby estate. Look out in the boggy patches by the side of the road for orchids.

When you reach the Langdon Beck to Cow Green road, turn left towards Cow Green, which is some 2½ miles away. The penalty for your enjoyment of Cauldron Snout and the fast flowing river is that you now have to regain all the height lost!

At the highest point, do look back down Teesdale. This is one of the best places to appreciate the strongly tilting nature of the Pennines. To the west, along the edge of the Pennine Fault, are the peaks of Mickle Fell, Meldon Hill, Great Dun Fell and Cross Fell. The land falls away towards the east at approximately 150 feet (45m) per mile.

Section 3: Landon Beck to Middleton in Teesdale

This must be a strong candidate for being one of the finest riverside walks in England, with marvellous waterfalls and a wealth of meadowland flowers at the riverside margins. If you wish to make rapid progress on this walk, leave your flower identification books at home!

Distance: 9 miles

Starting point: Langdon Beck Hotel. NY853312

Intermediate break point: Bowlees, 5 miles

Public transport: Langdon Beck may be reached by bus from Middleton in Teesdale.

Maps: 16.2 and 16.3 plus Landranger 91 or 92.

From the hotel, take the minor road down the side of the Langdon Beck to the junction with the Harwood Beck. Cross the beck and follow it downstream to join the Pennine Way at Saur Hill Bridge. Here you cross to the east bank.

The riverside meadows are not cut for hay until early July, and the riverbanks on the walk down to Cronkley have a wealth of flowers – in both number and variety. My wife and I met two ornithologists here. Their binoculars, tripods and long distance lenses were lying discarded in a heap on the ground and they were down on their knees, marvelling at the profusion of flowers.

After the junction with the Tees, the path crosses the bridge at Cronkley to the west bank of the river. A short climb takes you up onto Bracken Rigg, which is covered with Juniper, the remnant of a forest first established about 5-7000 B.C.

The strange "plantation" of space age bubbles which can be seen on the hillside from Bracken Rigg is the site of an environmental monitoring station. Descending from the Rigg, you come rather unexpectedly upon a large quarry. Unexpected, because it is completely hidden from the road going up Teesdale.

Half a mile after the quarry, you come to High Force, England's largest waterfall where the whinsill is exposed. Always spectacular, the fall is at its terrifying best after heavy rain. The most impressive view of the falls is to be had a little downstream.

Another 1½ miles downstream from the High Force brings you to Low Force, a series of spectacular falls. If you wish to visit the Bowlees Visitors' Centre, which has an excellent display on the natural history of Teesdale (including a comprehensive video), cross Wynch Bridge and go over the B6277 into Bowlees village.

From Wynch Bridge, Middleton in Teesdale is approximately 3½ miles downstream and is reached using the path down the west side of the river.

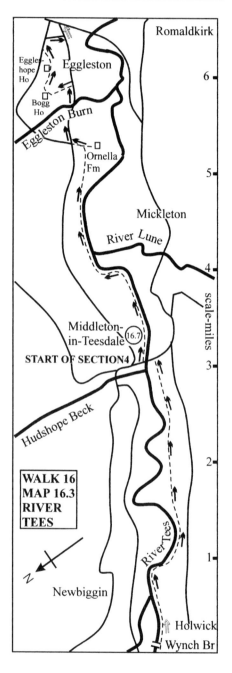

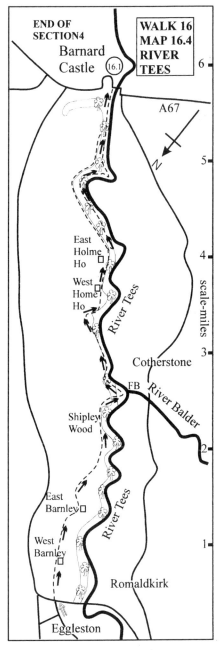

Section 4: Middleton in Teesdale to Barnard Castle

Although fairly long, this is a fine, easy walk, mainly along the riverbank. Lack of riverside paths around Eggleston forces the walk to higher ground, but this is rewarded by some excellent views over the valley below. The walk ends with a delightful section along the riverbank to come out in Barnard Castle, directly below the castle.

Distance: 11 miles

Starting point: Middleton in Teesdale, NY947255

Intermediate break points: Eggleston 4 miles, Cotherstone 7 miles.

Public transport: There is a bus between Barnard Castle and Middleton in Teesdale

Maps: 16.3 and 16.4 plus Outdoor Leisure 31 and Landranger 92.

In Middleton in Teesdale, go down to the river and take the path along the north bank. This is initially sandwiched between the river and the field boundary. After passing a small caravan site in just under a mile from the bridge, the river meets the hillside and the path goes into a wood, climbing occasionally to negotiate rocky promontories.

About a mile after the caravan site, the river turns south and the path leaves the riverbank, climbing gently uphill as it follows an ancient hollow-way. From the hillside there are some really excellent views looking up and down the river.

Towards the top of the rise, join the track coming up from Ornella Farm to the main road. Bear right at the main road, which you follow for about half a mile. With the exception of a short stretch, there are good verges.

After crossing Eggleston Burn, ignore a path on the left, but take a track on the left up to Bogg House. Go through the gate at the back of Bogg House, bear right and climb up to the house above. Bear right along the lane. When this splits, take the higher path, which takes you to the top of the rise. Here there is a seat which is strategically placed to allow you to sit and admire the views over the valley below.

This is a good vantage point to see the radical change in scenery which the valley is about to undergo as the river flows out of limestone (with volcanic intrusions) into gritstone. From Cow Green, the valley has been open, relatively broad and unwooded. Looking to the east, you can see that the river is about to enter a much more gorge-like and tree-lined valley. This will be the dominant nature of the valley down to Piercebridge.

Follow the path in front of Eggleshope House onto a lane which will take you down into the village. Pass the public house and church to come to a T-junction signed Middleton 3½ miles (on foot you have covered nearly 5 miles).

Turn left and follow the road to another T-junction. Here leave the road and take the farm road almost directly ahead to West Barnley. Pass on the left of first West Barnley and then East Barnley, after which a sign at a stile confirms that you are on the Teesdale Way. The Way keeps roughly to the 250 metre contour across the fields before descending to Shipley Wood. (The hollow which you should cross just before the wood marks the site of an ancient homestead.)

Follow the top edge of the wood. Just as you approach the end of the wood, a stile takes you over a wall into the woods for a short distance. As you emerge from the wood, Cotherstone is ahead and you descend towards the river. After a caravan site, a track takes you down to the riverbank where the Balder joins the Tees. Look out here for kingfishers and dippers flying low over the river.

If you wish to terminate your walk at Cotherstone, cross the footbridge over the river here. Otherwise, cross the meadow and make the steep climb up Cotherstone Crag above the river.

Follow the top edge of the wood for about half a mile. At the end of a long straight section of woodland, keep straight ahead as the woodland turns to the right. Pass through a gate and bear right down to a footbridge over a ravine. The footbridge takes you into a wood for a short distance.

Again, follow the top edge of the wood.

Pass two white Raby estate farms (West Holme House and East Holme House). Shortly after East Holme House, a path to the right takes you down the hillside to the riverbank. (If the weather has been very wet, you may wish to stay at the top of the woods since the path below can be muddy.)

There is a lovely, small, enclosed meadow at the river's edge. Cross the meadow to start a delightful 2 mile walk along the riverbank to Barnard Castle. The path brings you directly under the round tower of the castle. Turn left here and climb the hill. This will bring you onto Galgate, on the line of the old Roman road which crossed the Tees just above the castle.

Section 5: Barnard Castle to Winston

This is an easy walk, mainly along the riverbank or the terrace above the river, with Egglestone Abbey, Mortham Tower and Wycliffe providing historical interest.

The area around the confluence of the Tees and the Greta attracted many famous artists, including Turner and Cotman.

The walk ends at a bridge which, when it was built in 1765, was the largest single span bridge in Europe.

Distance: 8 miles

Starting point: Barnard Castle NZ050165

Public transport: There is a bus between Barnard Castle and Winston

Maps: 16.5 plus Landranger 92.

In Barnard Castle, cross the footbridge over the Tees at the bottom of Thorngate. Turn left and follow the riverside path. At the end of a small group of houses known as The Lendings, leave the riverbank to go to a caravan site. Walk through the caravan site then follow a track uphill and bear left before reaching a house. The path follows the terrace for just under half a mile to come out on the road to Egglestone abbey.

Just before the abbey, the road passes a small packhorse bridge spanning Thorsgill Beck. Pass the abbey, high above you on the right. Notice the 17th century mullion windows in some of the abbey buildings. (After the Dissolution of the Monasteries, as with most of the northern abbeys, part was converted into a house.)

From the abbey, Abbey Bridge with its impressive span is only a short distance downstream. It is possible to clamber down under the bridge to admire both the bridge and the limestone pavement below. The river must be an impressive site here when in flood – when I visited, the debris from the previous winter's floods was on ledges some 20 feet (6m) above the summer level.

Follow the path down the river's edge from Abbey Bridge to Rokeby Park, with the river running in a gorge below. Just before Rokeby you meet the road. Turn left here to follow the minor road at the bottom of Rokeby Park to the confluence of the Tees and the Greta. Known as the "Meeting of the Waters", the confluence was made famous by the paintings of Turner.

Cross the Dairy Bridge over the River Greta and follow the footpath to Mortham Tower, a combination of a 14th century peel tower and 18th century Hall. Unless you wish to see Greta Bridge, the view made famous by Cotman, which is about a mile further up the Greta, turn left just before Mortham Tower. Pass the edge of a wood and a derelict house at West Thorpe. When the track turns right, keep straight ahead and descend to the suspension bridge over the river. On the south side of the river there is a popular Lido and picnic area. Cross the suspension bridge and follow the riverbank downstream. (When I walked this section, the riverbank path was closed. The alternative is to climb up to the village of Whorlton and follow the top edge of the wood.)

As you pass Graft's Farm, Wycliffe is over the river, the 14th century birthplace of John Wycliffe, translator of the Bible. Both riverbanks are wooded for the next three quarters of a mile. When you leave the wood, you will see Ovington on the opposite bank. The next section, until Osmond Croft is on your left, is on an open terrace with unobstructed views to the river below.

From Osmond Croft, follow the edge of the woodland towards the river. Pass a group of chalets and bear right across a field to a stile

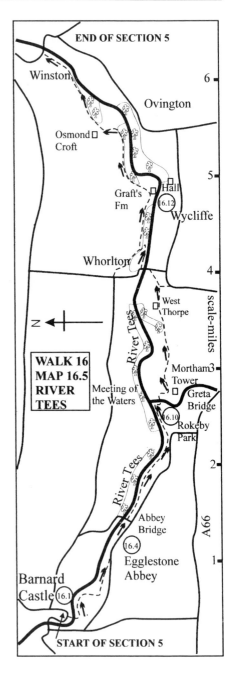

into woodland. You are now on a promontory above the river. Follow the woodland path to Winston Bridge. When built in 1765, this was the largest single span bridge in Europe. It was one of the few bridges over the Tees to survive an enormous flood in 1771.

Section 6: Winston to Piercebridge

This short walk, mainly along the riverbank, visits the attractive village of Gainsford and ends at Piercebridge, a village on the site of a Roman fort. At Piercebridge you may see the foundations of a Roman bridge (only rediscovered in 1978) and the pub which inspired the song "My Grandfather's Clock".

Distance: 5 miles

Starting point: The bridge, Winston NZ142163

Public transport: There is a bus between Winston and Piercebridge.

Maps: 16.6 plus Landranger 92 and 93.

There is some parking at the bridge at Winston. At Piercebridge, English Heritage and The George Inn share a car park which gives access to the Roman bridge.

From Winston Bridge, take the path down the north bank of the river. When you reach the A67, there is a new section of footpath along the riverbank, developed as part of the Teesdale Way. As yet not shown on maps, this section avoids the need to walk on the main road. When the path reaches the dismantled railway line, turn left up to the main road and then right towards Gainford.

In a short distance, take the bridle path on the right down to the river. Here you will find a fountain discharging sulphurous water. This disgusting brew was a major attraction in the 18th and 19th centuries and led to Gainford becoming a popular spa town!

Follow the path down the river to the road, and on entering Gainford, take the first road on the right, Low Row. On your right is a magnificent Jacobean hall with a 17th century dovecote in the grounds. (While the North-East may now be noted for racing pigeons, in the 17th century the interest was purely culinary!)

Walk through Gainford with its attractive greens and Georgian houses. When the main road is reached, pass a nursing home and two fields before turning right onto the path which takes you along the riverbank to Piercebridge.

At Piercebridge, cross the green (the site of the Roman fort), and go over the bridge. On your left is The George Inn, famed as the inspiration for the song "My Grandfather's Clock". The car park is shared with English Heritage and is the access point for the remains of the Roman bridge which was rediscovered in 1978.

Places of interest in the Tees valley

16.1 Barnard Castle

With its fine buildings and imposing castle, Barnard Castle, known locally as "Barney", is recognised as being one of the most historically and architecturally important towns in England.

The Romans crossed the Tees here, but in Anglo-Saxon times the capital of Teesdale was further down the river at Gainford. The Normans had the utmost difficulty in controlling the north of England, and this led them to choose the naturally defensive site at Barnard Castle for their fort. Guy de Baliol established the first wooden fort in 1093, but it was his nephew, Bernard, who built the first stone castle (modelled on Richmond Castle on the Swale) and, in so doing, gave his name to the town.

The 12th and 13th centuries were troubled times in the north, with frequent incursions by the Scots. However, with their strongly defended castle, the Baliols prospered at Barnard Castle, and became one of the most important families in the north. This very success was to lead to their downfall.

Through a marriage alliance, John Baliol ascended the Scottish throne and renounced his alle-

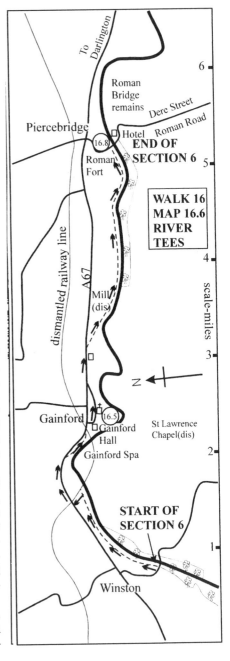

giance to the English Crown. In the ensuing war between England and Scotland, Baliol lost his Scottish support. He ended his life exiled in Picardy – on the estates his family had left two centuries earlier to come to England with William the Conqueror. John Baliol is best known today for the Oxford college his wife endowed in his memory, and for Sweetheart Abbey, in Scotland, where she buried his heart.

Following the demise of the Baliols, Barnard Castle temporarily passed to the Bishops of Durham (who had a claim on the estate going back to Anglo-Saxon times), but it was then given to the earls of Warwick, and through them to Richard III. Barnard Castle was no longer the main seat of a powerful local lord, but now a subsidiary estate of a figure of national importance.

Barnard Castle was itself, however, to take a last fleeting role in events of national importance. In 1569, the earls of Northumberland and West- moreland rose against the Crown, in what is known as the "Rising of the North". The aim of the rising was to overthrow Elizabeth I and replace her by the Catholic Mary Queen of Scots. Barnard Castle was held by Sir George Bowes for the Crown, and although he eventually surrendered the castle to its besiegers, the delay in capturing the castle caused the rising to falter. The Crown was able to regroup its forces and win the day.

In the 18th and 19th centuries, Barnard Castle settled down to the more prosaic business of making money. Textile and other manufacturing enter- prises crowded the Tees waterfront, and the prosperity generated was reflected in the many fine houses built further up the hill.

One of the joys of Barnard Castle is its very compactness. Within a small compass, it is possible to see:

- the castle (under the care of English Heritage),
- the central shopping area of Galgate, Horsemarket and Market Place,
- the Market Cross (actually a colonnaded buttermarket),
- the fine medieval County Bridge over the Tees,
- Bygraves House, a 16th century house where Cromwell stayed in 1648 (now a restaurant),
- The King's Head – where Dickens stayed in 1838 when researching "Nicholas Nickleby",
- the Bowes Museum.

The Bowes Museum was built in the French style for the Earl of Strathmore and his French wife. It houses a fine collection of paintings (El Greco, Goya and Canaletto) and has a life-size working model of a silver swan. The County Bridge was probably built in the 13th century and repaired in 1569. Before the Dissolution of the Monasteries, there was a small chapel at the middle of the bridge which performed illicit marriages – it was outside the jurisdiction of the two Bishops on either side of the river.

Barnard Castle is at its most colourful on market day (Wednesday).

16.2 Bowlees

Just off the B6277 at Bowlees, a Visitors' Centre provides a well-presented explanation of the natural history of Upper Teesdale. The waterfall, known as Summerhill Force, is up the side valley behind the Visitors' Centre. The water has cut back into the soft shale below the waterfall to form Gibson's Cave, and it is possible to stand in the cave behind the waterfall. Bowlees is a noted plant locality, particularly for a wide range of orchids.

16.3 Cow Green Reservoir

The rapid expansion of the steel and chemicals industries on Teeside in the 1950s and 1960s created a demand for water which threatened to outstrip the available supplies. Cow Green was chosen as the preferred site for a reservoir on the grounds of its large catchment area, high rainfall and low agricultural land value. Despite fierce resistance from conservationists, worried about the loss of a unique flora, the dam was eventually completed in 1970.

Against the background of Cross Fell, the highest Pennine peak, Cow Green has become a major attraction in its own right. From the car park at Weelhead Sike, a nature trail crosses an area of unique flora to Cauldron Snout, England's longest and most impressive cascade. The nature trail is one of several locations in the Cow Green / Langdon Beck area where the rare Spring Gentian may be seen. This remnant of the last Ice Age has a startling deep blue trumpet, flowers briefly in May, and opens only in bright sunlight.

16.4 Egglestone Abbey

This 12th century Premonstratensian abbey, impressively situated above the Tees, half a mile below Barnard Castle, demonstrates that medieval monks knew how to choose their sites!

As with many abbeys, Egglestone was sold at the Dissolution of the Monasteries, and the new owner converted the abbey into a home. The part of the abbey so converted is easily recognised from the many 17th century mullioned windows.

A small packhorse bridge, dating back to monastic times, crosses the Thorsgill Beck below the abbey.

16.5 Gainford

Gainford is a particularly attractive village with a 13th century church and Georgian houses around the village green. In Anglo-Saxon times, Gainford was the capital of Teesdale and had a monastery. Although no building fabric remains from the period, the large number of fragments of Anglo-Saxon stonework to be seen in and around the church suggest that there was a school of stonemasons at the monastery.

In the 9th century the Teesdale estates belonged to St Cuthbert of Lindisfarne (later to move to Durham). They were later mortgaged to the Earls of Northumberland and never returned. This resulted in an animosity and feuding between the Bishops of Durham and the secular Lords of Teesdale over land ownership. The dispute lasted several centuries. For a short period the Bishops actually took back ownership of the estate (see Barnard Castle).

Gainford Hall, at the west end of the village, is a fine Jacobean mansion built for the vicar in 1605. It has a 17th century circular dovecote in the grounds.

Half a mile to the west of the village there is a sulphurous spring on the riverbank which led to Gainford's popularity as a spa in the 19th century.

16.6 High Force and Low Force

Low Force is a series of picturesque waterfalls and, like High Force its larger counterpart upstream, is a result of the river meeting a hard outcrop of whinsill (dolerite).

Wynch Bridge, which crosses the Tees at Low Force, was, when built in 1704, the first suspension bridge in Europe. It collapsed into the river in 1802 with 11 people on it. All but one survived.

16.7 Middleton in Teesdale

The "capital" of upper Teesdale, Middleton is a large village in an attractive setting with a wide main street and green. First mentioned as being in the ownership of King Canute in 1030, Middleton was the market town of the forest of Teesdale in medieval times.

The London Lead Company bought the estate in 1815 and stayed until the decline of lead mining in 1905. The Quaker company took an active interest in nearly every aspect of their workers' lives – housing, schools, health and even brass bands – and were responsible for most of the buildings we see in Middleton today.

16.8 Piercebridge

The green of this small village is directly on the site of the Roman fort built to protect the bridge carrying Dere Street over the Tees.

A little further downstream, an earlier bridge was abandoned by the Romans when the river changed its course. The bridge foundations lay hidden until rediscovered in 1978. It is possible to visit the site, where display boards explain the history of both the bridge and the fort.

The present bridge was built in 1673 and rebuilt in 1797, following the flood of 1771 which destroyed many bridges on the Tees. The George Inn, next to the bridge, has the famous clock which stopped, never to go again, thus inspiring the song "My Grandfather's Clock".

16.9 Raby estate and castle

The northern side of Teesdale has been run as a single estate since early medieval times. The most visible evidence of the estate are the many white farms which make such a feature of the dale (the Raby tenants are required to whitewash their properties each year).

Lord Barnard lives in Raby Castle, for centuries the home of the Nevilles, one of the most powerful families in the country. Despite many 18th and 19th century additions, Raby Castle retains much of its original 14th century character. The main features of interest include works of art, medieval kitchens, a deer park and walled garden.

16.10 Rokeby Park

Rokeby, a fine Palladian style hall, was designed by its owner, Thomas Robinson, in 1730. Robinson's commitments kept him away from Rokeby for long periods (he was governor of Barbados for 5 years), and in 1769 he sold the estate to J.S. Morritt, whose descendants still retain Rokeby.

Sir Walter Scott was a frequent visitor to Rokeby, and he used it as the setting for his ballad of the same name. The house, which has recently been opened to the public, contains a unique collection of needlework by Ann Morritt, eldest sister of J.S. Morritt.

Mortham Tower, a 14th century peel tower (with later extensions), which is just over the River Greta, is also part of the Rokeby estate.

16.11 Stanwick

About 4 miles south of the Gainford, Stanwick (176113) is one of the most important historical sites in England. Here the Brigantes, under their leader Venutius, built an enormous fortification around their 850 acre site, in an attempt to defend themselves against the Romans. Their efforts were in vain, and in around AD70, the Romans defeated them to complete the conquest of northern England. In total there are some 6 miles of ramparts and ditches. Parts of the fortifications, which are 20 feet (6m) high, are open to the public.

16.12 Wycliffe

Wycliffe was the 14th century birthplace of John Wycliffe, translator of the Bible and one of the forerunners of the Protestant Reformation. Wycliffe was the first to put forward the view that the Church had become too worldly and should be disendowed by the King. (Wycliffe was not himself above benefiting from the Church's worldly wealth by holding down several church "livings" at the same time as he was advising its disendowment.) Two centuries later, Henry VIII followed Wycliffe's advice, and the result may be seen 3 miles upstream in the ruins of Egglestone Abbey.

Walk 17: River Tyne

Section 1: Alston to Haltwhistle, 16 miles

Section 2: Haltwhistle to Bardon Mill, 9½ miles (circular walk, 15 miles)

Section 3: Bardon Mill to Haydon Bridge, 5 miles

Section 4: Haydon Bridge to Hexham, 9 miles

Section 5: Hexham to Corbridge, 4½ miles

Information Centres: Haltwhistle 01434 322002; Hexham 01434 605225; Corbridge 01434 632815

This walk, which is in five sections, follows the Tyne valley from Alston to Corbridge. There was little settlement in the Tyne before the coming of the Romans, but it was then to become a fiercely contested border region for some 1500 years. Peace was to come to the region only with the union of the English and Scottish crowns in 1603. The walks include much evidence of the frontier nature of the valley including:

- one of the best stretches of Hadrian's Wall,

- several Roman forts and roads,

- medieval forts,

- pele (peel) towers.

The towns of Hexham and Corbridge, which are of considerable historical interest, are on the walks. This historical interest is matched by superb scenery, including the quiet upper reaches of the South Tyne, the exquisite section of Hadrian's Wall perched on an outcrop of whinsill and the delightful deciduous woodlands of Allen Banks on a tributary of the Tyne (sections 3).

The Tyne is particularly accessible and is perhaps better served by bus and rail than any other of the northern dales. The starting and end points of all the sections are joined by public transport, making it easy to plan linear walks.

Section 1: Alston to Haltwhistle

For those not deterred by the prospect of a 16 mile walk, an early bus from Haltwhistle gives a good start for this excellent all-day walk. (The walk could, of course, be shortened to any desired length by leaving the bus before Alston).

Because of the elevation, there is little settlement in the upper reaches of the South Tyne valley. Alston was established as a mining town, and the few settlements seen on the hillsides were built to supplement the miners' incomes by the raising of a few cattle, rather than as self-supporting farms.

The main attraction of this walk is the remote and rugged countryside. For much of the stretch of the South Tyne between Alston and Haltwhistle, there is a choice of footpaths on opposite sides of the valley. Although the Pennine Way keeps to the west side of the valley, my preference is for the eastern side of the valley below Slaggyford.

The site of a Roman fort with some exceptionally well-developed ramparts is passed at Whitley Castle, while lower down the valley Featherstone Castle, which dates back to the 12th century, is seen.

Distance: 16 miles

Starting point: Alston. NY718465

Public transport: Wright Bros. bus from Haltwhistle railway station.

Maps: 17.1 and 17.2 plus Landranger 86.

From the centre of Alston, take the road down to the river. Cross the bridge and turn right onto the A689, and right again onto the Pennine Way. In about three-quarters of a mile down the Pennine Way, pass Harbutt Lodge and follow the lane up to the A689. Turn right and pass Harbutt Law, dated 1869, but with its mullioned windows and cornices echoing a building style of two centuries earlier.

Immediately after Harbutt Law, go into the fields on the left, where the path climbs steeply up hill. When you reach the top of the ridge, there are excellent views down the valley. About a mile away, just behind some farm buildings, you should be able to see the site of the Roman fort of Whitley Castle.

Follow the path across the Gilderdale Burn and skirt to the left of the fort. The fort has a most impressive set of ramparts on its western side. Climb a stile into the field containing the fort and descend to the A689, which is reached between a farm building and a small wood.

Cross the road and follow the path past a farm building to Kirkhaugh, about half a mile away. At Kirkhaugh, bear left uphill. Turn right at the top of the farm buildings to cross the fields to Lintley. Just before reaching

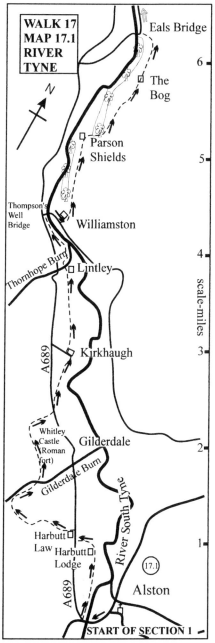

Lintley, the line of the Roman road which is being followed is clearly seen as it crosses some low-lying ground.

Follow the path under the disused railway and down the Thornhope Burn to the Tyne. When Thompson's Well Bridge is reached, leave the Pennine Way and cross the Tyne. Go through the first farm buildings on the left (Williamston), and climb the track which goes steeply above the wood. Take the path on the left, which leaves the track and follows the contour before descending to Parson Shields. ("Shield" is a pre-Norman word used in the Tyne valley to describe a summer pasture.)

After the farm, follow the track which climbs above a wood. Pass a well-preserved limekiln on the right, and when the track levels out, you are now on a green way with some excellent views of the river below.

Follow the path to the next farmhouse, The Bog, after which a metalled road takes you to Eals Bridge. ("Eals", which is pre-Norman for river flat, suggests that there was a settlement here in Anglo-Danish times.)

Go through Eals and follow the track down the riverbank to Towsbank Wood. Here you climb upwards across a steeply inclined hill, and some care is necessary until you reach the level. For the next three-quarters of a mile the trees block the view of the valley below, but when you come out of the wood you will see the railway viaduct crossing a gorge below.

A minor irritant is that shortly the way ahead is not a right of way. You have to detour to the right, climbing half a field upwards before crossing a stile and returning to your previous line. The hidden benefit is that the short climb gives some good views over the valley below.

Descend the hill. At the corner of the second field, a path will take you steeply down to meet the river under the viaduct in the Lambley Gorge. The Lambley Gorge is the result of the river meeting the Stubblick Dyke, an exposure of hard igneous rock. This is the local section of the fault which lies along the three sides of the northern Pennines (see geology appendix for further explanation).

As a result of the fault, younger Coal Measure rocks are exposed at the surface and are responsible for a line of coal deposits which lie along the east-west axis of the fault. In the 1860s, a railway line was opened from Lord Carlisle's Lambley colliery to join the Haltwhistle to Alston line at the west side of the Lambley Viaduct.

After a fair amount of climbing and descending over the last few miles, you may be pleased to know that the next three miles is strictly along the valley bottom.

From the viaduct follow the path downstream. Divert to the right to avoid a stream before rejoining the riverbank down to the next bridge. After the bridge, follow the riverbank. The rather austere brick

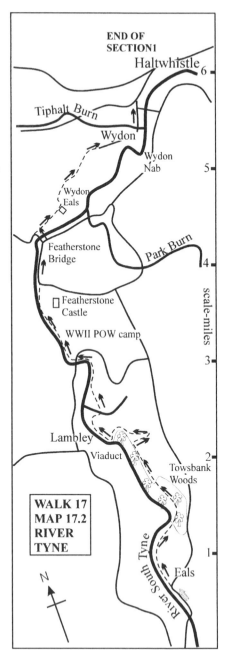

buildings you pass are of a World War II German prisoner of war camp. About half a mile after the camp, you will pass Featherstone Castle. Nearly everything you can see of this impressive building is Victorian Gothic, but at its heart there is a 12th century pele tower. The river has changed course considerably here, and at one time flowed much closer to the castle.

After the castle you will join the road for a short distance down to Featherstone Bridge. Cross this elegant humpback bridge of 1778 and take the farm road on your right to Wydon Eals.

At Wydon Eals the path climbs through a wood and a stile is crossed over a fence. Follow the edge of the fields to another stile. When you go through a gate into the next field, there are good views of Haltwhistle on the north side of the river.

Skirt the field down to Wydon where you follow the farm road which takes you into Haltwhistle. To the right of this farm road, the river encounters another exposure of igneous rock at Wydon Nab. Above the igneous rock there is a layer of limestone, and above that 50 feet (15m) of boulder clay. The boulder clay is a reddish colour, having been brought by ice from the area of red sandstone rocks in the Eden valley.

Section 2: Haltwhistle to Bardon Mill

This section of the walk includes a truly classic walk along Hadrian's Wall and visits military roads built by Agricola in the AD 80s (Stanegate) and General Wade in the 1740s (the Military Road). The Roman fort of Vindolanda is directly on the walk and Housesteads could be included by extending the walk by two miles.

The walk may be either linear, using public transport to return from Bardon Mill to Haltwhistle, or circular, with a return leg along the south side of the valley.

Distance: linear walk 9½ miles, circular walk 15 miles

Starting point: Haltwhistle, NY705640

Public transport: There is a regular bus service along the valley which stops at Haltwhistle and Bardon Mill. Only a few of the Newcastle to Carlisle trains stop at Bardon Mill.

Maps: 17.3 plus Landranger 86 or 87.

From Haltwhistle, follow the minor road up the west bank of the Haltwhistle Burn. In about a mile the road skirts to the right of Lees Hall before reaching the B6318. The straightness of this road and the Roman forts along its length might persuade you that this was one of the many Roman roads

Whinsill crags and Hadrian's Wall

in this area. In fact, it is the Military Road which was built by General Wade after the Jacobite rebellion of 1745.

Take the small road across the other side of the Military Road. When it swings left, just after a gate, take the path on the right. Cross a stile and go over the line of the vallum associated with Hadrian's Wall. At the top of the field you will reach Hadrian's Wall, which you follow to the right.

The next few miles along the wall are a marvellous undulating section. You will pass in turn:

- a lake (a disused quarry) and picnic site at 0.4 miles,
- milecastle 42 at 0.6 miles,
- milecastle 41 at 1.6 miles,
- Windshields Crag trig point at 2.4 miles,
- Crag Lough at 4 miles.

From Windshields Crag trig point there is a splendid panoramic view which includes the waste lands to the north, limestone ridges to the north-east, the line of the wall along the whinsill and to the south, the valley of the south Tyne.

At the end of Crag Lough, you bear right (If you wish to visit Housesteads fort you should carry on along the wall for about another mile, returning along the Wall to Crag Lough).

In only a few metres along the track from the wall, you will come to a

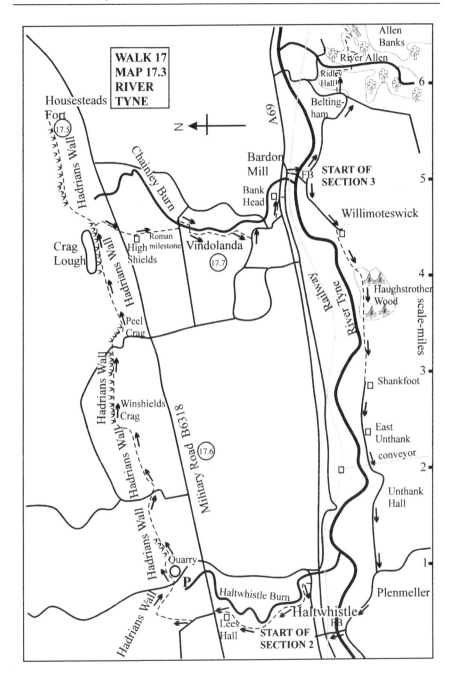

WALK 17
MAP 17.3
RIVER
TYNE

N

Housesteads
Fort
17.5

Hadrians Wall

Chainley Burn

Crag
Lough

Hadrians Wall

High
Shields

Roman
milestone

Vindolanda
17.7

Peel
Crag

Hadrians Wall

Winshields
Crag

Military Road B6318

17.6

Hadrians Wall

Hadrians Wall

Quarry

P

Hadrians Wall

Lees
Hall

Haltwhistle Burn

START OF
SECTION 2

Allen
Banks

River Allen

Ridley
Hall

Belting-
ham

A69

6

Bardon
Mill

FB

START OF
SECTION 3

5

Bank
Head

Willimoteswick

Railway

River Tyne

Haughstrother
Wood

4

scale-miles

Shankfoot

3

East
Unthank

conveyor

2

Unthank
Hall

1

Plenmeller

Haltwhistle
FB

signpost to Vindolanda 1¼ miles which you follow. The path across the field is not very distinct and you should aim for the farmhouse on the other side of the Military Road (High Shields). When you hit the vallum which crosses the field, follow it to the road. The path forward is on the other side of the road and passes to the left of High Shields.

Once past High Shields, Vindolanda is laid out below you in plan view. Follow the path down the fields to reach a road just to the east of Vindolanda. (Just before reaching the road look out for the Roman milestone in the corner of the field.)

The road is Stanegate which predates Hadrian's Wall by about 40 years, having been built by Agricola during his conquest of northern Britain in the AD80s. Unless you are visiting Vindolanda, turn left on reaching the road, and then in a few metres, turn right onto a track which will take you through the woods to Bardon Mill.

In just under a mile from Vindolanda you will pass under the line of an electricity power line. Bear right here, away from the burn, and make for the corner of the field which gives access to a road. Follow this road downhill until just before making the final descent to the main road at Bardon Mill. Here you bear left. Pass to the right of a house (Bankhead) and cross the A69 onto a path which takes you into the yard of a pottery factory.

If you intend to walk back to Haltwhistle (not catching a bus or train), follow the road through Bardon Mill, and at the end of the village take the track downhill over the railway line and the footbridge over the Tyne.

Over the river, the road to the right will take you to Willimoteswick, the ancient fortified home of the Ridleys, in about three-quarters of a mile. Pass to the right of Willimoteswick and follow the path which descends to the plain.

When you reach Haughstrother Wood, ignore a path going down towards the river on the right and take the path into the wood. The path divides in the wood and you should take the right fork. Although the path gets close to the river twice over the next couple of miles, the views are largely obscured by the trees.

In about 2 miles after Haughstrother Wood, after passing Shankfoot, East Unthank and Unthank Hall, you will pass under the line of a conveyor which crosses the river. This is bringing coal from an open cast mine high up the valley side to a railway loading station on the other side of the river. (The mine is on the same coalfield as that encountered at Lambley on the first section of the walk.)

At Plenmeller you come to a T-junction and turn right along a road which takes you to the footbridge over the Tyne into Haltwhistle. (Plenmeller has recently sprung to fame as a possible centre of gravity of the United Kingdom. Personal computers have renewed interest in calculating the country's point of balance and, seemingly, depending on which off-shore islands are or are not included in your calculation, Plenmeller is a candidate for the trophy.)

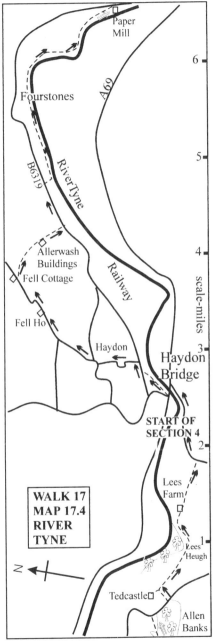

WALK 17
MAP 17.4
RIVER
TYNE

Section 3: Bardon Mill to Haydon Bridge

This short walk along the quiet southern side of the South Tyne valley takes in the delightful deciduous woodlands at the National Trust property of Allen Banks. From the highest points on the walk there are glimpses, on the skyline, of the crags on which Hadrian's Wall is built.

Distance: 5 miles

Starting point: Bardon Mill, NY782647

Public transport: There is a regular bus service along the Tyne valley which links the end points of the walk.

Maps: 17.3 and 17.4 plus Landranger 86 or 87.

Take the lane at the east end of Bardon Mill, which goes down to the railway crossing. Cross the railway and river. Bear left onto the minor road which passes a nature reserve before climbing up from the river plain to the delightful village of Beltingham.

Follow the road to a T-junction and turn left towards Ridley. Take the first track on the right, in about 100 metres (unmarked). The track crosses the bottom end of the grounds of Ridley Hall. For part of the way this follows a haha (a type of sunken park surround which was popular in the 18th century as a means of giving uninterrupted views of the surrounding countryside from within a park).

At the end of the ha-ha, you will come to the National Trust property of Allen Banks. Turn right here and follow the river upstream. When you draw level with a suspension bridge, the hillside is too steep to descend to the riverbank. Go upstream a little before doubling back along the riverbank path and crossing the footbridge.

From the footbridge, climb the steps ahead and then zigzag up the hillside through the woods, ignoring the intermediate level paths which you cross.

This part of the walk, through the deciduous woodlands of Allen Banks, is particularly attractive.

Just before leaving the woodlands, the path doubles back to a small tarn before leaving the wood at a higher level. There are now fine views up and down the valley. Behind Bardon Mill you should be able to see the small valley leading up towards Vindolanda. Behind that, on the horizon, you can see the crags on which Hadrian's Wall sits.

When you reach a road, turn right and climb upwards. In about 5 minutes, you will reach a footpath sign to Lees and Haydon Bridge on the left. This is a farm track down to Tedcastle. Just before Tedcastle, bear right, away from the farm track. Be careful here as the most used track across the fields is a farm track, and is not the one you want. Your path is a subsidiary track, which climbs uphill towards a stile (which you should be able to see).

From the stile, cross the next field, climbing upwards towards the top corner of the woodland at Lees Heugh. Being the highest point of the walk, from here you should now be able to see rather more of the crags along Hadrian's Wall on the skyline. At the right-hand end of the section of crags, you should be able to see a small deciduous woodland. This marks the position of Housesteads Fort.

The OS maps show the path from the woods proceeding ahead and descending to Lees Farm. If you follow the maps strictly, you will find a wall in front of you which you are unable to cross, there being neither stile nor squeeze posts. What you should do is to follow the edge of the wood downhill, go through a gate and then proceed to Lees Farm. From the farm, follow the farm road and then a minor road into Haydon Bridge.

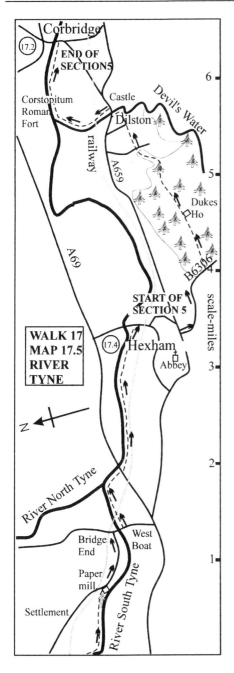

WALK 17
MAP 17.5
RIVER
TYNE

Section 4: Haydon Bridge to Hexham

The first half of this walk leaves the riverbank for the plateau on the north side of the valley. The climb of 500 feet (150m) from the valley bottom is rewarded with some good views, not only of the valley below, but northwards to the Cheviots.

With the exception of two short stretches of road walking, the second half of the walk is along paths directly adjacent to the riverbank. There is a delightful approach to Hexham – down an avenue of trees, with the river on the left and a golf club and Hexham Abbey on the right.

Distance: 9 miles

Starting point: The bridge, Haydon Bridge, NY843643

Public transport: There are good bus and train services along the Tyne valley which connect the end points of this walk.

Maps: 17.4 and 17.5 plus Landranger 87.

In Haydon Bridge, follow the path along the riverbank from the bridge. Go under the railway and bear right down the B6319 for about 200 metres, then take the minor road up the hillside. Climb through Haydon, ignoring roads to the left and right. After climbing about 500 feet from Haydon Bridge, you will reach the plateau above the valley and will come to a T-junction. Bear right here along an unmade road.

At the highest point, just after Fell House, look to the north. If visibility is good, you should be able to see the Cheviots on the far horizon. As you start your descent, the countryside ahead of you is now more rolling.

At Fell Cottage, take the footpath on the right, signed to Allerwash Hall. You should now be able to see the steam rising from the saw-mill in Hexham, and on the hilltop behind Fourstones, the outline of an ancient hillfort.

At the end of the field, cross a stile, and after jumping across a small burn, follow the edge of the field to a gate. Go through the gate and follow the track past Allerwash Buildings down to the B6319. Bear left here and follow the road for nearly a mile to a track on the right which goes down to the riverbank. Although the road is fairly narrow, it is usually quiet, traffic preferring the main road on the other side of the river.

Follow the riverbank downstream for two miles, passing Fourstones on the way to a paper mill. At the paper mill, the river meets the hillside and you are forced back on the road for a half mile stretch down to the bridge at West Boat. Cross the river here, and take the lane on the left. At some houses you will come to a notice board on the left which advises you that you have reached the Tyne Green Trail. For the next two miles you follow the riverbank down to the bridge at Hexham.

Section 5: Hexham to Corbridge

Although it is not possible to walk directly down the riverbank between these two historic towns, a detour to the south allows a short interesting walk to be devised.

Both Hexham and Corbridge are extremely interesting in their own rights, and the walk passes Dilston Castle and the Roman fort of Corstopitum (on the other bank of the Tyne).

Distance: 4½ miles

Starting point: Hexham, NY936639

Public transport: There are good bus and train services between Corbridge and Hexham.

Maps: 17.5 plus Landranger 87.

From the centre of Hexham, take the B6306 uphill (towards Blanchland) for about three-quarters of a mile. There is a good footpath at the side of the road all the way.

When you reach the crest of the hill, take the track on the left leading into the wood. In about half a mile down this track you will pass Duke's House, a Victorian extravaganza with a large number of chimneys.

At the end of the woods, the path goes through a long strip of wood and is, in places, in a deep hollow-way.

Cross two small roads coming up from the valley bottom to come to Dilston, where the track follows the Devil's Water to the left, down to the main road. High on the hill is Dilston Hall, built in 1835. The third Earl of Derwentwater built an earlier hall here in 1714, but had little time to enjoy his new home. In 1715 he took part in the abortive Jacobite rebellion and paid the price for being on the losing side – he was executed.

Cross the A695 bridge and take the path down the east side of the Devil's Water to its confluence with the Tyne.

As you follow the riverbank down to the magnificent bridge at Corbridge, the Roman fort of Corstopitum is on the hilltop on the other side of the river. (The fort can be reached from Corbridge and is well worth a visit.) Although I was unable to find it, it is said that in low water the line of the Roman road (Dere Street) may be seen crossing the river to the fort.

Places of interest in the Tyne valley

Alston

Alston is attractively situated and has a sloping, cobbled main street and distinctive covered market. Lead was the reason for the establishment of Alston. It is the highest market town in the country (1154ft). At the peak of its prosperity, a navigable drainage level stretched 5 miles into the hillside from Alston.

The town was devastated by the economic depression of 1828-31, with some 2000 inhabitants leaving, many emigrating to Canada. The coming of the railway to Alston in 1852 was too late to benefit the lead mining industry.

17.2 Corbridge

Corbridge was at one time the capital of Saxon Northumbria, owing its importance to its situation at the cross road of two highways established in Roman times – Dere Street (York to Edinburgh) and Stanegate. Stanegate was originally Agricola's fortified line, and later the supply line to Hadrian's Wall. Until General Wade built his Military Road in the 18th century, this was the main road between Newcastle and Carlisle.

The town was burnt three times by Scottish raids. In more settled times, Corbridge's position at a crossing of the Tyne led to it becoming one of the most important centres of the droving trade (see appendix). At great fairs on Stagshaw Bank, as many as 100,000 animals were to be seen at one time.

Corbridge, with its wide main street, is now an important tourist centre, with many places of historical interest. The Roman fort of Corstopitum, just to the west of the town, has some of the best remains of Roman granaries in Europe. St Andrew's Church was built of stone taken from the Roman fort and some parts of the church date back to its establishment in the 8th century. The Vicar's pele was situated in the church yard as a retreat for the Vicar during Scottish raids and is now probably the most complete pele tower in existence. Low Hall is another pele tower with a Jacobean hall attached. The grandson of the builder of the hall lost his life (and the hall was forfeit to the Crown) when he joined the unsuccessful Jacobite rebellion of 1715. The magnificent seven-arched bridge of 1674 was the only Tyne bridge to survive the great flood of 1771. It is said that the flood was so great that it was possible to touch the floodwater from the bridge above.

17.3 Haltwhistle

As with nearly all pre-Norman settlements in the South Tyne valley, Haltwhistle is situated on the north side of the valley to catch the sun. A post-Roman earthwork was situated on castle hill, which also had a pele tower (demolished in the 1960s).

Woollen mills were established on the Haltwhistle Burn in the late 18th century, but Haltwhistle's main growth was as a result of coal mining and quarrying in the 19th and early 20th centuries. The grey slate terraces reflect this mining heritage. With the opening of the Haltwhistle to Alston railway in the 1850s, Haltwhistle overtook Brampton as a market town.

Although perhaps not as obviously attractive as Hexham, Haltwhistle is a good centre from which to explore the Tyne valley and Hadrian's Wall.

17.4 Hexham

Hexham has had a more turbulent past than most towns. In AD 674, Queen Etheldreda of Northumbria gave land at Hexham to build a church of which it was said that " none north of the Alps could compare". The church was burnt to the ground by Halfdane in AD 875, during the Viking conquest of northern England.

The Normans established an Augustinian priory at Hexham in the 12th century, but the town was razed with much savagery by the Scots in 1296. (They boarded up the school and burnt the scholars alive.)

Hexham was one of the main centres of the Pilgrimage of Grace, the unsuccessful rebellion against King Henry VIII's Dissolution of the Monasteries. For his part in the pilgrimage, the Abbott was hung outside his abbey.

Although a number of important landowners in the Tyne valley supported the Jacobite rebellion of 1715, Hexham itself was little affected by the rebellions of 1715 and 1745. It suffered, however, in 1761 when there was a riot in protest against the perceived unfairness of recruiting for the military – 51 people died when the troops opened fire.

In 1725, during excavations to strengthen the abbey tower, the Saxon crypt was rediscovered. This important Saxon structure, which may be reached from the nave of the abbey, is built in stone from the nearby Roman fort of Corstopitum. The Roman inscriptions were deliberately placed on the inside to act as a key for plasterwork.

Today Hexham is a bustling and prosperous market and tourist town. The main interest is the centre of the town with the abbey, the market square (market held on Tuesdays) and the Moot hall cum manorial prison all in close proximity to one another.

17.5 Housesteads (Vercovium)

Housesteads is the most dramatically sited and best preserved of the forts on Hadrian's Wall. The 5 acre site has been well excavated, allowing you to see on the ground:

- the HQ building,
- the C.O.'s house,
- some barracks,
- the granaries,
- the only example of a Roman hospital in Britain.

Look out for the 24-seater flushed latrines, and the wheel ruts at the east gate.

Until the 18th century, the Armstrongs, a family of border reivers (cattle rustlers) operated from the site. They emigrated to the USA!

17.6 The Military Road

During the Jacobite rebellion of 1745, General Wade was unable to move troops from Newcastle to Carlisle, and Carlisle Castle quickly capitulated to Bonnie Prince Charlie's army. A new road was therefore surveyed as soon as the rebellion had been suppressed.

The turnpike, much of which follows Hadrian's Wall, was opened in 1753. This was possibly the first scientifically engineered road since the Roman roads (also built for military needs).

17.7 Vindolanda

This site was built by Agricola to defend Stanegate, forty years before the building of Hadrian's Wall. It would be worth a visit even if it were only to see the well excavated building foundations. These include a fine HQ building, a military bathhouse, a Roman Inn and a civilian settlement.

What is unique and absolutely outstanding about Vindolanda, however, is that the anaerobic conditions in the soil have preserved large volumes of fragile personal effects, not seen at all on other sites:

- textiles,
- leather goods,
- the largest archive of early Roman written material.

Do visit the museum to see these artefacts before visiting the site.

The replica stone and turf walls and the stone milepost which is just to the north of the site are also worth seeing.

Walk 18 : River Ure

Section 1: Urehead to Hawes, 9 miles

Section 2: Hawes to Bainbridge circular, 13 miles

Section 3: Askrigg to Aysgarth circular, 10½ miles

Section 4: Aysgarth to Jervaulx, 12 miles

Information Centres: Hawes 01969 667450; Leyburn 01969 23069

Unlike most of the dales, Wensleydale is not named after its river, but after a small village which was the main market town in early medieval times. Yoredale, an earlier name for the dale, is now reserved for describing the geological sequence of rocks which is so characteristic of the valley. It is this sequence of alternating hard and soft rocks which is responsible for Wensleydale's best known features – its waterfalls.

The valley has much of historical interest from pre-historic times onwards, but it was in the 15th century that it was the home to figures of national importance – the King's Chancellor, Richard Scrope, who lived in Bolton Castle, and Richard of Gloucester, who left his home at Middleham Castle to become Richard III.

The valley has an abundance of excellent walks. Four are described which take the walker from the source of the river to Jervaulx Abbey, where the valley runs into the plain. Two of the walks are circular, and there is public transport to enable the other two to be carried out as linear walks.

Section 1: Ure Head to Hawes

This high level walk along an ancient green road gives splendid views of the empty upper Wensleydale valley below.

Lady Anne Clifford used this route in the 17th century when travelling between her many northern castles, and mentions it several times in her diaries. Later it became an important drove road down which Scottish cattle were brought to English markets.

Distance: 9 miles

Starting point: Aisgill Moor Cottages SD778963

Public transport: On certain days in the summer months there is a bus from Hawes to Garsdale station. From the station, either take the road to Aisgill Moor Cottages or shorten the route by taking one of the many paths from the B6259 which climb up to the High Way above.

Maps: 18.1 and 18.2 plus Outdoor Leisure 30 and Landranger 98.

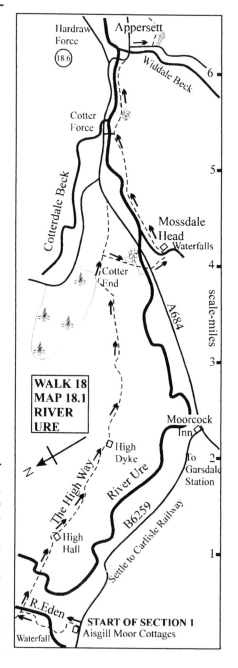

The Ure and Eden rise next to each other on Lunds Fell and the two valley walks have a common starting point at Aisgill Moor Cottages.

At the cottages, cross the railway line and bear left to the fine waterfall on the Eden. Follow the river upstream, past a farmhouse, until Hell Gill Bridge is reached, spanning Hell Gill Beck. Turn right here onto the High Way, an ancient greenway. Almost immediately, the path divides and you should take the higher path.

In a few hundred metres, you will cross a stream which is the infant river Ure coming down from its source some 800 feet (242m) above you at Ure Head.

Over the next three miles, you will climb gently a further 300 feet (91m) only. For most of the way there is a wall immediately to your right. Do look over the wall from time to time for there are some wonderful views over the valley below. To the south you should be able to see Whernside and Ingleborough. The ruined buildings you pass at High Hall and High Dyke were inns when this was an important highway.

On reaching the highest point, you start your descent to the corner of a wood at Cotter End. Here there is a small limestone quarry and limekiln. There is a bench seat and this is a lovely secluded spot to take a break and admire the view over Hawes and the Wensleydale valley beyond. It is difficult to believe that the main road up the valley once came up this hill. Lady Anne Clifford's carriage and retinue of several hundred must have been quite a sight coming up the steep gradient in the 17th century on her way from Skipton to her castles in the Eden valley.

From the quarry, follow the wall-line downhill for about 400 metres until you reach a stile on the right, which you cross. The path ahead is indistinct, but you should make for the top edge of a wood which is shaped as a reversed L. Here there is a stile which you cross before making for another stile near the lower edge of the woodlands. A hollow-way now takes you down to the road.

Across the road, a sign points to Appersett 2½ miles. Follow a hollow-way uphill, and cross some undulating ground towards the bridge over Mossdale Beck at Mossdale Head. Mossdale Head was one of the places visited by Turner on his tour of 1816, and his watercolour of the falls may be seen in the Fitzwilliam Museum, Cambridge.

Pass to the left of the farm and follow the yellow marker posts across the fields down to the river's edge. In about two thirds of a mile, join a farmtrack and follow this towards the A684. Unless you wish to visit Cotter Force, which is up the beck opposite, do not go onto the road, but follow the footpath down the south side of the river. At a bend in the river, climb up into a small wood and follow the river down to Appersett.

If you wish to terminate your walk at Appersett, there is a space facing the green where a few cars may be parked. Otherwise, follow the small road along the east side of the Widdale Beck. Immediately after passing under a redundant railway viaduct, take the path on the left marked Ashes ¾. When you reach the A684 at Ashes, bear right and follow the road into Hawes.

Section 2: Hawes and Bainbridge circular

The first leg of this circular walk is over the fells to visit Semer Water, one of only two natural lakes in the Yorkshire Dales. On the way to Semer Water, a green road is crossed which was the Roman road to the fort at Bainbridge. The view looking down this road is regarded as one of the classic "Roman" views in England.

From Semer Water, the walk follows the River Bain, the shortest river in England, to Bainbridge. The return leg is along the north side of the valley.

Distance: 13 miles

Starting point: Hawes SD875898

Intermediate break point: Bainbridge, 8½ miles

Public transport: No public transport is required for the circular walk. If you wish to complete one leg only, between Hawes and Askrigg, there is a Postbus on weekdays and a Dalesbus at weekends in the summer.

Maps: 18.2 plus Outdoor Leisure 30 and Landranger 98.

Take the A684 out of Hawes towards the east. Just before leaving the town, take the footpath to the right marked Burtersett. The path is flagged all the way to Burtersett (in some places the flags are obscured by a covering of grass). The flags are an indication of the former industry of Burtersett, which was quarrying. In the fells above, the miners quarried a sandstone which cleaved well and could be made into paving slabs and roofing tiles. Chert, a glazing material used by the ceramics industry, was also mined.

In Burtersett, take the road uphill and after bearing right, follow the track marked Wether Fell 2m. This track climbs some 700 feet (212m) and as you climb higher, excellent views open up, not only of Hawes, Burtersett and Askrigg below, but also of more distant hills – Wild Boar Fell and Whernside to the west, and the North Yorkshire Moors on the far horizon in the east.

After passing a small hut, continue to climb upwards along a much used sunken hollow-way. When the track divides, almost at the crest of the hill, take the lesser track to the right. This will bring you in about 400 metres to the Roman road. Turn left here and follow the road down to the straight section. You can now look all the way down this magnificent straight road to the fort at Bainbridge, 4 miles away.

After only a very short distance along the Roman road, take the bridleway to the right marked BW Crag Side Road, which leads towards Countersett. The path crosses three walls. At the third, turn right and follow the footpath sign to Semer Water. As you come over the brow of the hill, there are excellent views over Raydale and Semer Water below.

The path goes directly down hill to Marsett. Marsett is the third village

The Roman road descending to Bainbridge

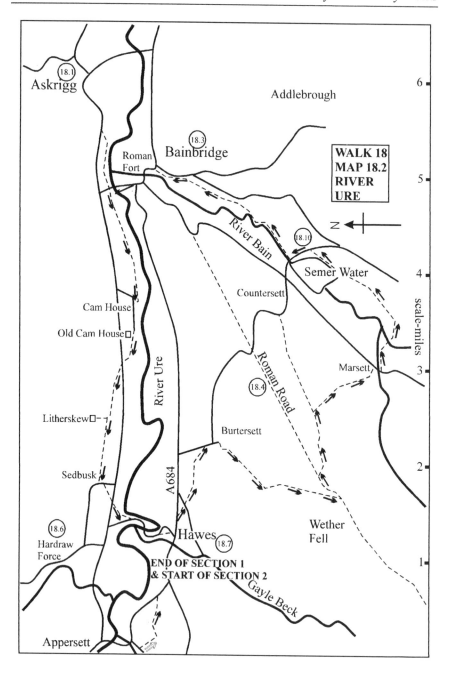

Askrigg

18.1

Addlebrough

6

18.3

Bainbridge

Roman
Fort

WALK 18
MAP 18.2
RIVER
URE

5

River Bain

N

18.10

Semer Water

4

Countersett

scale-miles

Cam House

Old Cam House

River Ure

Roman Road

Marsett

3

18.4

Litherskew

Burtersett

Sedbusk

A684

2

Wether
Fell

18.6

Hardraw
Force

18.7

Hawes

END OF SECTION 1
& START OF SECTION 2

1

Gayle Beck

Appersett

we have come across in this short walk with the suffix – "sett". "Saetr" is Norse for summer pasture, and suggests that the whole area was settled by people of Scandinavian origin in the 10th century.

On reaching Marsett, cross the beck and follow it downstream. Cross two footbridges and cross the old lake bed to the hillside. Bear left at a barn and follow the line of stiles towards Semer Water. Enter the Semer Water Nature Reserve just after passing the remains of a small chapel. The path goes along the edge of Semer Water, one of only two natural lakes in the Yorkshire Dales.

Follow the road to the bridge where the River Bain flows out of the lake. On the foreshore you will pass the Carlin Stone, a massive limestone glacial erratic which Turner painted on his tour of 1816. Follow the path along the slowly moving river Bain for approximately three quarters of a mile. Just after the path leaves it, the river flows in a wooded ravine below you. As you descend to Bainbridge there are good views of the site of the Roman fort below.

Go through the village, passing The Rose and Crown, to come to Yore Bridge. Here you take the path to the left (if you wish to finish your walk at Askrigg, take the path on the right). In a short distance, the path up the field goes onto the dismantled railway line. Follow this to Cam House. Here leave the track and proceed onto a small road to the right. Follow this to Old Cam House.

When the road bears right to Old Cam House, go across the cattle grid, but immediately turn left into the field. The exit from this field onto the road is at the other end of the field. Cross the road and follow the footpath sign towards Litherskew.

Just before Litherskew, join the track coming away from it to Sedbusk. At Sedbusk, bear left down the hill, but almost immediately take the footpath on the right which goes across the fields. Firstly, you go down to the road below, and then past a small packhorse bridge to the bridge over the River Ure. Cross this bridge (Haylands) and a short, flagged path across the field will take you towards Hawes.

Section 3: Askrigg to Aysgarth circular

This circular walk on the north side of the river has a high level section with excellent views over the valley, and a return leg along the valley bottom.

A Bronze Age stone circle is seen under Ivy Scar, and the 15th century Nappa Hall, just to the east of Askrigg, is one of the earliest examples of a domestic house in Yorkshire.

Distance: 10½ miles

Starting point: Askrigg church SD947910

Intermediate break point: Aysgarth, 5½ miles

Public transport: No public transport is required for the full circular walk. If you wish to complete one leg only of the walk between Askrigg and Aysgarth, there is a Postbus on weekdays, and a Dalesbus on summer weekends.

Maps: 18.3 plus Outdoor Leisure 30 and Landranger 98.

From the church, climb steeply out of Askrigg to the north. At the top of the first rise, follow the footpath sign to Newbiggin. Here, follow the road uphill. In the late spring and early summer, look out for early purple orchids on the verge at the right-hand side of the road. About 400 metres above Newbiggin, take the turning to the right, and at the brow of the hill follow the footpath sign, Bolton Castle 5¾.

This straight track along the terrace gives fine views over the valley below and Addlebrough opposite. Particularly striking is the Roman road coming down from Wether Fell to the fort at Bainbridge. As you progress along the hillside, it is worth looking back occasionally at the Roman road to catch the view when you are directly in line with this remarkably straight road.

About half a mile along the terrace, you will come to a building, Heugh, where the track divides. Take the track to the left, which climbs slightly before descending towards Woodhall. Just before Woodhall, take another track on the left. This climbs slightly before crossing the beck at the edge of Haw Bank Wood.

The track now traverses the long terrace under Ivy Scar which was settled in the Bronze Age. Under the Scar there is much evidence of former lead mining. Look out here for the beautiful, diminutive mountain pansies which grow well in poor soil conditions and are tolerant of lead contamination. To the left of the path there is a Bronze Age stone circle.

The land under the Scar is not enclosed, but when you reach the first wall, go through the gate and bear right. Follow the wall round to join a track which goes down over the escarpment towards Carperby. As you

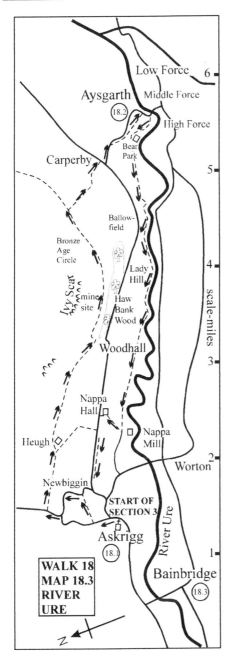

Low Force

Aysgarth Middle Force

18.2

High Force

Bear
Park

Carperby

Ballow-
field

Bronze
Age
Circle

Lady
Hill

Ivy Scar

mine
site

Haw
Bank
Wood

Woodhall

Nappa
Hall

Nappa
Mill

Heugh

Newbiggin

START OF
SECTION 3

Askrigg

18.1

WALK 18
MAP 18.3
RIVER
URE

Bainbridge

18.3

River Ure

Worton

scale-miles

descend, you will see on your left a mine opening. Gritstone roofing slates were mined here, and on the right of the track there is an enclosure with some very large slates which must have been left here when the mine closed.

At the bottom of the escarpment, the track goes away from the hillside. The walls here are typical of 17th/18th century enclosures, and there is a line of fine barns, built at the same time, stretching away towards Bolton Castle in the distance.

As the track begins to descend over the next escarpment, take the stile on the left and cross the field diagonally before descending into Carperby. From Carperby, take the road towards Aysgarth for a short distance before going into the field on the right. The path first follows the road closely, but leaves it when the road drops to the left towards the river. Head towards a small coppice surrounded by an iron fence, where you will find a stile.

Cross the next field and descend over the disused railway line to Aysgarth Bridge. At the bridge, you may wish to make a short diversion into Freeholders Wood, on the left, to visit the Middle Force, and Lower Force beyond. Middle Force, a waterfall of 16 feet (5m), is viewed from a special platform.

The path above the bridge leads to High Force, where there is a charge if you wish to approach the riverbank. From High Force, take the path towards Askrigg. This climbs upwards before meeting a dismantled railway line. The first section of the line is privately owned, and the path detours to the right around Bear Park.

When the path rejoins the railway, it initially skirts it on the right before eventually going onto the line for a short distance. Just before Ballowfield, take the track on the left which goes down to the riverbank.

Follow the riverbank for about a mile, passing the pronounced rounded drumlin on the right, Lady Hill, which in spring is a sea of blue-bells.

After leaving the riverbank, the path follows the former railway track to Nappa Mill. The path directly ahead at the mill is to Askrigg, but it would be a pity to miss the 15th century Nappa Hall, originally a peel tower and now a farm. To reach the hall, take the path on the right which goes diagonally back across the field you have just come through.

The path skirts the left of the hall and goes up to the road. Join the road only as far as the sign towards Nappa Scar, and then take the path onto the limestone terrace on your left. Follow the terrace for about half a mile to its end, before going back onto the road which will take you into Askrigg.

Section 4: Aysgarth to Jervaulx Abbey

This is mainly a riverbank walk, much of which is wooded, along both the River Ure and its tributary, the River Cover. Both rivers are crystal clear and there are a succession of attractive pools, rapids and waterfalls.

Between the two rivers, the delightful village of Middleham, with its castle and strong historical connections, is visited. The walk ends at the ruins of Jervaulx abbey.

Distance: 12 miles

Starting point: Aysgarth Falls, SE011886

Intermediate break point: Middleham, 8½ miles

Public transport: On Thursdays there is an early bus from Carperby (just to the north of Aysgarth) to Jervaulx, and a return bus in the afternoon (the Ripon to Hawes bus), allowing this section to be walked in reverse.

Maps: 18.4 and 18.5 plus Outdoor Leisure 30 (to Middleham), Landranger 98 and 99.

From the Falls, take the road uphill to the church. The path downriver starts in the churchyard. After a small wood, the path descends to the river and follows the rim of Lower Force before descending to river level.

Cross the Bishopdale Beck at Hestholme Bridge, and take the gate into the field on the left just after the bridge. The path passes to the left of a

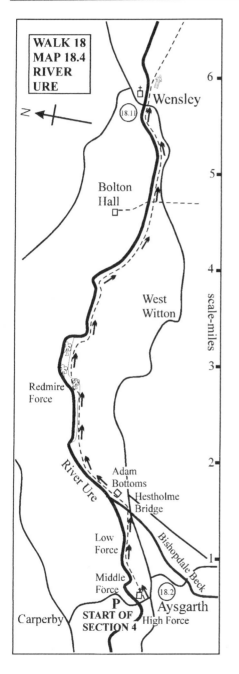

WALK 18
MAP 18.4
RIVER
URE

N

Wensley

18.1

Bolton
Hall

West
Witton

scale-miles

Redmire
Force

River Ure

Adam
Bottoms

Hestholme
Bridge

Low
Force

Bishopdale Beck

Middle
Force

18.2

Carperby

START OF
SECTION 4

P

Aysgarth
High Force

farmhouse at Adam Bottoms before reaching the River Ure. The river here has a delightful streamy character – a succession of pools and rapids.

In just over half a mile, the path comes to the edge of a strip of woodland above the river's edge. Several stiles invite you to go down to the river, but all are private until you reach a sign directing you into the wood. The path now takes you down to Redmire Force. Leaving the rim of the gorge, bear sharp right. From the Force, the path is in close proximity to the tree-lined riverbank, although not always directly adjacent to it.

Just over 2 miles after Redmire Force, you will cross an avenue going down to Bolton Hall and then enter a flower rich woodland which takes you to Wensley bridge in about another mile.

Crossing the road at the bridge, you will notice a distinct change in the scenery:

- the hilltops are now much lower,

- there are no longer tree belts along the riverbank,

- the walls of the upper valley have now largely given way to hedges.

It is clear that the river is now close to leaving the valley for the plain.

Follow the path down the riverbank, passing two small copses. When an ox bow is reached about 1½ miles below Wensley Bridge, the path leaves the riverbank to skirt a field. Immediately the river is rejoined, take the gate into the field on the right (not signposted) and climb the hill. At the top of the field, Middleham comes into view.

The paths are not well signed here, but you follow the gates towards Middleham, which you reach through the churchyard. Climb up the hill and cross the attractive square to the castle. It is well worth a visit. The path to the Cover is directly ahead from the castle, but if time allows, it is worth taking the short detour to the right to visit the motte and bailey which was the earliest fort at Middleham. From here there are good views down over the castle.

Return to the main path and climb the hill away from the castle before descending the hillside to the path along the River Cover. There is now a delightful woodland walk of about a mile down to Cover Bridge. Pass the Coverbridge Inn, where the beer garden beckons, and cross the bridge onto the path on the other side of the river. Shortly, the Cover joins the Ure and you follow the riverbank for about 1½ miles to Jervaulx Abbey. It is easy to see why the early monks, originally established at Fors in Upper Wensleydale, persuaded themselves to move to the richer living down the valley at Jervaulx.

Just down the main road to the left is a car park for the abbey (there is an entrance charge to the abbey). If you have resisted the

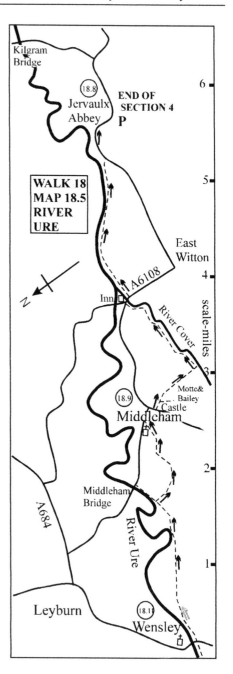

beer garden at Cover Bridge, further temptation awaits you at the car park in the form of a tea room.

Places of interest in Wensleydale

18.1 Askrigg

After Wensley had been devastated by plague in 1563, Askrigg took its place as the market town for upper Wensleydale. It maintained this position until Hawes superseded it when the first turnpike came through the valley in the 18th century.

The centre of this attractive town of mainly 17th and 18th century houses is the 12th century church. Here is the stepped market cross, and a bull ring set in the cobbles. Across the street is Skeldale House, used as the set for the TV series "All Creatures Great and Small". Up the gill behind the church are two fine waterfalls – Mill Gill Force and Whitfield Force.

Askrigg has given its name to one of the southern of the two geological blocks into which the northern Pennines is divided by the Stainmore pass. (The other is the Alston block.)

18.2 Aysgarth

A feature of Wensleydale is its many waterfalls. None is more famous than those at Aysgarth. The Great Scar Limestone is responsible for High Force, Middle Force and Low Force being at Aysgarth. This thick band of hard limestone, which is so visual a feature of more southerly dales (for example, Malham Cove and Kilnsey Crag), occurs in Wensleydale only in the valley floor between Appersett and Aysgarth.

In the 10 miles above Aysgarth, the river is unable to erode this hard rock, but when it meets the more vulnerable Yoredale series at Aysgarth, it produces several falls. In the two miles which include the three falls at Aysgarth and Redmire Force downstream, the Ure descends a third of the total height lost across the entire 30 miles length of the valley.

The village of Aysgarth is mainly 19th century, and is of little interest. The church, although itself mainly 19th century, is of a much older foundation and has some fine carved woodwork, said to have come from Easby Abbey in the 16th century.

Aysgarth Bridge, originally built for packhorses, was widened in 1784. The adjacent mill was built in the same year and has been put to a variety of uses. Once a supplier of tunics to Garibaldi's army, today it houses a museum of horse-drawn carriages.

18.3 Bainbridge

The Romans established a fort on the drumlin just to the east of the River

Bain in AD 80 during their campaign to conquer Brigantia. They remained there for 300 years.

The Normans had more leisurely objectives. The Lords of Middleham established 12 foresters at Bainbridge to administer the forest which stretched from Bainbridge to the Westmorland border in Mallerstang. The tradition of blowing a horn at 9 o'clock on winter nights dates from that period, and was to guide travellers stranded on the hills. During the summer months, the horn resides in The Rose and Crown, an inn which dates back to the 15th century.

Most of the houses which today line the attractive village green were built in the 18th and 19th centuries.

18.4 Bainbridge Roman road

The green road seen descending from Wether Fell to the Roman fort at Bainbridge was built by Agricola around AD 80 to supply his fort in the valley below. The road probably originated in Lancaster, although today we may only trace its route to Ingleton (where it is seen on the Doe/Twiss walk).

We know much about how the Romans built their roads, a complete surveyor's staff, or Groma, having been recovered from Pompeii. By projecting the line of the road coming down the fell backwards, and doing the same for the more southerly sections, it is possible to work out exactly where the Roman surveyors stood on Cam Fell and Dodd Fell when laying out the road.

As with other Roman roads, this road has probably been in continuous use for more than 1900 years. In medieval times it was known as Devil's Causeway, and in 1751 the route was adopted as part of the Richmond to Lancaster turnpike. However, in 1795 the turnpike was re-routed through Hawes, and the track up Wether Fell was relegated, first to being a minor road, and later to the delightful green road we see today.

What, one wonders, would the Roman surveyor who marked out his road from Dodd Fell have thought, had he known that his road would still be in use 1900 years later?

18.5 Bolton Castle

The building of this fortified manor house for Richard Scrope, Chancellor to Richard II, took 19 years from 1379. It is said to be the best preserved medieval castle in the country.

Mary Queen of Scots was held captive here in 1568/9 and her room may be seen in the south-west tower. She lived in some style, with a retinue of 40, but this was the beginning of a captivity which, 19 years later, was to lead to her execution.

The castle was held for the Crown during the Civil War, until it was starved into surrender in 1645. One of its corner towers was damaged in the fighting and later collapsed. There are magnificent views over Wensleydale from the roof.

Hardraw Force

There are many waterfalls in Wensleydale, both on the River Ure and its many tributaries. At 96 feet (29m), Hardraw Force is England's highest single drop waterfall. The glen through which the waterfall retreated makes a natural amphitheatre, and is the venue for an annual band concert.

The historian Whittaker recorded what must have been a remarkable sight in the winter of 1739/40. The waterfall froze as a hollow column of ice, the unfrozen water continuing to flow down the tube in the centre.

A fine painting of the waterfall was made by Turner in 1816 and is now in the Fitzwilliam Museum, Cambridge. Access to the waterfall is through The Green Dragon Inn, and a charge is made.

18.7 Hawes

Although Hawes was documented as far back as 1307 as Le Thouse (mountain pass), its development was held back for many centuries because of its position in the Norman forest of Wensleydale. It was only a growing packhorse trade which stimulated the granting of a market charter in 1700.

The re-routing of the Lancaster turnpike through Hawes in 1795, confirmed Hawes as the main market town of upper Wensleydale (The White Hart was a coaching inn). The town's growth increased rapidly when the railway arrived in 1878. Although nothing today survives of the industry, much of Lancashire was paved with stone quarried around Hawes and exported by rail.

With its attractive mixture of 17th, 18th and 19th century stone buildings, Hawes is today the main commercial and tourist centre of upper Wensleydale. Grouped together around the old railway station car park are the National Park Visitors' Centre, the Dales Countryside Museum and a rope factory (which is open to visitors). The museum contains a core of granite taken from Raydale in 1973. This rock, not seen anywhere on the surface in Wensleydale, is largely responsible for the stability of the Yoredale series. Its existence had been predicted before it was proved by drilling.

18.8 Jervaulx Abbey

Originally founded at Fors in upper Wensleydale (on the site of the present village of Grange), Jervaulx (Norman French for "Yore valley") moved to its present, more favourable site in 1156.

In common with other Cistercian foundations, Jervaulx's main wealth came from sheep. It owned considerable land in the lower valley, on the north side of the valley above Askrigg (known as Abbotside) and in other dales (for example, Studholme in Ribblesdale). At the Dissolution of the Monasteries, the Abbot joined the Pilgrimage of Grace. Although he took refuge on Witton Fell, he was hunted down and executed as an example to others who might be thinking of defying the king.

Jervaulx was much damaged at the Dissolution, and only in the chapter house are there substantial remains. Although the abbey is privately owned, there is public admission. Two former monastic activities are still of economic importance to Wensleydale today:

- the making of cheese (Wensleydale),
- the breeding and training of horses (Middleham).

18.9 Middleham

Middleham was originally a Saxon settlement, the middle village between East and West Witton. A Saxon princess, Alkeda, is said to have been martyred by the Danes in Middleham, and the church is dedicated to her.

Alan Rufus, Lord of Richmond, established a motte and bailey on William's Hill, and a century later a magnificent stone castle was built nearby. In the 13th century, Middleham came into the ownership of the Nevilles of Raby Castle through marriage. Over the next two centuries, Middleham became one of the major centres of power in England, being known as the "Windsor of the North".

When the Earl of Warwick, the last of the Nevilles, died in battle in 1471, Richard of Gloucester inherited Middleham through his wife. He became Richard III in 1483. Although cast as a villain by Shakespeare, Richard was a popular figure in the north.

Although Middleham became a market town in 1389, it later failed to compete with other towns and the market was lost. However, during the period of the droving trade, Low Moor, just to the west of Middleham, was one of the greatest of the northern cattle fairs.

Its Georgian houses today give Middleham the aire of a town rather than the village its population of 600 would suggest. Its business is now the training of race horses, an activity which traces its origins back to the monks of Jervaulx abbey.

18.10 Semer Water

This 90 acre lake in Raydale is one of only two of the many post-glacial lakes in the dales to have survived to the present time. The other is Malham Tarn. Raydale was blocked by a moraine and the River Bain, England's shortest river at two miles in length, flows through this glacial debris to its confluence with the Ure at Bainbridge.

The Carlin Stone, an enormous limestone glacial erratic, sits on the foreshore, and is in the foreground of Turner's painting of 1816 – now in the British Museum.

An ancient legend which tells of a sunken city beneath Semer Water may have some basis in fact. When the water level was reduced in 1937 to recover a strip of land, a piled timber structure was uncovered which turned out to be from the Iron Age. Other Bronze Age and Iron Age artefacts have also been found close by.

18.11 Wensley

For about 100 years from 1202, this tranquil village was the only market town in the dale, and as a result gave its name to the valley.

It suffered particularly badly from the plague in 1563, and never managed to regain its former pre-eminent position.

The church is particularly fine. Although the earliest building fabric is of the 1240s, there are two pre-conquest grave stones which have Anglian inscriptions – Donfrid and Eadberehct. Other interesting artefacts include 14th century wall paintings, 14th century brass, choir stalls of 1527 and an oak screen saved from Easby Abbey at the Dissolution of the Monasteries.

Walk 19: River Wear

Section 1: St John's Chapel to Stanhope, 12 miles
Section 2: Stanhope to Wolsingham, 7 miles
Section 3: Wolsingham to Witton-le-Wear circular, 15 miles
Information Centres: Stanhope: 01388 527650; Bishop: Auckland 01388 604922

Although there is a long distance walk, the Weardale Way, between the source of the river and the sea, not all parts of the walk are of equal merit. In my view, the best walking lies between St John's Chapel and Witton-le-Wear, and the three walks described in this book lie between these two towns. Only the first section confines itself to the Weardale Way, the other two sections deviating considerably from the long distance walk, mainly to take in more riverbank walking.

The regular bus service up the valley is very useful as a means of getting between the starting and end points of the first two sections, and makes it easy to plan these linear walks.

Sadly, the most interesting historical sites in Weardale – Durham (Cathedral), Bishop Auckland (Castle and Binchester Roman fort) and Escomb (rare Anglo-Saxon church) do not coincide with the most interesting walking. They have not been included in the walks described, although they are referenced in the Places of Interest at the end of the walk description.

Section 1: St John's Chapel to Stanhope

This walk, on the north side of the valley, combines sections across open moorland and paths down tributary streams. There is much evidence of former lead mining activity and the Middle Hope Burn is particularly floriferous.

At the side of the road in Eastgate there is a replica Roman altar, found near Rookhope Burn, which shows that the Romans hunted in Weardale.

Distance: 12 miles

Starting point: St John's Chapel, NY885380

Public transport: There is a regular bus service between Stanhope and St John's Chapel.

Maps: 19.1 plus Landranger 87 and 92, and Outdoor Leisure 31.

From the A689, take the lane down the east side of the tributary stream. Cross the stream and then take the footpath down to the footbridge over the river Wear.

Cross the meadows and climb the hill. Cross one road, and at the second, turn right. Across the other side of the valley you should be able to see the road climbing the hillside on its way to Langdon Beck in Teesdale.

Follow the road, which keeps to an almost constant level, passing several farmhouses, to the end in about a mile. Here take the track on the left, which you follow for about half a mile before following the sign on the right which reads Middle Hope Mine ½ mile.

Cross the Middle Hope Burn. Here there is much evidence of former mining activity. Follow the burn downstream. There is a series of pools as the burn goes down to Westgate, and this tributary valley is very floriferous. If in the right season, expect to see flowers which are tolerant of lead – spring sandwort, thyme and mountain pansy – together with orchids, cranesbill and ragged robin.

As you approach Westgate, you will meet a road. Do not go into the village, but turn left here, climbing steeply for about 300 feet (91m) before leaving on the lane to the right. The path now zigzags up the hillside to Heights Pasture. When you reach the pasture, make towards the top edge of a small wood which you should be able to see on the skyline.

The first stile is reached after going round the edge of a new wood, and the hilltop is reached at a stile which is midway between the wood and the field boundary on the left. From this high point, there are good views looking down over the Wear valley, and ahead you should be able to see the line of a dismantled railway. Make for this railway, aiming to join it at the point where the curve joins a straight section.

Follow the line of the railway for about a mile (about half a mile before Rookhope). Here you take the footpath into the field on the right. At the

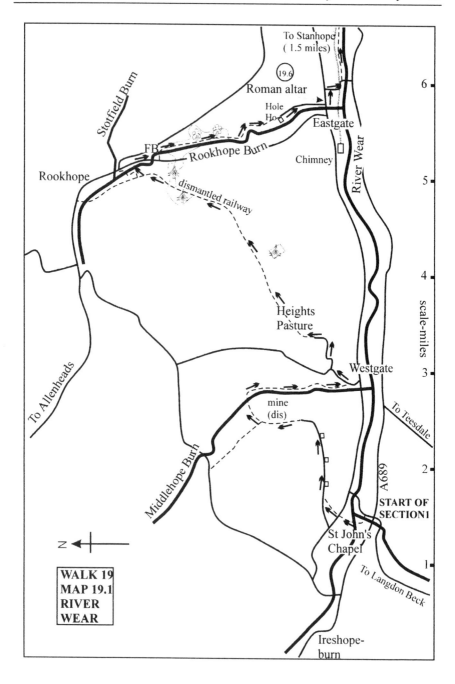

To Stanhope
(1.5 miles)

19.6

Roman altar

Hole
Ho

Eastgate

Stotfield Burn

FB

Rookhope Burn

Rookhope

Chimney

River Wear

dismantled railway

6

5

4

scale-miles

Heights
Pasture

Westgate

3

To Allenheads

To Teesdale

mine
(dis)

Middlehope Burn

A689

2

START OF
SECTION1

z

St John's
Chapel

WALK 19
MAP 19.1
RIVER
WEAR

To Langdon Beck

1

Ireshope-
burn

bottom of the field, follow the wall-line to the left before passing to the right of a derelict cottage. Cross the burn and go along the side of a cemetery to reach the Rookhope road at Stotfield Burn.

Turn right here and follow the road until, just after crossing the Rookhope Burn, you take the footpath on the left, which goes over a footbridge (signed Eastgate 2 miles). The path follows the burn until it reaches a river meadow. Here it climbs almost to the top of the hillside before descending to Hole House.

When you reach Eastgate, turn left onto the A689 where you will see a replica of a Roman altar found 300 metres to the north, near Rookhope Burn in 1869.

Take the first road on the right towards the river, and follow the path between the railway and the riverbank towards Stanhope. One of the advantages of walking the Weardale Way in this direction is that you are walking away from the 300 feet (91m) cement works chimney on this section!

Just before reaching Stanhope, you will cross the railway and pass a bridge. Notice that the west side of this bridge is of the ribbed arch monastic design, showing that it was built before about 1600. At the bridge, you will also see that the river has cut down to an exposure of the whinsill, the igneous intrusion which lies under much of the northern Pennines. The only exposure in Weardale is here, and you will see a disused quarry over the road, where the rock was mined.

Section 2: Stanhope to Wolsingham

The first part of this section follows the Weardale Way as it climbs across the south side of the valley from Stanhope to Bollihope Burn.

In preference to the higher route which the Weardale Way then takes, this walk follow the Bollihope Burn down to the River Wear, where there is an excellent walk along the riverside meadows to Wolsingham.

Distance: 7 miles

Starting point: Stanhope Market Place, NY996393

Public transport: There is a regular bus service between Stanhope and Wolsingham.

Maps: 19.2 plus Outdoor Leisure 31 and Landranger 92.

At your starting point in the Market Place, notice in the churchyard wall the magnificent fossilised stump of a tree which lived some 250 million years ago. Take the road at the east end of the Market Place towards the river, and then follow the path downstream along the riverbank.

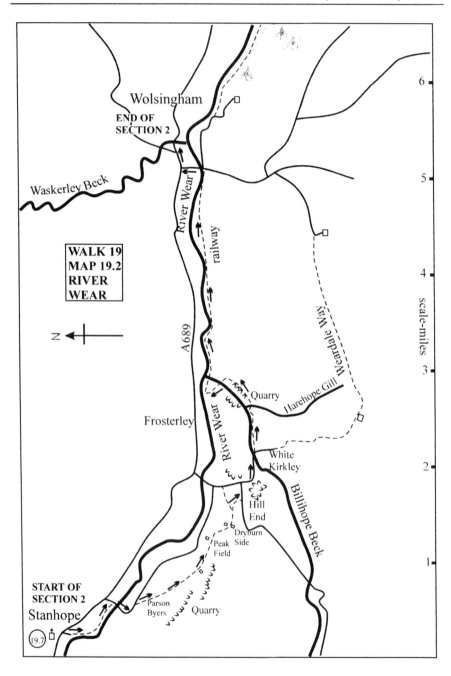

Wolsingham

END OF
SECTION 2

Waskerley Beck

River Wear

railway

WALK 19
MAP 19.2
RIVER
WEAR

N

A689

Weardale Way

Harehope Gill

Quarry

Frosterley

River Wear

White
Kirkley

Billhope Beck

Hill
End

Dryburn
Peak Side
Field

START OF
SECTION 2

Stanhope

Parson
Byers

Quarry

19.7

6

5

4

scale-miles

3

2

1

When you reach the road bridge, cross the river and follow the road for a short distance until you reach a row of cottages on the left. Here take the path on the right, which climbs diagonally up the hill to Parson Byers. From Parson Byers, pass through several gates to reach a large field with a single tree at its centre. Leave the track across the field, climbing diagonally upwards to the top wall. When you are about level with the single tree below, you will find an exit into the next field.

The path ahead descends to cross a small steam before climbing to the bottom of a quarry spoil heap and a derelict building (deserted at the beginning of the 20th century when the farmhouse moved to the valley bottom). Proceed along the hillside and cross a meadow to a small stream. Follow the stream and pass about 50 metres to the right of the farm buildings at Peak Field.

Cross the stream. In the second field after the farm, climb diagonally upwards across the meadow to the buildings at Dryburn Side. Go through the gate just above the lowest of the buildings, and follow the track, which climbs steeply upwards to the hamlet of Hill End. On reaching Hill End, bear left downhill. At the T-junction, bear right and follow the road through Low Bishopley.

As you cross the Bollihope Burn, the Weardale Way follows the road ahead, but you should go through the gate on the left and follow the burn downstream. The burn is attractive, with deep pools in the limestone gorge.

When you reach Harehope Gill, the track is forced away from the riverbank up to a crossing of the gill. The path now passes along the top rim of a large, attractive, disused limestone quarry of impressive dimensions. The flatness of the quarry floor shows how well bedded is the limestone, and in places you can see where large blocks had been broken away from the floor, but never further processed.

At the end of the quarry, bear left onto the track which you follow down to the river. There is now a most pleasant 2½ mile walk along the valley bottom to Wolsingham, sometimes adjacent to the river, sometimes next to the railway line. The river itself is clear, fast flowing and most attractive.

As you approach Wolsingham, do not go through the white gate at the river's edge, but rather the gate adjacent to the railway line. The road across the river will take you to the centre of Wolsingham.

Section 3: Wolsingham to Witton-le-Wear circular

One of the finest stretches of the Wear valley lies between Wolsingham and Witton-le-Wear. As the public transport between Wolsingham and Bishop Auckland does not follow the valley bottom, the walk described is circular.

Distance: 15 miles

Starting point: Wolsingham Square NZ075373

Public transport: Not available.

Maps: 19.3 plus Landranger 92.

The way to the river bridge starts just to the east of The Square in Wolsingham. After crossing the bridge, take the lane on the left. At a T-junction bear right, and crossing the railway line, follow the lane until it swings to the right. Here follow the yellow waymarkers into the field on the left.

Follow the bottom of the fields until the path goes into the woodland adjacent to the river. There is now a most attractive section through deciduous trees at the river's edge. As the deciduous trees give way to a mixture of conifer and deciduous woodland, the track climbs away from the river up into Black Bank Plantation.

Pass a house on your right, at the edge of the wood, and bear left at the track above. Ignore a track on the left going down to Black Bank House and follow the track as it turns right through 180 degrees. Now take the track on your left and follow this to the edge of the wood, where it turns sharply to the right. At the next sharp right turn (back into the woods), take the stile on the left before following the wall-line.

(Some sections of the plantation are being felled and others replanted. In future the wood may look different, but the tracks should remain as described. There are no waymarkers in the plantation.)

The pasture here is scrub. At the end of the field there is a dense thicket of silver birch. Go though the gate at the end of the field and bear left onto the track which descends the hillside. There are good views down the valley from here. In early summer the meadow is a blaze of buttercups, and the silence is broken only by the calls of curlew, plover and cuckoo.

When you reach Monkfield, bear left following the waymarker which you will find between the two sets of buildings. Follow the edge of the field to its bottom left-hand corner, where there is a path to the footbridge over the river.

After the bridge, the path follows the river upstream for a short distance before bearing right across the railway line to Low Harperley. Bear right at Low Harperley, a fine 18th century building with mullioned windows, and follow the track towards the police training centre at Harperley Hall.

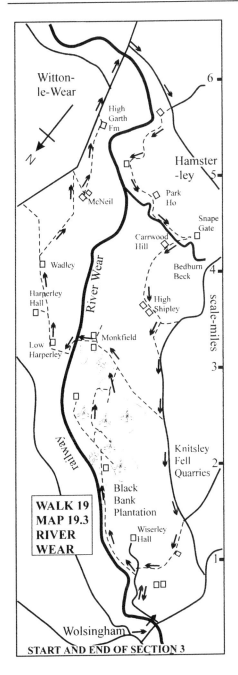

WALK 19
MAP 19.3
RIVER
WEAR

START AND END OF SECTION 3

As the track bears left, just before the hall, your path carries straight on in front of the hall, making towards the top edge of a strip of woodland which marks a gorge.

The stile near the top end of the woods leads to a footbridge. Emerging from the wood, follow the edge of the field to the farm ahead (Wadley). Pass to the left of Wadley. About 100 metres after a small stream, take the stile on the right and head for the large tree two fields away on the skyline.

After the tree, there are good views looking back up the valley and across the valley to Hamsterley Forest. Although the map shows a path directly ahead to the farm at McNeil, this is best avoided as one of the fields is very hard going when there are standing crops. Instead, follow the track up to the main road, and then double back down the farmtrack leading to McNeil.

As you approach McNeil, just after the friendly advice to beware of the dog, and just before the house on the left, go through the gate on the left (unsigned). The path now follows the hillside to Witton-le-Wear. If you do as I did and follow the wrong sheeptrack too high up the hillside, you will have some difficulty getting down to the correct path which is below a fence. In just over half a mile after McNeil, you will pass High Garth Farm. Follow the farm road up to the main road.

You must now follow the main road down to and over the river, a distance of just over half a mile. Although the road is busy and is not ideal walking, the verge is broad, and you should be able to get it behind you quickly. After the river take the minor and quieter road on the right, and follow this for about three quarters of a mile to a cross roads. Take the road on the right marked Park House 1 mile.

At Park House the road becomes private for a short distance, and you take the path which starts at the white gate on the right. There is now a pleasing stretch following the Bedburn Beck. Pass a bridge over the beck marked private, and just before Snape Gate, cross the stile in the corner of the field into the woods. Some care is now needed in choosing the right path. The most used path goes down a cul-de-sac to a bend in the beck. You should take a lesser track on the right which goes through a conifer wood to a footbridge.

When you cross the stile out of the wood, make for the farm on the right (Carrwood Hill). Go around the left-hand side of Carrwood Hill and through the gate which leads to the path climbing directly uphill. Follow the track through High Shipley, and when it bears left downhill to the road, cut the corner by bearing right at the bend. Go through the gate into the next field, and then make for the top left-hand corner of the field. Here you will find a gate onto the road.

Follow the road across Knitsley Fell, with its many disused quarries, for just over a mile. When you reach a road on the left coming up from Bedburn, take the field path on your right directly opposite this road.

Follow the path down to a derelict cottage where you will pick up a track going downhill. Do not take the track which goes to the hamlet on the left, but follow the waymarkers downhill. Bear left when you meet the track from Wiserely Hall, and this will take you back to Wolsingham.

Places of interest in the Wear valley

19.1 Auckland Castle, Bishop Auckland

Auckland Castle has been the main country residence of the Bishops of Durham since Norman times, but became the Bishop's principal residence in the 19th century when the residence in Durham was given to the university.

The Chapel (said to be the largest private chapel in Europe), the State rooms and Throne room of the castle are open to the public.

19.2 Binchester Roman fort

One and a half miles north of Bishop Auckland are the remains of Binchester, a Roman fort built to control a river crossing of Dere Street, the supply route to the north. Because of its strategic importance, Binchester was manned throughout the Roman occupation of Britain.

The fort has been partly excavated (the excavations continue) and the military baths are the best to be seen in Britain. Finds from the fort may be seen at the Bowes Museum, Barnard Castle.

Escomb Church

The Anglo-Saxon church at Escomb is thought to have been built around AD 680 with material taken from the Roman cavalry fort at Binchester. A number of stones in the walls have clearly identifiable Roman inscriptions, and the chancel arch is thought to be a reassembled Roman archway. The church somehow survived the attentions of the Danes, and is regarded as one of the finest and least changed examples of an Anglo-Saxon building in the country. .

The village in which the church is situated is unprepossessing, but there is a pub next to the church which, conveniently for walkers, has outdoor tables.

Anglo-Saxon church at Escomb

19.4 Durham

On a promontory above the Wear, Durham Cathedral provides one of England's best known skylines. Most of Durham's interest lies in the area around the Cathedral, and is ideally suited to exploration on foot.

In addition to its imposing position, Durham Cathedral is perhaps

England's finest Norman building. It is often thought that English Cathedrals merely ape French designs, but a feature introduced by its architect makes Durham a major landmark in European architecture.

Early Norman cathedrals have barrel roofs, a feature inherited from Roman designs (what we call Norman architecture should be called Romanesque), and one which precludes the introduction of light at roof level. By replacing the barrel roof with ceiling vaults suspended on ribs, the Durham architect was able not only to make a significant reduction in building weight, but also to luminate the building by introducing windows at roof level. Durham, therefore, stands at an important transition between Romanesque architecture and the more elegant Gothic designs which were to follow. The natural extension of the ribbed roof concept introduced at Durham was eventually to be the glorious Perpendicular churches, such as King's College, Cambridge, where the whole church becomes a rib cage, allowing the solid walls to be replaced by glass.

Durham's patron saint is St Cuthbert, a 7th century Bishop of Hexham, who retired to a contemplative life on Lindisfarne. During the Danish raids, the monks of Lindisfarne carried St Cuthbert's body around Northumberland. Only after 250 years on the move were the remains finally brought to Durham and placed behind the altar.

In medieval times, the Bishops of Durham, in addition to their religious powers, wielded enormous civil powers throughout the Palatinate of Durham – the area between the Tees and the Scottish border. This included the raising of armies and the minting of coins. Successive Kings found Bishops of Durham more reliable than other northern Lords who were often tempted to found powerful dynasties and attempt to seize the Crown (or the Scottish Crown). Being celibate, the Bishops were unable to found dynasties!

Durham Castle, which is adjacent to the Cathedral, last saw siege during the Civil War, when it was held for the Crown. After being the official residence of the Bishops of Durham, it became part of Durham University in the 19th century.

19.5 Killhope Mine

Between 1853 and 1910, Killhope, at the head of Weardale, was one of Britain's richest lead mines. The waterwheel, crushing mill and washing floor have been restored and opened to the public, but perhaps the most important feature of the site is the Visitors' Centre. Here, a collection of personal correspondence gives a vivid presentation of the life of families involved in the lead mining industry in 19th century Britain.

19.6 Roman altars dedicated to Silvanus

Weardale was clearly a favourite hunting area in Roman times, two altars having been found dedicated to Silvanus the God of hunting.

A replica of one of the altars is to be seen by the side of the road at the east side of East Gate (the original is in the Durham University Museum). Another altar dedicated to Silvanus was found in 1747 on the Bollihope moors, and celebrates the capture by Gaius Tetius Macarius, prefect of a cavalry regiment, of an enormous bear. This is now in the Stanhope parish church.

9.7 Stanhope

Although Weardale is not in general noted for its prehistoric artefacts, in 1859 a quite exceptional find was made in Heather Burn Cave (989415), about two miles north of Stanhope on a tributary of the Stanhope Burn. The possessions of a wealthy Bronze Age family were found. They appeared to have inhabited the cave for a considerable period before perishing in a flood which scattered their remains over the cave floor. Among the finds were:

* human bones and the bones of beef, mutton and game;
* parts of a four-wheeled horse drawn cart;
* a bronze bucket, gold ring and bracelet;
* a mould and tongues for the making of bronze axes.

Sadly, the cave was destroyed, but the artefacts are to be seen in the British Museum as the Heather Burn Collection.

Although Stanhope lost the Heather Burn Collection to the British Museum, it has a fine 250 million year old fossilised tree found near Edmondbyers Cross, which is now incorporated into the Stanhope churchyard wall.

Stanhope Church is itself of the 13th century, and has some medieval glass in the west window. The river bridge at the west of Stanhope is 15th century, widened in 1792. The older portion may be identified by the arch ribbing under the west side of the bridge.

Walk 20: River Wharfe

Section 1: Buckden to Littondale circular, 14 miles

Section 2: Buckden to Grassington, 10½ miles

Section 3: Grassington to Bolton Abbey, 10 miles

Section 4: Bolton Priory and Bolton Bridge circular, 2 miles

Section 5: Bolton Bridge and Addingham circular, 5½ miles

Section 6: Addingham and Ilkley circular, 7 miles

Information Centres: Grassington 01756 752774; Ilkley 01943 602319

With its lovely river, limestone terraces and villages, upper Wharfedale is the very essence of a Yorkshire Dale. At Burnsall, the river flows out of the limestone and into gritstone. Although quite different in character from the upper valley, the gritstone valley between Burnsall and Ilkley would be considered by many to be the equal of its limestone counterpart.

Wharfedale has been continuously occupied since the Bronze Age and, for those with an eye for past times, there is much to see:

* Bronze Age cup-and-ring markings on Ilkley Moor (and in the Ilkley Museum), and Bronze Age stone circle at Yockenthwaite;

* the outline of Iron Age settlements on the limestone terraces in upper Wharfedale;

* a Roman fort at Ilkley (artefacts from the fort may be seen in the adjacent museum);

* Anglo-Saxon and Viking stone carvings in the churches at Burnsall and Ilkley;

* strip lynchets where early medieval arable farming was practised;

* Bolton Priory, one of the monastic foundations which dominated the economy of the Pennines until the Dissolution of the Monasteries;

* the 17th and 18th century field barns and dry stone walls which were built when the pastoral farming displaced arable farming, and which today are the hallmark of the Dales.

The walks described are in six sections and cover the whole valley between Beckermonds and Ilkley. Because of the tremendous variety of both river-bank and hilltop walking, I have made four of the six sections into circular walks. You could, of course, make quicker progress down the valley by linking together adjoining segments of the circular walks.

Section 1: Buckden to Littondale circular

A strenuous, but very satisfying way to reach the source of the Wharfe from the highest car park in Wharfedale (Buckden) is to take the circular walk which crosses over to Littondale before returning to the Wharfe at Beckermonds.

The walk requires two climbs to 2000 feet (over 600m), but the reward is some superb hilltop views. A Celtic settlement is passed in Littondale, and a small Bronze Age circle at Yockenthwaite. Hubberholme Church has a rare rood loft.

Distance: 14 miles

Starting point: Buckden car park SD942774

Maps: 20.1 plus Outdoor Leisure 30 and Landranger 98.

From the car park in Buckden, cross the road and take the minor road past the 17th century Manor House to the river. Cross the bridge, and just before the road reaches the side of the valley, take the track on the left which climbs steeply up the hillside between ashwoods. (You are now on the corpse way, used in medieval times to carry the dead from the upper Wharfe down to Arncliffe for burial.)

From the top of the woodland, there are good views looking back towards Buckden. The track climbing diagonally from the car park in Buckden is a Roman road established by Agricola in the AD 80s when conquering northern England. Above the woodlands, take the path which leaves the track on the right, following a line of blue-topped posts. This climbs over Birks Fell to Old Cote Moor.

The hilltop is flat and, initially, the views are unremarkable. However, when you reach the edge of the hillside above Littondale, there is a wonderful panorama. You should be able to see:

• Rylstone Fells (just above Skipton),

• Pendle Hill (in the Ribble valley),

• Fountains Fell,

• Penyghent,

• Whernside.

As you descend towards Littondale, you will cross undulating terraces of Yoredale rocks – repeated sequences of gritstone, limestone and shale. It is noticeable how much poorer the drainage is on this side of the valley, supporting only reeds, heather and peat. The limestone scar on the other side of Littondale is well drained and supports short green grass. In early summer the meadows in the valley below are a sea of yellow buttercups.

In Litton, pass the pub and take the path down to and over the river. At

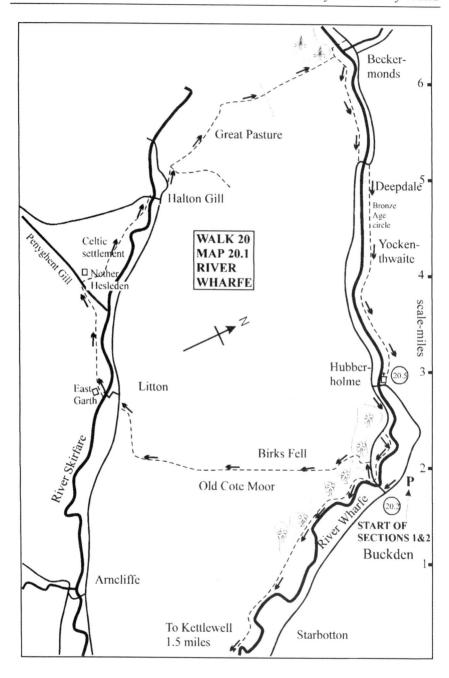

Beecker-
monds

6

Great Pasture

5
Deepdale

Bronze
Age
circle

Halton Gill

Yocken-
thwaite

4

Celtic
settlement

**WALK 20
MAP 20.1
RIVER
WHARFE**

□ Nether
Hesleden

Penyghent Gill

N

scale-miles

Hubber-
holme

20.5   3

East □
Garth

Litton

River Skirfare

Birks Fell

2

Old Cote Moor

P

20.2

River Wharfe

**START OF
SECTIONS 1&2**

Buckden

1

Arncliffe

To Kettlewell
1.5 miles

Starbotton

East Garth, a path takes you up the valley to Nether Heslenden, where you cross the Penyghent Gill. ("Heslenden" is Old English for "hazel valley") Follow the path signed to Foxup and Cosh.

The name Penyghent is Celtic, and in the second field after Nether Heslenden, earth mounds in the field to the left (just under the hillside) are the remains of a Celtic settlement and field system.

Halton Gill is reached in just under a mile from Nether Heslenden. At the west end of the hamlet, take the track which climbs steeply upwards. This was an old packhorse route from the Ribble (Stainforth) to Yockenthwaite and Beckermonds. Leave the main track at the first bend and follow the footpath which crosses Great Pasture. In just under a mile, the path bears sharp right just after a small stream, climbing steeply to a wall at the crest of the hill.

There is a stile in this wall, but because the track is indistinct, you may reach the wall at a point other than the stile. Many footprints along the line of the wall show that finding this stile can be a problem! As a bearing, use the wall-line coming up from the edge of the wood at Beckermonds. The stile is about 400 metres to the right of the intersection of this wall-line and the hilltop wall. Ingleborough and the top of the quarries in Ribblesdale are visible, and on a clear day you should be able to see the Langdales, 40 miles away in the Lake District.

After the stile, follow the path down to Beckermonds where the Oughtershaw and Green Field Becks meet to become the Wharfe. Do not cross the river, but follow the Dales Way downstream. The riverbed here comprises horizontal limestone strata and in summer has a habit of disappearing underground for short distances. The water is clear and you will see trout darting for cover as you approach their pools. Two of my favourite flowers are to be seen in profusion here in early summer. They are the bird's eye primrose and common butterwort, a delicate, blue- flowered, insectivorous plant (the name reflects the flower's ancient usage as a butter preservative).

In just over a mile from Beckermonds, cross to the other side of the river at Deepdale Bridge, and in a further half mile the path passes a small Bronze Age circle. Yockenthwaite is about half a mile beyond the circle, and a further 1½ miles brings you to Hubberholme with its interesting church.

Cross the bridge at Hubberholme, and follow the road for about half a mile before taking the path which leads along the riverbank to Buckden.

Section 2: Buckden to Grassington

This walk comprises two distinct parts. The first part is to Kettlewell along the riverbank, with woodlands of an old estate clothing the bottom of the hillside.

The second part, from Kettlewell to Grassington, is over stark but attractive limestone terraces. The elevation here gives good views over the glacial U-shaped valleys of Wharfedale and Littondale below.

Just before entering Grassington, the walk passes the sites of Celtic and medieval settlements.

Distance: 10½ miles

Starting point: Buckden car park SD942774

Intermediate break point: Kettlewell, 4½ miles

Public transport: There is a morning bus on Mondays and Fridays from Grassington to Buckden.

Maps: 20.1 and 20.2 plus Outdoor Leisure 10 and Landranger 98. (These maps omit the short section between Starbotton and Kettlewell which is straightforward.)

From the car park, cross the main road and go down the small road to the river. Just over the bridge, the path down the valley is on the left. The lower hillside on the right of the footpath is wooded, being part of a former estate but now belonging to the National Trust.

Starbotton, on the other side of the river, which is passed about halfway to Kettlewell, had to be almost totally rebuilt after a disastrous flash flood in 1686.

In Kettlewell, take the lane along the south side of the beck. At the top of the village, a path leads into the fields on the right. The fields here are very narrow so the stiles come thick and fast. The path leads onto the road to Conistone, but you stay on this only until just after Scargill House, where you take the path on the left, Highgate Leys Lane. When the lane reaches the top of the wood, turn right to walk along the limestone terraces (the footpath is not signed). The field boundaries are now very widely spaced.

After just over a mile, you come to a small hillock to the right, topped with a cairn, Conistone Pie. From the cairn there are excellent views of:

- Wharfedale and Littondale below;

- Mastiles Lane, the medieval monastic road from Malham which may be seen descending to Kilnsey, where the monks of Fountains Abbey sheared their sheep;

- the overhanging limestone scar at Kilnsey Crag which is a dominant feature.

The Wharfe near Beckermonds

Shortly after Conistone Pie the path deviates slightly when it crosses a path coming up from Conistone below. On the terrace edge to your right, just after passing the path from Conistone, there are faint outlines of Celtic hut and field systems. Grassington is now about 2½ miles further down the path. On the way to Grassington you pass over Lea Green, the site of Celtic settlements, and just before Grassington, the site of a medieval village.

The first building you reach on the outskirts of Grassington is Town Head Farm with its two storied porch, mullioned windows and hood mouldings. The farm belongs to the trustees of Fountaines Hospital in Linton, the rent going towards the upkeep of the almshouse.

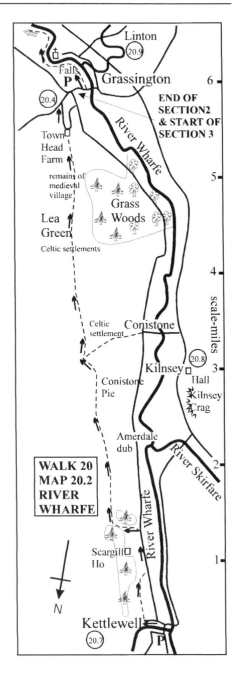

Section 3: Grassington to Bolton Abbey

The riverbanks between Grassinton and Bolton Abbey are accessible to the motorist and are, therefore, popular with walkers. The top half of the walk is typical limestone countryside, but gritstone is reached at Burnsall and the hillsides then become more rounded and wooded.

Geological features seen on the walk include:

* the Craven Fault at Linton Falls,
* reef knolls, just south of Burnsall,
* the strid, a narrow gorge through which the river flows.

Places of general interest include:

* Burnsall, an attractive mainly 17th and 18th century village with Anglo-Saxon and Danish artefacts in the church;
* Barden Tower, one of the many Clifford castles;
* the ruined Augustinian Bolton Priory.

Distance: 10 miles

Starting point: Grassington centre, SE003638

Intermediate breakpoint: Burnsall 3½ miles, Strid Wood 8 miles.

Public transport: On Tuesdays, Saturdays and Sundays in the peak summer season, there is a bus from Bolton Abbey to Grassington.

Maps: 20.2 and 20.3 plus Outdoor Leisure 10, Landranger 98 and 104.

From the centre of Grassington, go down to the river. Just before the bridge, take the path to the left. The bridge was originally a packhorse bridge, and has been widened and flattened. If you look under the arches you will see evidence of some of these modifications.

Pass a weir and you will reach a footbridge at Linton Falls, where the river flows over the Craven Fault. The falls are very impressive when the river is in flood. There are houses here now, but until the 1950s there was a working mill.

Beyond the falls you will come to Linton Church, thought to be built on an earlier pagan site. The church serves Grassington, Threshfield and Hebden as well as Linton. Another 1½ miles brings you to a suspension bridge which you cross. Follow the riverbank down to Burnsall. Cross the 17th century Burnsall Bridge, and take the path to the right down the river. In front of you is Kail Hill, the last of the line of reef knolls stretching across Craven. The path crosses a footbridge and skirts Kail Hill before passing below the village of Appletreewick.

When Fir Beck is reached, the path is diverted away from the riverbank to the road. However, immediately after the bridge, the path follows the beck down to rejoin the river. Barden Bridge is now just over a mile downstream. Just before the bridge, there is a path between the road and the river. Erosion has caused the path to collapse. Ignore the path and follow the road.

Here you may wish to cross the bridge to see Barden Tower, one of the many castles which belonged to the Cliffords of Skipton. Follow the path down the east side of the river to a Gothic structure spanning the river. This is an aqueduct taking water from Nidderdale to Bradford.

You may now proceed down either side of the river, but the path down the west side gives the better access to the Strid. You may climb down the bank to view the Strid, but do remember that over the centuries many people have been drowned here.

The Strid Wood brings you to the Devonshire Pavilion which serves refreshments. Cross the footbridge and in another mile you will come to the ruins of the Augustinian Bolton Priory and its car park, beyond.

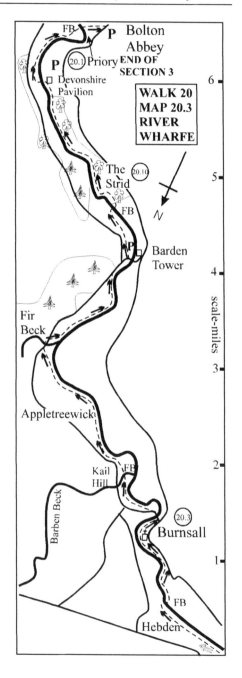

Bolton Abbey
END OF SECTION 3
P (20.1) Priory
Devonshire Pavilion

WALK 20
MAP 20.3
RIVER
WHARFE

6

The Strid (20.10)

FB

N

5

Barden Tower

4

scale-miles

Fir Beck

3

Appletreewick

Kail Hill

FB

2

Barben Beck

(20.3)
Burnsall

1

FB

Hebden

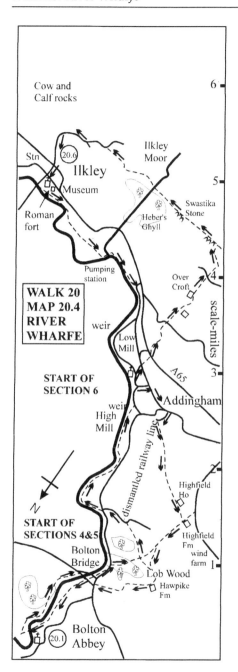

Section 4: Bolton Priory and Bolton Bridge circular

This short stroll along both banks of the river is, to my mind, by far the best way to visit Bolton Priory.

Distance: 2 miles

Starting point: Bolton Bridge, SE071529

Maps: 20.4 plus Landranger 104.

Although you can visit Bolton Priory by parking at the main Bolton Abbey car park, I much prefer the alternative of starting from the small lay-by on the Addingham road, just to the south of Bolton Bridge. From this starting point you have the advantage of approaching the Priory across the meadows, with the river in the foreground. An added attraction, to a Yorkshireman at least, is that the parking is free!

From the lay-by, take the path along the riverbank, which goes under the new road bridge to the old bridge. Although there were several early medieval bridges on this site, they were presumably all lost in floods. (The only medieval bridge to survive on the Wharfe is at Otley, where the river is more sedate.) The present elegant structure is probably of the late 1770s, a period when many fine bridges were built in the Pennines. In comparing the old and new bridges, it is reasonable to wonder why we appear to have lost the art of building structures which please the eye.

From the bridge, follow the riverbank upstream to the Priory. To return from the Priory, cross the footbridge and follow the footpath uphill before doubling back along the cliff top. From the cliff edge, there is an excellent view of the Priory below on the bend in the river. The path now follows the riverbank to Bolton Bridge.

Section 5: Bolton Bridge to Addingham circular

This excellent circular walk includes some fine stretches of riverbank, together with a high level section which gives panoramic views of the valley between Bolton Priory and Ilkley.

Distance: 5½ miles

Starting point: Bolton bridge, SE071529

Maps: 20.4 plus Landranger 104.

From the lay-by just to the south of Bolton Bridge, take the road towards Addingham. At the first bend in the road, cross the road and take the path into Lob Wood. (Some maps still show the Dales Way going down the road. This is narrow, without pavement, and unpleasant to walk on.) The path goes under the viaduct of the dismantled railway line before climbing steeply upwards, a climb greatly assisted by some wooden stairs.

At the top of the wood, cross a stile and follow the wall-line towards the top corner of the next wood. At the top of this wood, Ilkley comes into view, with Ilkley Moor behind and the Cow and Calf rocks on the skyline. From the corner of the wood, descend diagonally over the next field to join the track which crosses the dismantled railway line to a farm. Follow this track down to the road, bear left for about 50 metres and then turn right onto the path down to the river.

There is now a delightful fast-flowing section of river to follow. When the river bends back to meet the road again, the path is forced to the top of a steep bank. When the path returns to river level, the river has completely changed its character. It is now a slow moving mill-pond, the change being caused by the downstream weir at High Mill.

Pass the mill and continue down the riverbank until a suspension bridge is reached. The path now comes out onto the road near the church. Follow the road to the right to a T-junction, where you bear right towards the centre of Addingham.

Even before the Industrial Revolution, Addingham was an important wool spinning centre, and as you follow the road, you will pass some interesting 17th and 18th century buildings. In about half a mile you will come to the line of the old railway. Turn right into Chapel Lane and follow the lane past the school before turning left onto the footpath which climbs up the hill ridge.

In a short distance the lane becomes a private road. The path goes into the field on the left, and continues to follow the lane uphill. When the lane passes a farmhouse, it deteriorates into an impenetrable sunken hollow-way. The reason for this dereliction is soon seen when you reach a derelict farmhouse. Continue straight ahead from this farmhouse, crossing a golf course, and making for the right-hand side of a large house beyond it (Highfield House).

After Highfield House, make for Highfield Farm, where you will find a stile on the right just before some outbuildings. There is a line of wind generators directly beyond the farm. From the stile, make for two derelict barns, where you will join a track. You can now put your navigation on auto-pilot as the track will take you all the way to Bolton Bridge, passing between some farm buildings at Hawpike Farm.

There are wonderful views of the valley below from this track, none better than from the highest point, where you go through a gate. Here you can see down the valley to Ilkley, Ilkley Moor and the Cow and Calf, and up the valley to Bolton Priory. If visibility is good, you should be able to see Great Whernside further up the valley. From here you can see why the Celts named their river the Wharfe – the "winding river".

Section 6: Addingham to Ilkley circular

This walk includes a high level section along the edge of Ilkley Moor, where the Bronze Age Swastika Stone is seen, and a return leg along the riverbank.

Remains of a Roman fort may be seen in Ilkley, together with artefacts from the fort in the adjacent museum. Next door, the parish church houses some fine Anglo-Saxon crosses.

Distance: 7 miles

Starting point: Addingham Church, SE085497

Public transport: There is a regular bus service between Ilkley and Skipton, which stops at Addingham. This can be useful if you want to do only one half of the walk.

Maps: 20.4 plus Landranger 104.

From the church, take the road which passes Low Mill Lane on its way to a T-junction (with the road through the centre of Addingham). Cross the road and take the left-hand of the two footpaths signed. Climb up to and over the A65, where you bear left to cross the next field diagonally to a gate. The path passes through a peaceful little wooded valley, where a footbridge takes you across a stream. At the top of the wood, bear right slightly to cross a field to a minor road. On the other side of the road, take the farm track (signed to Keighley). When the track divides, take the left fork to Over Croft.

The track terminates at Over Croft. The path follows the left bank of a stream in a hollow until you reach a track above. This serves the highest farms on the hillside. Bear left here and when the track divides, take the right fork into the fields.

Cross the field ahead diagonally to reach the wall at the bottom of the moor. Climb up the moor, and bear left when you reach a track which runs along the moor's edge. In just under half a mile you will reach a stone outcrop guarded by iron railings. This is the Swastika Stone and, like a number of other stones on Ilkley Moor with cup and ring markings, is of the Bronze Age. (Until a climatic deterioration in the early Iron Age, most of the habitation in the Pennines was on the moor tops.)

Leaving the Swastika Stone, the path skirts the top edge of a wood, where a footbridge takes you across Heber's Ghyll. After passing to the right of a small reservoir, the highest houses in Ilkley are reached. When you reach a road follow it down into Ilkley.

Just before the river, you will find the site of the old Roman fort of Olicana. Worth visiting on the site are the parish church, with three fine Anglo-Saxon crosses (8th/9th century), and the adjacent Manor House Museum which has artefacts from the Roman fort amongst its exhibits. A remnant of the fort wall may be seen behind the museum.

From the museum, go down to the riverside meadows and follow the riverbank path. Pass a fine 17th century hump-backed bridge, and when the path leaves the riverbank, follow the road to the tennis club. At the clubhouse, the footpath goes into the field on the left. The riverbank is rejoined just before a pumping station.

When you meet the Addingham road, which is adjacent to the riverbank, follow this for a short distance before taking the drive on the right to the old mill. Go past the mill and the millworkers' cottages (now converted into smart houses) and follow Low Mill Lane up towards Addingham. The church and the old rectory at the other end of Low Mill Lane are in an idyllic setting by a stream running through the meadows. The grandeur of the rectory suggests that in earlier days vicars were numbered amongst those who had their prayers answered!

Places of interest in the Wharfe valley

20.1 Bolton Abbey

Augustinian monks founded a priory at Embsay in 1120, but moved to Bolton in 1154 to land given to them by Lady Alice de Romily.

Twice raided by Scots in the 14th century, the abbey passed to the Cliffords (and then to the Devonshires) following the Dissolution of the Monasteries. Unusually, the nave was saved from destruction to become a parish church.

The 14th century abbey gatehouse was converted into a house and is now the Devonshires' shooting lodge. The abbey setting by the river has attracted many famous artists, including Turner. The area around the abbey has been turned into an attractive woodland setting by the Dukes of Devonshire, and public access has been given to some fine walks.

20.2 Buckden

No village existed at Buckden at the time of the Domesday survey. Buckden was established later by the Normans to control hunting in their forest of Langstrothdale Chase.

The footpath which climbs from the car park through Rakes Wood was a Roman road, and in the 17th century was frequently mentioned by Lady Anne Clifford as her route from Craven to Westmorland.

20.3 Burnsall

This is an extremely attractive village, comprising mainly 17th and 18th century buildings and a fine bridge in a river setting. In the 17th century, Sir William Craven was Burnsall's "Dick Whittington". A local boy who became Lord Mayor of London, he returned to Burnsall to repair the church and the bridge and build a grammar school (now a primary school).

The church is in the Perpendicular style, but has a much older history as may be seen from its Anglo-Saxon crosses and Danish hog-back tombstones.

Burnsall has an annual Feast. The main event is a race to the top of the local fell. There are excellent views of the valley below from Burnsall Fell.

20.4 Grassington

With its cobbled square and fine 17th and 18th century houses, Grassington is the main residential and tourist centre for upper Wharfedale.

Its early prosperity was based on textiles and lead mining, and the simultaneous collapse of both these industries caused the population to be halved between 1850 and 1900. However, the opening of a branch line from Skipton in 1901 brought commuters and tourists, and Grassington has never looked back.

The Wharfe near Grassington

20.5 Hubberholme

Hubberholme was first settled by the Norse in the 10th century, but was unable to grow since it was incorporated into the Norman forest of Langstrothdale Chase.

In medieval times, the church was merely a chapel of ease and the dead from upper Wharfedale had to be carried down the corpse way to Arncliffe for burial. The church, which is mainly 12th century, has a rare rood screen. Because of Hubberholme's remoteness, the screen survived Queen Elizabeth's edict that such ornaments should be destroyed. It is recorded in the church that the river once rose to such an extent that fish were swimming in the aisle.

On New Year's Day, a ceremony with a 1000 year tradition takes place in Hubberholme. A 16 acre field is let for the benefit of the poor of the parish.

20.6 Ilkley

During their campaign to conquer northern Britain in AD 80, the Romans established the fort of Olicana at Ilkley. The purpose of the fort was to control the crossing of the Wharfe by the important road from Ribchester to York.

Today the parish church and Manor House Museum stand on the site of the fort, and part of the fort's wall may be seen in the grounds of the museum. The museum, which is a fine early medieval building, houses a collection of artefacts from the fort. Three finely carved Anglian crosses, which may be seen in the church, suggest that Ilkley was an important centre in Anglo-Saxon times, perhaps having a monastery and a school of carving.

Above the town, on Ilkley Moor, there are a number of stones with cup and ring markings which show that the moor was populated in the Bronze Age, a time when the weather was better than it is today.

Ilkley is perhaps best known for the Cow and Calf rocks and Yorkshire's unofficial National Anthem – "On Ilkla Moor baht 'at" (sadly, written by a Lincolnshireman).

20.7 Kettlewell

In early medieval times most of the land around Kettlewell was owned by monastic foundations. To meet their needs a market was established at Kettlewell in the 13th century. Lead mining brought prosperity to Kettlewell in the 18th century and many of the buildings are of that period.

With its attractive setting, three pubs and adequate parking, Kettlewell is a popular tourist village.

20.8 Kilnsey

The dramatic overhanging limestone scar above Kilnsey is one of Wharfedale's most prominent features.

Today Kilnsey is perhaps best known for its visitors' centre and annual show (which includes a race to the top of the crag). In medieval times, Kilnsey was on an important monastic route between Fountains Abbey and the abbey estates at Malham. The monks established a grange at Kilnsey where their sheep were sheared and reeds for thatching were produced. (At the time there was still the remnant of a post-glacial lake in the valley bottom.)

At the Dissolution of the Monasteries, the estate at Kilnsey passed to the Wade family. In her diaries, Lady Anne Clifford records staying with Cuthbert Wade at Kilnsey Hall in the 17th century, on her travels between Craven and Westmorland. The hall is now in a ruinous state and is used as a farm shed. Adjacent to the hall is a small building which is said to be the gatehouse of the medieval monastic grange.

Despite attempts to have the monastic road to Malham tarmaced, Mastiles Lane remains a green road and is a fine walk.

20.9 Linton

Linton is a particularly attractive village of mainly 17th and 18th century houses around a beck which is spanned by a clapper bridge and a 14th century packhorse bridge.

The village is built on a glacial moraine, and until the 1850s a tarn backed up from the moraine to Cracoe. Flax was grown around the tarn for linen manufacture and accounts for the village name – Lin(flax) tun(place).

The most striking building in the village is the almshouse of Fountaines Hospital. Richard Fountaine, born in Linton in 1640, was a timber merchant. He had the good fortune to be in London at the time of the Great Fire of 1666. The reconstruction of London made him a very wealthy man and when he died in 1721, he left a will which provided for both the building and endowment of the almshouse. The trustees invested in many farms in Wharfedale, and today the endowment of the almshouse is still funded from the rents.

20.10 The Strid and Strid Woods

Part of the Bolton estates between Barden Tower and Bolton Abbey has been designated a Site of Special Scientific Interest. About 30 miles of paths have been laid out as a nature trail through the mixed woodlands.

About a mile north of the Cavendish Pavilion, the river has cut a 30 feet (9m) deep white water channel through the gritstone. It is known as The Strid. Do not be tempted by the name, which means the stride, to jump over this deceptively narrow gorge – many who have tried to do so have drowned. The first recorded drowning was in the 12th century when a young boy who was heir to the Romille estates was pulled into the water when out hunting. According to the story, the boy cleared the river, but his greyhound pulled him back into the water.

A brief history of the Pennine Dales

On Queen Victoria's Coronation Day, a cave was discovered above Settle which has provided many insights into the life of the earliest inhabitants of the Dales. In addition to many fine man-made implements, Victoria Cave had three distinct layers of animal remains.

The deepest and oldest layer contained the bones of animals such as lion, hippo and elephant. These animals were older than the last Ice Age and had roamed the dales in a warm, interglacial period.

The next layer contained woolly rhino and bear, which used the cave during a much colder period.

The youngest deposits, from around 8000BC, were of reindeer, bison and deer; animals hunted by the Old Stone Age people who came across the land bridge which still connected Britain to the Continent.

The Middle Stone Age, from about 5000BC, was still a period of nomadic hunting. Extensive use was made of the small flints which are to be found widely spread on higher ground throughout the Pennines. The Middle Stone Age people were great fishermen in the lakes which were trapped behind glacial moraines in nearly every valley, and harpoons have been found in both Victoria Cave and other caves nearby.

Following an improvement in the climate, the first farmers came to the Pennines in about 3000BC. These New Stone Age or Neolithic people were users of fine grained axes from the Lake District. Towards the end of the Neolithic period, these

Victoria Cave near Settle

people started to build stone burial chambers and henges. The large henge, Long Meg and her daughters, seen on the Eden valley walk, is of this period.

From about 2000 BC, Bronze Age people, also known as Beaker people because of their fine pottery, arrived from the continent. They were prolific builders of stone circles. The largest in the dales is seen on the Wensleydale walk at Ox Close (990903), and a small circle is passed at Yockenthwaite on the Wharfe valley walk (900794).

If Victoria Cave produced the best collection of early prehistoric finds, a cave at Heather Burn in Weardale holds the same position for the Bronze Age. Here axes, spears, gold jewellery and a four-wheeled cart were found (The Heather Burn collection is now in the British Museum).

The contents of a Bronze Age burial at Rilston, now displayed in the Craven Museum, Skipton, show that the wealthy at least were now wearing fine woven cloth.

The start of the Iron Age, in about 700BC, coincided with a significant deterioration in the climate. This made many of the Pennines areas settled in the Bronze Age uninhabitable. Iron Age settlements, which are mainly small fields with a single hut, are confined to the drier limestone scars, and the remnants of these settlements may still be seen in Wharfedale and Ribblesdale.

About 100BC, a military caste of Celtic-speaking chariot drivers settled in the Pennines, ruling over a confederacy known as Brigantia, which stretched from the Trent to the Tyne. It was the Brigantes whom Tacitus tells us constituted the largest of the British tribes when the Romans arrived in Britain.

Apart from a few bumps in the fields, representing outlines of huts and fields, and a few henges, there is very little on the ground from the first 8000 years of human occupation of the Dales to excite the visitor. The best place to view the material from this period is not in the valleys themselves, but in the Craven Museum at Skipton.

If the traces from the first 8000 years of man's presence are sparse, this is not true of the following 400 years. The Romans have left us a cornucopia, including some of the best remains in Europe of the Roman Empire.

When the Romans first invaded Britain, they were at first happy to settle the agriculturally rich south of England, leaving the Brigantes as friendly neighbours on the northern border. However, when an anti-Roman faction under Venutius came to power in Brigantia, it was apparent to Romans and Britons alike that conflict was inevitable. Venutius marshalled what must have been an enormous labour force to build many defensive sites through-out the Pennines. His redoubt was the massively defended 600 acres site at Stanwick, between the Tees and the Swale at (185116).

Despite these preparations, the Brigantes were no match for the Roman war machine. Venutius was defeated at Stanwick in AD 74 by Cerialis (governor from AD 71-74).

Agricola, governor from AD 78-88, then set about consolidating the Roman gains, establishing forts along three defensive lines:

- Stanegate on the north side of the Tyne valley,

- Stainmore (Greta Bridge to Brough),

- the Wharfe, Aire and Ribble gap (York to Ribchester).

These lines of defence linked the two important north-south roads from Manchester to Carlisle and York to Corbridge.

While this was the main skeleton of the Roman control over Brigantia, in common with their normal practice, they built additional forts about a day's march apart (10-12 miles), and the roads to link them. Most of what we know about the early Roman campaign in northern Britain is from the writing of Tacitus. He gives Agricola particularly good reviews, but it must be remembered that Tacitus was Agricola's son-in-law!

It was not the Romans' initial intention to freeze their conquest along the Tyne valley, and for 50 years they campaigned vigorously in Scotland. However, when Hadrian, an Emperor who by nature was a consolidator rather than a campaigner, visited Britain in AD 122, he decided to build an 80 mile wall along the line of the Tyne valley, just to the north of the earlier defensive line of Stanegate. In doing so, he was defining what was to be the northern border of the Roman Empire for the following 250 years.

Although there appears to have been a general rising in the Pennines in around AD 155, when forts from Hadrian's Wall to Derbyshire were destroyed, this must have been a temporary setback. The many third century Roman Altars dedicated to the hunting god Silvanus which have been found suggest that the Romans were then able to devote a good deal of time to leisure pursuits.

By the 4th century, however, the Picts and Saxons were beginning to take advantage of a weakened Roman Empire. Around AD 385, Hadrian's Wall had been destroyed and the Romans had retreated to their defensive line across Stainmore. Some 20 years later, they were to withdraw from Britain.

Many of the Roman sites are seen on the walks, and some of the delightful green ways incorporated into the walks are themselves former Roman roads. Whilst not directly on a walk (since it is in the plain rather than in a valley), Stanwick (180115), the site of the defeat of the Brigantes, and therefore of one of the most important events in English history, is well worth a visit.

Since Bede, the earliest of the English chroniclers, was not born until AD 673, our knowledge of the early centuries after the Roman withdrawal is sketchy. It would seem that there was a Celtic kingdom of Rheged which included south-west Scotland and the Pennine dales. Although no known place names have survived from this period, many names of hills and rivers are of Celtic origin – Pendle, Penyghent, Tyne and Wharfe. (Such names have much more longevity than names of settlements which are more likely to change when new tribes arrive.)

Battles were certainly fought between the Celts and the new Anglo-Saxon immigrants from the continent, and the legendary prowess of King Arthur and his knights is of this time. Pendragon castle, seen on the first section of the Eden walk, is reputed to be the birthplace of King Arthur. Sadly for the story, archaeologists have dated the building of the castle to around 400 years after Arthur's death.

From an analysis of their place names and their cemeteries (unlike the Romans before them, the Anglo-Saxons did not bury their dead by the roadsides), it would seem that the Anglo-Saxons established widespread settlements throughout the south and east of England in the 5th and 6th centuries, but that it was not until the 7th century that they settled the Pennines.

The first wave of the Anglo-Saxon settlement was in the Aire, Wharfe and Ribble valleys, where many villages have the suffix "-ley", describing the clearings they created in the woods.

The Anglo-Saxon epic poem "Beowulf", composed about the end of the 7th century, gives an insight into life at that time, and paints a picture of many small kingdoms vying with each other for territorial dominance. These gradually coalesced, until England was effectively controlled by three kingdoms: Northumbria, Mercia and Wessex. The country was prosperous, and from about AD 800, this prosperity started to attract the interest of the Vikings in the form of almost annual raids.   •

By AD 873, the Danish army had subjugated Mercia. Overwintering that year at the sacked Mercian royal centre of Repton, the Danes decided to split the Army. The northern army under Halfdane was to settle Northumbria, and the southern section under Guthrun was to lead the onslaught on Wessex.

Halfdane quickly conquered Northumbria, and Guthrun's objective was almost achieved, with Wessex control under Alfred being reduced to a small area in the Somerset marshes. However, in a remarkable reverse, Alfred defeated Guthrun and forced him to accept the Treaty of Wedmore (AD 886). Under the treaty, the Danes were to confine their influence to an area to the north and east of the line which ran roughly from London to Chester. The Pennines were, therefore, firmly under Danelaw, with York being the capital.

In the 10th century, the Norse, Danish who had earlier settled in Ireland, came to the Pennines from the west, creating an even larger Danish kingdom ruled from York and Dublin.

The English did not stand by the Treaty of Wedmore and started a campaign of attrition to recapture the land under Danish control, taking Chester (AD 907), Stafford and Tamworth (AD 913), Derby (AD 917), Thelwall and Manchester (AD 920), Bakewell (AD 920) and finally York

(AD 954). The capture of the Danish capital of York and the killing of the Danish leader, Eric Bloodaxe, in Stainmore in the same year ended the first period of Danish rule in Britain.

For a period after their expulsion from England, the Danes concentrated their attention elsewhere, but from about AD 990 they started raiding England again, extorting vast tributes in the form of Danegeld. Indeed, these tributes became so onerous that England eventually fell directly under the control of the Danish king.

There are few physical remains from the Anglo-Saxon and Danish periods. Anglo-Saxon churches were mainly of wood, and have not survived, and most of the few which were of stone were destroyed by the Danes. Those that have survived are:

• the crypt at Hexham Abbey,

• the crypt at Ripon Cathedral,

• the lovely small church at Escomb, in the Wear valley.

Although the Danes were pagan when they came to Britain, they converted to Christianity and started to emulate the Anglo-Saxon custom of building stone crosses. Throughout the Pennines, there are large numbers of stone crosses to be seen in churchyards. Some, such as the wonderful cross at Bewcastle (565746), may be identified as purely Anglian; or the Loki stone at Kirkby Stephen as Danish (because of its representation of a Danish devil), but many can only be called Anglo-Danish. Hog-back tombstones such as those at Burnsall Church (Wharfe valley) and Addingham Church (Eden valley) are Danish, and are thought to represent their long-houses.

When an Anglo-Saxon or Danish king died, succession was not assured, and often had to be fought for. On Edward the Confessor's death, there was a three-cornered fight between the English Harold, Tostig the Dane and William the Norman.

Although William prevailed, the Danes continued to represent a serious threat, particularly in alliance with the north which had been under Danish rule for so long. William was ruthless in neutralising this threat, and mounted a campaign known as the Harrying of the North. Following the campaign, the Domesday survey records much of the north as "wasta est". Arguments have long raged about whether these two words mean that the whole population had been put to the sword or had escaped to the hills.

To consolidate their hold of the north, the Normans built a large number of castles. Nearly every dale of any size has its Norman castle guarding the entry to the valley, strategically placed to benefit from the better arable land in the plain, whilst controlling the communication routes through the dales.

Anglo-Saxon and Danish landowners were, almost without exception, dispossessed, and the land was divided between the King, the barons and the church. Many of the upper dales became royal forests, strictly reserved for hunting by the king.

Until the Union of the Crowns in 1603, the border between England and Scotland was never really defined. Particularly after the Scots success at the Battle of Bannockburn in 1314, they raided the north of England with impunity, often as far south as Craven. Life could only be protected by the building of impregnable fortresses, and most of the building in the northern dales during the 14th to 16th centuries was of bastles and pele towers. The Scots were no respectors of churches. Staward Peel (Allen walk) was a retreat for the monks of Hexham, and in Corbridge even the vicar lived in a pele. Many of the bastles and pele towers seen on the walks were, in more peaceable times, converted to farms.

Throughout the first half of the second millennium, the church continued to accumulate enormous endowments of land, becoming the biggest landowner in the dales. The monasteries and abbeys not only owned massive estates of land, but also mines and manufacturing facilities. By the 16th century the church was perceived by many to have become worldly and decadent. Henry VIII, a profligate himself, took full advantage of the church's unpopularity to engineer an appropriation of the church's assets for himself and his followers.

Perhaps because of the church's large land holdings, there was more resistance to Henry's Dissolution of the Monasteries in the north than in the south, and there was a rising of 30,000 men in what was known as the Pilgrimage of Grace. The rising was disarmed by promises from the king to consider the grievances, and the granting of a full pardon to the participants. These promises, however, were tactical expedients and, when the participants had dispersed, Henry had the 200 leaders rounded up, hung, drawn and quartered.

Not only were the Abbots of most of the northern monasteries executed, but so too were the heads of many of the leading families in the dales, their lands being forfeit to the King. The redistribution of wealth which resulted from the Dissolution of the Monasteries and the Pilgrimage of Grace, created a new, wealthy yeoman class. It was not long before these yeomen had accumulated sufficient capital to build themselves the fine halls which we see in most of the dales.

A somewhat poignant example of this redistribution of wealth is one Stephen Proctor of Gargrave. The Proctors had for many years been monastic agents, the family name reflecting this employment. At the time of the Dissolution, Stephen Proctor's father was living in Gargave. By the 1580s we see Stephen building Friars Head, an exquisite small hall at Winterburn near Gargrave, (Airedale walk). Some twenty years later Stephen Proctor had prospered to such an extent that he was able to build himself one of the most magnificent mansions in the north, Fountains Hall (Skell walk), in the grounds of Fountains Abbey. Stone for his hall he "quarried" from the abbey itself, thereby dismantling the very building which his forebears had served for generations.

Nearly all of the abbeys and monastic houses seen on the walks have similar Yeoman houses built adjacent to the foundations which were their source of building material.

Although few houses in the dales pre-date the Dissolution, many of the bridges are considerably older. Unlike the south, where medieval bridges were predominantly wooden, the lack of trees in the north and regular winter floods, dictated that Pennine bridges were of stone. As the largest landowner, the monasteries built many of the bridges. The bridges built between the 12th and 16th centuries mostly have ribs underneath their arches, a design feature first seen in the building of Durham Cathedral.

The innovation of using ribs was a most important breakthrough. The heavy barrel roof design of the Cathedrals, a roof design which had been unchanged since Roman times, could now evolve into the much lighter and more elegant Gothic, and later, Perpendicular designs. The advantage for bridge design was that a much lighter scaffold might now be used in the construction, the woodwork being moved from rib to rib as the construction progressed.

On the walks, medieval "ribbed arch" bridges are to be seen at:

- Eden valley (Warcop),
- Lune valley(Kirkby Lonsdale),
- Ribble valley(Settle),
- Tees valley(Barnard Castle),
- Wear valley(Stanhope).

Plain arches replace ribbed arches as the standard design shortly after the Dissolution of the Monasteries.

In addition to the medieval "ribbed arch" bridges, there is a marvellous collection of other bridges in the Pennines. These would make a fascinating subject for study in their own right:

- Roman bridge abutments (Tyne and Tees valleys);
- packhorse bridges, built mainly between 1650 and 1750;
- elegant late 18th century designs, such as those by John Carr of York.

One of the reasons for the large number of late 18th century bridges is that there was a massive flood in 1771 which swept away most of the bridges over a wide area in the northern Pennines. The dawning of the Industrial Revolution justified their speedy replacement.

Following the Union of the Crowns in 1603, there was a reduction in the lawlessness which had been the way of life on the northern border for several centuries. However, when the Scots crossed the Tyne in 1638 and occupied the north, Parliamentarians became deeply concerned about the

King's inability to control his Scottish subjects. This unrest was one of the primary causes of the outbreak of the Civil War in 1642.

In the north, which was mainly for the King, the Civil War was largely a matter of defending your garrisons and destroying those of the your opponents. Many of the castles, such as Carlisle and Skipton, withstood lengthy sieges before capitulating.

In the second phase of the Civil War, Cromwell's defeat of the Scots at Preston in 1648 was one of the critical events in establishing him as Protector. Cromwell's Bridge, where he decided to commit to battle in Preston, is seen on the Ribble valley walk.

During the Civil War, Lady Anne Clifford had become the High Sheriffess of the County of Westmorland, inheriting the castles of Skipton, Barden, Pendragon, Brough, Appleby and Brougham. It was too dangerous for her to visit her inheritance until 1649, after the King's execution, but she then spent most of the rest of her life travelling between and restoring the many castles damaged during the Civil War.

Her recently published diaries, ("The Diaries of Lady Anne Clifford" by D.J.H. Clifford) describe her journeys. The routes include the delightful green way known as Lady Anne's Way which has been included in the first sections of the Eden and Wensleydale walks.

Today, the dales are nearly entirely pastoral and few of the river valley walks see crops other than hay. It has not always been thus, particularly in the southern dales. North of Stainmore, the poor quality of the soils has always dictated that the land be used mainly for stock rearing. In the medieval period, it was this stock that attracted the "reivers"; cattle raiders from the even poorer areas further north.

In the southern dales, however, the best quality land in the valley bottoms was still reserved for crops in the 16th century, following a farming pattern set by the Anglo-Saxons almost a thousand years before. The medieval strip lynchets where arable farming was practised may still be seen in many of the valleys and are particularly prominent in Wharfedale below Grassington and Ribblesdale above Settle.

During the 17th century, two factors combined to revolutionise this pattern of land use – growth of a market for cattle in the south of England which could not be satisfied locally, and the establishment of markets for corn which allowed the dales people to buy corn, which they had previously had to grow.

Reversing the previous "trade" in cattle which the "reivers" had driven north, a new supply chain was established, based on cattle bred in Scotland, fattened in the Pennine Dales and then sold in the south of England. To support this trade, the southern Pennine dales had to change from arable to pastoral farming. The common fields were broken up and enclosed by the drystone walls which are today one of the hallmarks of the dales.

The many exquisite stone barns we see throughout the dales are also from this period, as are the limekilns built to produce the lime used to reclaim large areas of previously barren land.

Cattle were brought from Scotland down a few major drove roads, some of which are now delightful green ways. Several have been incorporated into the walks, including:

- Maiden Way (South Tyne valley),
- High Way (Eden valley),
- Thorn Gill (Ribble valley),
- Hunters Bark (Ribble valley).

Although first established in the 17th century, the real growth in the "droving" trade followed the explosive growth in the 18th century of cities such as Nottingham. The "droving" trade ceased in the 19th century with the coming of the railways, but the predominantly pastoral land use established in the dales in the 17th and 18th centuries remains today.

In late medieval times, textile production was a major employer in the dales, particularly hand knitting in the Sedbergh, Kirkby Stephen, Richmond and Kendal areas. By the end of the 18th century, textile production was becoming automated, but employment was maintained by the large number of water-powered mills established on the fast flowing rivers of the dales. However, the life of most of these mills was relatively short, for the smaller ones in particular could not compete with the more economical steam-powered mills being built close to the coal fields.

To agriculture and textiles, lead mining must be added as the third of the three major economic activities of the dales. Mining was particularly prosperous in the 18th century, and many of the dales towns and villages of that period which we find so attractive today, were financed by this lead prosperity (Grassington and Kettlewell in Wharfedale, Richmond and Reeth in Swaledale).

At the end of the first quarter of the 19th century, an unusually severe economic depression caused the population in some dales to be halved.

The immediate cause of the depression was a collapse of the lead mining business, which could not compete with cheaper Spanish lead. The problem was, however, compounded by reductions in demand for labour in the other two traditional areas of employment: textiles and agriculture.

Textiles collapsed in the unequal competition between steam and water power, and agriculture, while in itself viable, was much less labour intensive after the move from crop production to cattle.

Not until the 20th century did the rise in commuting and the holiday trade start to restore the dales population to levels seen a century before. The medieval traveller would not have understood the modern fascination with the Pennines. For him the Pennines were a dangerous, forbidding place, to be travelled through quickly, if at all. In 1724, most would have agreed with Defoe when he wrote of "high mountains which had a terrible aspect....especially Pen-y-ghent."

The change in attitude was largely a by-product of the Napoleonic War. No longer could writers and artists travel to their favourite continental watering holes, and they came instead to places such as the dales. Perhaps the person who did most to popularise the Pennines was Turner, who paid several visits to the dales. In 1816 he did a 550 mile, 25 days tour on horseback, producing no less that 450 sketches, often in the most appalling weather. On his return to London, Turner made 20 finished paintings which are acknowledged as being amongst his greatest masterpieces. Of his finished works, only two did not contain a river, a lake or a waterfall, and it therefore comes as no surprise to learn that Turner was a fanatical fisherman, even having an umbrella which converted into a rod.

The reason Turner had need of his umbrella was that just over a year before he set out, the largest volcano ever recorded erupted at Tambra in Indonesia. The volcano injected an estimated 100 cubic kilometres of rock into the atmosphere, severely disrupting the world's weather system for at least two years and ensuring almost continuous rain for Turner.

It is likely that the volcano affected the outcome of the Battle of Waterloo in 1815, the waterlogged fields impeding the mobilisation of Napoleon's canon, and there was snow in North America in June 1816 which caused the crops to fail. It would have been the same North American weather system which caused Turner to write to a friend a month later – "weather miserably wet, I shall be web-footed like a drake".

Turner's travels through the dales are chronicled and many of his pictures are reproduced in David Hill's very readable book "In Turner's Footsteps". Many of the views painted by Turner are seen on the walks, including:

- Semer Water, Wensleydale,
- Hardraw Force, Wensleydale,
- Aysgarth Falls, Wensleydale,
- Marrick Priory, Swaledale,
- Richmond, Swaledale,
- Junction of the Greta and the Tees,
- Egglestone Abbey, Teesdale,
- Crook of Lune,
- Kirkby Lonsdale.

Unlike the unfortunate Turner, I completed my walks along the Pennine river valleys during the glorious summer of 1995. The moral is clear – before setting out for the Pennines, check the previous year's volcano records!

Also by Tony Stephens:

PEAKLAND RIVER VALLEY WALKS

This is the companion volume to 'North Country River Valley Walks', covering the network of almost 20 rivers in the Peak District. Some 250 miles of walks are included, all along the river valleys with diversions to higher ground in order to reach the source of the river or to admire the wide panoramas of river systems from a lofty vantage point. Routes ranges from a modest 8 miles along the Hope Valley to the 63 miles along the Derwent: truly a collection for walkers of all abilities! £7.95

More books for northern walkers:

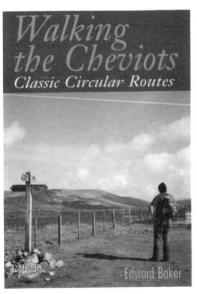

WALKING THE CHEVIOTS: Classic Circular Routes

This book by local author **Edward Baker** provides an excellent introduction to this solitary, wild countryside. Everyone is catered for – from weekend family groups to the experienced hill walker. Each route contains details of the natural history, geology and archaeology of the area. For ease of reference, the book is in two sections, covering the northern and southern Cheviots - distinct areas with their own unique character. In all, there are almost 50 walks - by far the most comprehensive collection published for the Cheviots. £7.95

BEST PUB WALKS IN NORTHUMBRIA
Stephen Rickerby   £6.95

BEST PUB WALKS IN THE YORKSHIRE DALES
Clive Price   £6.95

PUB WALKS IN THE YORKSHIRE WOLDS
Tony Whittaker   £6.95

PUB WALKS ON THE NORTH YORK MOORS AND COAST
Stephen Rickerby   £6.95

BEST PUB WALKS IN & AROUND SHEFFIELD
Clive Price   £6.95

BEST PUB WALKS IN & AROUND LEEDS
Colin Speakman   £6.95

All of our books are available from your local bookshop. In case of difficulty, or to obtain our complete catalogue, please contact:

Sigma Leisure, 1 South Oak Lane, Wilmslow, Cheshire SK9 6AR
Phone: 01625 – 531035;
Fax: 01625 – 536800
E-mail: sigma.press@zetnet.co.uk
Web site: www.sigmapress.co.uk

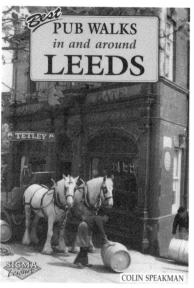

ACCESS and VISA orders welcome – call our friendly sales staff or use our 24 hour Answerphone service! Most orders are despatched on the day we receive your order – you could be enjoying our books in just a couple of days. Please add £2 p&p to all orders.